# ON HER GAME

## CAITLIN CLARK
### AND THE REVOLUTION IN
### WOMEN'S SPORTS

# CHRISTINE BRENNAN

**SCRIBNER**

New York  Amsterdam/Antwerp  London
Toronto  Sydney/Melbourne  New Delhi

Scribner

An Imprint of Simon & Schuster, LLC
1230 Avenue of the Americas
New York, NY 10020

First Scribner hardcover edition July 2025

SCRIBNER and design are trademarks of Simon & Schuster, LLC

Simon & Schuster strongly believes in freedom of expression and stands against
censorship in all its forms. For more information, visit BooksBelong.com.

For information about special discounts for bulk purchases,
please contact Simon & Schuster Special Sales at 1-866-506-1949
or business@simonandschuster.com.

The Simon & Schuster Speakers Bureau can bring authors to your live event.
For more information or to book an event, contact the Simon & Schuster Speakers Bureau
at 1-866-248-3049 or visit our website at www.simonspeakers.com.

Interior design by Kyle Kabel

Manufactured in the United States of America

1   3   5   7   9   10   8   6   4   2

Library of Congress Cataloging-in-Publication Data has been applied for.

ISBN 978-1-6680-9019-0
ISBN 978-1-6680-9021-3 (ebook)

*For Helena, my favorite athlete,*
*and Peter, my favorite robotics engineer*

# Contents

# 2024 Indiana Fever Roster

| Name | # | Position | Height | Weight | Birthdate | College/Home Country |
|------|---|----------|--------|--------|-----------|----------------------|
| Grace Berger | 34 | Guard | 6'0" | 160 | 06/03/1999 | Indiana/USA |
| Aliyah Boston | 7 | Center | 6'5" | 220 | 12/11/2001 | South Carolina/USA |
| Caitlin Clark | 22 | Guard | 6'0" | 152 | 01/22/2002 | Iowa/USA |
| Damiris Dantas | 12 | Forward | 6'3" | 214 | 11/17/1992 | Brazil |
| Temi Fagbenle | 14 | Forward | 6'4" | 180 | 09/08/1992 | USC/United Kingdom |
| Lexie Hull | 10 | Guard | 6'1" | 155 | 09/13/1999 | Stanford/USA |
| Kelsey Mitchell | 0 | Guard | 5'8" | 160 | 11/12/1995 | Ohio State/USA |
| Katie Lou Samuelson | 33 | Forward | 6'3" | 163 | 06/13/1997 | Connecticut/USA |
| Victaria Saxton | 5 | Forward | 6'2" | 181 | 11/10/1999 | South Carolina/USA |
| NaLyssa Smith | 1 | Forward | 6'4" | 185 | 08/08/2000 | Baylor/USA |
| Kristy Wallace | 3 | Guard | 5'11" | 157 | 01/03/1996 | Baylor/Australia |
| Erica Wheeler | 17 | Guard | 5'7" | 143 | 05/02/1991 | Rutgers/USA |

# Introduction

L ike many of you, I was introduced to Caitlin Clark by a stunning three-point shot.

It was February 26, 2023, and I was watching an ESPN broadcast of the Indiana–Iowa women's basketball game on my iPad in my kitchen in Washington, DC. I wasn't watching the game to see Clark. All three of my siblings graduated from Indiana, as did a niece and brother-in-law, and the Hoosiers were having a terrific season, so I was watching to see this good team my family loved.

Of course I had heard about Clark, but I hadn't particularly followed her. I missed much of her freshman year in 2020–21, a year marred by COVID-19 and, for me, a year of preparation for the postponed Tokyo Olympics, which had been moved to the summer of 2021. I certainly was aware of her exploits and had seen highlights of her play during her sophomore year, including a few clips on social media of a monster shooting night at Michigan while I was in Beijing covering the 2022 Winter Olympics, but by no means had I focused on her.

In fact, after her sophomore year, on June 23, 2022, Title IX celebrated its fiftieth anniversary. I wrote 5,000 words for *USA Today* that day on the huge impact the law that opened the floodgates for girls and women to play sports has had on our nation. I told the inspiring stories of Billie Jean King and the 1999 US women's soccer team, and

I wrote about girls like me who played sports at a time when gyms were empty because no one cared about our games except our moms and dads.

Five thousand words. Not one was either Caitlin or Clark. How quickly things can change in sports, and in our culture.

•

So now it was Clark's junior year at Iowa, and I was watching Indiana play, and the Hoosiers had just taken the lead, 85–83, with 1.5 seconds left. Iowa was inbounding the ball, and everyone knew the pass was going to Clark. She broke free. Her defender slipped. The ball was in her hands beyond the three-point arc. Clark launched a wild shot from a ridiculous position, off-balance, left leg askew. It was crazy and almost laughable. There was no way on earth something like that could go in—until it did.

The announcers yelled. The home crowd in Iowa City erupted. Clark had won the game, 86–85. She joyously ran off the court and tore through the photographers and camerapeople sitting on the end line to reach the stands behind the basket, where she was swallowed up by her jubilant teammates.

I've been fortunate to play sports my entire life, and cover sports for more than 40 years around the world, which means I've seen a lot, but I couldn't take my eyes off this. I watched all the replays ESPN showed, then happened upon a few on social media and watched them again. The Indiana alums in the family did the same. How could they not? As we texted, I commiserated with them over the loss even as I was shaking my head. What had we just watched?

What happened next has become part of the lore and legend of American sports. Clark led Iowa into the NCAA Tournament, and pretty soon into the Final Four. On Friday night, March 31, friends I hadn't heard from in months—male friends, sports-loving guys—were texting, asking if I was covering the Iowa–South Carolina game at the

Final Four in Dallas, or, if not, was I watching? No man had ever asked me questions like this before about women's basketball.

Although I've covered quite a few Women's Final Fours over the years, I wasn't in Dallas for that one because I was preparing to cover the Masters golf tournament. But yes, I was watching. Of course I was watching.

Clark scored 41 points to upset defending national champion South Carolina, 77–73, and take her underdog Iowa team to the finals against LSU. I started to wonder: When had we ever seen a female athlete quite like this, especially in a team sport?

In addition to her once-in-a-generation—perhaps once-in-a-lifetime—talent, Clark was assisted in her ascendance by timely developments in the NCAA. She was now in her third year of four playing college ball at Iowa, with her games regularly being shown on national television—on the networks, on cable channels, or on streaming services. There was no one-and-done on the women's side as there was on the men's—women didn't play just their freshman year and bolt to the pros—meaning Clark's staying power allowed audiences the opportunity to get to know her, while the top male college players disappeared quickly to the NBA. Social media, of course, gave us a window into Clark's life, making her all the more accessible. And there was the new power of NIL: name, image, and likeness. By the time Clark was done with college, she reportedly had at least 11 NIL deals worth more than $3 million, including TV commercials such as her ubiquitous State Farm spots that made her even more recognizable.

Off to the national championship game Clark went, and what happened there set the stage for one of sports' most fascinating new rivalries. As LSU built an insurmountable lead near the game's end, Tigers star Angel Reese walked up to Clark, waving her hand in front of her own face in the "You can't see me" gesture made famous by actor and professional wrestler John Cena, mocking a move Clark had made in Iowa's Elite Eight game a week earlier with Louisville, although not to an opponent, as many thought, but just to her own bench, as we later found out.

Reese also pointed to her fourth finger, indicating where her NCAA championship ring would go. Clark ignored her, but the nation did not, and an important conversation ensued about what we expect from female athletes, and about race, since Clark is white and Reese is Black.

It's rare for me to be on a national news show talking about women's team sports, but this story was different, so I traveled to New York to be on the CNN set Monday morning to discuss it—to talk about women's basketball rather than the men's basketball championship game coming up that evening. I was back on CNN again that night. Same subject: women's hoops. Some thought the back-and-forth was terrible for women's sports, that we weren't focusing on the athletes' exceptional play, but rather on their behavior. I thought it was terrific. Women's sports are always about more than sports: the relative newness of our fandom, the explosion in national interest, how it all relates to the girl next door. This had it all.

Three days later, on Thursday morning, I was at the Masters. Tiger Woods was about to tee off at Augusta National Golf Club, but I wasn't outside at the first tee. No, I was inside the press center, on an ABC News Live Zoom, still talking about Caitlin Clark and Angel Reese. With good reason: The TV viewership for the Iowa–LSU game was massive, 9.9 million, the largest audience to watch a women's basketball game in nearly 40 years. Caitlin and Angel were quite a pairing.

Or were they? Was this really about both of them? The answer was yes, and no. Reese is a terrific rebounder and presence around the basket, as well as an intriguing personality and successful pitchwoman—and the defending national champion—but the 2023–24 women's college basketball season was built around Clark, a highly visible and confident point guard with a foundational fan base ready and willing to tune in to anything she did, making her the driving force behind what would become the greatest days in the history of women's team sports, and perhaps women's sports as a whole.

While she was selling out arenas in the midst of her barnstorming run to break the NCAA Division I scoring record for both women and

men, Clark was becoming one of the nation's most famous athletes—
perhaps the most famous. She appeared in multiple big-time commercials. Her games became must-see viewing across various broadcast and
cable networks. Her interviews were polished and insightful. She signed
autographs for boys and girls before and after games. Newspapers and
news organizations were covering her in a way no female basketball
player—no female team sport athlete—had ever been covered: wall to
wall, every day, with respect, even reverence.

Yet I still had never interviewed her, never written a word about her,
never met her. In fact, I finally saw Clark for the first time in person
not with a press pass, but with a general admission ticket.

My family and I bought tickets to the Iowa game at the University
of Maryland, in the DC suburbs, on Saturday night, February 3, 2024.
Sitting among thousands of spectators far from press row, I watched
Clark receive a pass, dribble once, and effortlessly launch a three-point
shot from a jaw-dropping distance that we might exaggerate and call the
parking lot. It went in. The game was 15 seconds old. I laughed out loud.

This wasn't just sports. It was entertainment. Clark was the high-
wire act at the circus. She was the diva at the opera. She was a show.
She was *the* show. What in the world was she going to do next? A
sellout crowd of 17,950 had packed the Xfinity Center not to see the
game, per se, but to see her. That's why my family was there. It was all
about Clark. And she delivered. She made 7 three-pointers in all and
finished with 38 points in a 93–85 Iowa victory.

Even people who weren't there were affected, and impressed. Friends
who were driving on the Beltway who had forgotten that Clark was
in town saw the massive traffic jam for the university exit and figured
there was some big entertainer performing on campus that night. They
were not wrong.

I soon wrote my first column on Clark for *USA Today*, reporting
on her prospects for the 2024 US Olympic women's basketball team
and on whether she would stick around for a fifth COVID year at
Iowa or go pro.

Quickly, I found that while covering other sports stories in the course of my daily work, I was writing and talking more about Clark for my various media outlets. And why not? She had become a huge national story, the Iowa high school girl who never left home to go to college, now a coast-to-coast sensation drawing 4 million more people to watch the women's NCAA championship game against South Carolina on April 7, 2024, than watched the men's NCAA final the next night: 18.9 million to 14.8 million.

That's a sentence I never thought I would write. Women's college basketball being more popular than men's college basketball? In 21st-century America? How was this possible?

The answer was Clark.

•

There was so much to tell. As I watched videos of this well-known personality walking through baggage claim at Dallas Fort Worth International Airport for a WNBA preseason game in early May, I checked with an NBA source to ask why the WNBA was allowing Clark, and all of the league's players, to fly commercially. Within a few days, I broke the news that the WNBA would finally be instituting private charter flights for all 12 of its teams, a policy change that had come about because of Clark's popularity and fame, and concerns for her safety. Charter flights should have come much sooner for all the WNBA players—especially after Brittney Griner's unjust imprisonment in Vladimir Putin's Russia—but Clark's presence made it happen, basically over one May weekend.

A month later, I broke another story on a beat I've covered since 1984, the Olympics: the controversial news that Clark was not going to be given a spot on the 2024 US Olympic women's basketball team.

As Clark was turning the page from college to the pros as the No. 1 pick in the 2024 WNBA Draft by the Indiana Fever, I was fascinated by the possibilities that this new young star would offer to a league I've covered since 1999, whether it be for Lifetime TV, *USA Today*, CNN, or ABC News. My overriding thought was that the WNBA, so often ignored and even scoffed at by the male-dominated mainstream sports media, deserved this moment, deserved this attention, deserved her.

But then I began to see signs of just how unprepared the WNBA was for Clark's arrival, and how some in the league wanted to minimize her impact, even predicting her failure. Basketball is a physical game, and rookies in all sports often get a rude welcome, but there were some truly jarring reactions to Clark's arrival from some of the biggest names in the women's game. This was especially surprising considering how many new fans Clark was bringing to a league that desperately needed them, illustrating the possibilities of the old adage "a rising tide lifts all boats."

What was going on? Was this because Clark is white and straight in a league that is 74 percent Black or mixed-race, with a sizable gay population? Was it because she played at Iowa rather than one of women's basketball's blue bloods—schools like UConn, South Carolina, Notre Dame, and Stanford? Was it because the WNBA did so little to help its players understand what was about to happen when Clark entered the league? Was it because of her eight-year, $28 million Nike shoe deal, as reported by *The Wall Street Journal*, when established Black stars had never received that kind of a contract? Was it jealousy? Was it all of the above?

Questions abounded. I moderated a panel called "The Caitlin Clark Effect and the Future of Women's Sports" at the University of Maryland's Shirley Povich Center for Sports Journalism on March 26, 2024, with sports editors Roxanna Scott of *USA Today* and Jason Murray of *The Washington Post*, as well as longtime WNBA player and assistant coach LaToya Sanders and 1999 US soccer star Briana Scurry. All four are people of color. As we talked about the issues involving Clark's star power, I asked this question: "If everything about Caitlin Clark is the same, except her skin color, if she is Black instead of white, how would this story be different?" The answers touched on issues of race and racism, TV ratings and national interest, but everyone agreed that a Black woman would not be getting the same kind of attention that Clark was receiving.

As all these issues surrounded Clark upon her arrival in the WNBA, she surprised the naysayers by becoming every bit the sports and cultural star in the pros that she was in college: breaking records, winning awards, filling massive arenas, attracting historic TV viewership, and continuing to be a role model for thousands, probably millions, of girls and boys in the United States, and in other nations as well. She handled every question and controversy, manufactured or real, with respect, dignity, and a level of maturity that went well beyond her 22 years. She seemed to be 22 going on 40, or 50.

•

This book came about quickly. As fascinated as I was with the story of Caitlin Clark, and what it meant for women's sports and our culture, I wasn't planning to write a book about it until a July 10 Zoom conversation with Scribner editor Rick Horgan. The next day, we had a deal. A week later, I flew to Paris to cover the 2024 Summer Olympic Games. I came back in mid-August. I was home in Washington, DC, for three days, then flew to Indianapolis.

For the next six weeks, I was on the road with Clark and the Indiana Fever. I covered games, practices, and press conferences. I interviewed players, coaches, administrators, and fans. I asked questions of a lot of people—including Clark, of course. Sometimes the questions I asked were more newsworthy than others. When the WNBA players association wanted to ban me in late September for asking a question and a follow-up of the Connecticut Sun's DiJonai Carrington—two questions I would ask any athlete, male or female, anytime, to give them a chance to clear the air on a controversial topic—the players' action revealed just how unprepared they were for the new national scrutiny the league was receiving.

Just to be clear, that attempt failed. I was not prevented from covering the WNBA.

That unusual incident should not for a moment distract from what this book is about. This is a story about a groundbreaking, historic, immensely popular, but also at times controversial cultural figure, made for the moment, and how she is dramatically altering one of the last great bastions of male superiority: sports. It's about her talent, her intelligence, her competitiveness, her sense of humor, and her sense of responsibility, especially toward young girls who love sports.

It's a remarkable story, one I truly did not think I'd see in my lifetime, which makes it all the more interesting to tell.

# CHAPTER ONE

# A Dad and His Daughter

The father read the tweet and didn't particularly like it. Many dads might have shrugged it off, but not this one.

The Big Ten Network had sent out a promotional graphic showing the logos of all the various schools playing in the Big Ten/ACC Challenge, a kaleidoscope of letters and symbols and school colors:

> The B1G/ACC Challenge is set. How many wins for the good guys do you see? It's on, @accnetwork. 😼

The father who was about to type a short reply on Twitter the afternoon of October 30, 2020, was, like so many millions of dads in America, a father with an athletic daughter, a girl dad. Because of that, he looked at the tweet and noticed what millions of sports fans never would: that no one from the Big Ten Network had bothered to make the distinction that they were referring to men's basketball and had not mentioned the women's game.

The tweet was about the men's version of the basketball challenge between the Big Ten and the ACC, but that was left unsaid, as it almost always was, because to the Big Ten Network it was a foregone conclusion that an adjective wasn't necessary in the biggest of big-time men's sports, which Big Ten and ACC basketball certainly was.

That didn't mean it should be that way, so the father typed a simple reply: ". . . hmmm. What about the women's teams? WBB matters too."

He then sent his words out into the world, which instantly became attached to the Big Ten Network's original tweet. No one liked his post. No one retweeted it that day, or the next, or the next. On that October day, this father's words went unnoticed.

The name of the man who decided to tweet because he thought women's basketball deserved better was Brent Clark.

His daughter would soon be starting her freshman season in the Big Ten.

Her name was Caitlin. She would not go unnoticed.

•

Caitlin Clark was in the eighth grade, she was on a basketball court, and she was in trouble. She was playing with and against a court full of older girls at an AAU basketball tournament in Hampton, Virginia, and she was trapped in the backcourt, in a corner, and out of any reasonable options. Playing "up" two years on All Iowa Attack coach Dickson Jensen's sophomore team because she already was so good, she was cornered by two defenders and no one from her team was coming to help. More than 100 college coaches were in the gym, watching, recruiting, peering into the future.

Stymied, young Caitlin Clark pictured one way out of the mess she was in. She decided to pass the ball to the only person she could. Herself. With one quick motion, she bounced the ball between the legs of one of her defenders, then pushed her way through both of the players guarding her and grabbed the ball again.

"She caught her own pass," Jensen said, still marveling at the moment nearly a decade after it happened. "Then she was off and running down the court."

The two girls defending her were not off and running down the court. "They were kind of frozen, still standing in the corner, guarding a shadow," he said. "Caitlin was there one second and gone the next. It was like they were guarding a ghost."

Jensen doesn't remember how the possession ended—if Clark scored, even if his team scored. That's because he wasn't watching. "I turned around to my coaches," he said, "and was like, 'Did we all just see what we just saw?' I turned my head and missed whatever happened."

All these years later, he still smiles at the moment. "It was phenomenal. I've never seen anything like it in my life. I mean, from an eighth-grade girl, just tremendous. And everybody's watching, the whole place was like, 'Okay, this kid, this kid's insane.' That's just instinct, that's desire, that's wanting to win, that's creativity, all these things that are making Caitlin so different than any other player we've ever seen in the women's game."

And the best part? "It was a legal basketball play."

•

A year later, magic happened again. In an AAU game against a highly regarded team from Philadelphia, All Iowa Attack was down by 11 points with 1:10 remaining in the game. In other words, the game was over. Clark was now a ninth-grader playing up again, this time with Attack's 17-year-olds. Miraculously, they went on a wild 13–0 run in the final 70 seconds.

All 13 points were scored by Clark.

"There were 2 three-balls, both deep bombs, and she got fouled on both and made the shots, so that's eight points," Jensen said. "And another three-ball for 11. And a layup. And we win the game to get to the Final Four at Nike nationals.

"Everybody in the gym is just like, 'What happened?' Caitlin was not looking for her teammates one ounce in that last run. She said, 'I'm taking this over. I'm gonna win the game because if we lose, we're gone, right? So I'm not gonna lose.' And so, that was her mindset. And in my mind, as a coach, I'm like, 'You go, girl.' I didn't say a word.

I'm just watching it unfold, because you just don't see that kind of stuff. There's a look in her eye. There's a way that she goes about it, just really, really strong."

•

Much of this could have been predicted from the goings-on in gym class and recess a few years earlier in West Des Moines, Iowa.

A call from the elementary school, Saint Francis of Assisi Catholic School, came to the Clark home. Caitlin had been too competitive in gym class. Again. Recess also was an adventure—playing with the boys, keeping up, or more likely even beating them, in everything they did. "I don't want anyone to be better than me," she says now with a sly smile.

She appears to have been born with that mindset. Young Caitlin played anything and everything: soccer, tennis, softball, volleyball, track and field, golf, and, of course, basketball. She was good at all of it. Had she not turned her full-time focus to basketball as a high school junior, soccer could have been her sport. As a freshman at Dowling Catholic High School, she scored 26 goals in only six games (she missed a good portion of the season while representing the United States at an international basketball under-16 championship in Argentina), becoming the only freshman to be named first-team all-state, according to *The Des Moines Register*.

Clark credits her soccer experience with making her a better passer on the basketball court. "I think soccer helped me a lot in reading angles and understanding angles."

Despite spending all this time playing sports and traveling to games, Clark also was a strong student, becoming a member of the National Honor Society and making the Presidential Honor Roll. During the many times that her sports achievements are drawing raves, Clark tries to sneak in a mention that her mother, in particular, is proud of her academic record too.

•

Clark was five when she told her parents she wanted to play basketball, but there were no teams in the area for girls that young, so she joined a boys team her father was coaching. Soon Clark was taking over games with her impressive early skills. This was an adjustment for the boys she was playing against.

Iowa men's basketball player Payton Sandfort was in the same league and remembers losing to Clark's team in the semifinals of a tournament in the first or second grade.

"I was like, 'Oh my gosh, is this what all girls are like?'"

Caitlin continued to play basketball against the boys until the fifth or sixth grade, quite a bit longer than most girls, Jensen said. "At that age, fifth grade, sixth grade, the boys really can be bigger and stronger. What did that mean for her? It just helped her to advance quicker. She was pretty similar size-wise to the boys, but little boys are quicker and faster, and they're a little tougher and a little meaner. We need the speed, we need the quickness, we need the competitiveness, we need the toughness, and you can do that all against boys."

•

Clark was born into a world of sports. Her father, Brent, played basketball and baseball at Iowa's Simpson College and is a member of the Division III school's athletics hall of fame. Her mother, Anne Nizzi-Clark, also grew up in a sports-loving home; her father is former Dowling Catholic football coach Bob Nizzi.

Caitlin has two brothers, one older, one younger. Blake Clark, who grew up to play football at Iowa State, is two years older than her. She wanted to do everything Blake did, and being Caitlin Clark, she often could. Colin Clark, who participated in track and field and basketball, is three years younger.

When Blake had the training wheels taken off his bike, Caitlin protested to her parents that she wanted hers taken off, too, so off they came. She immediately began racing around the family driveway, a bit precariously, on two wheels.

Like millions of other American homes, that driveway was a centerpiece of the Clark kids' sports life. It had a basketball hoop, but one thing it didn't have, because of the way it was slanted, was a full three-point line. Clearly, that had to be rectified, so the Clarks removed some grass and added more concrete to take care of the problem.

Caitlin not only couldn't get enough of playing sports, she also spent hours watching them. "I grew up loving every kind of sport, watching whatever it was that was on TV," she said. Going to high school games when she was little was a dream for her. She had the gear, too, whether it was a miniature Iowa Hawkeyes football uniform, complete with helmet, matching Kansas City Chiefs shorts and shirt, or a pink Peyton Manning Indianapolis Colts jersey. Most important, unlike some families even to this day, she had parents who encouraged and wanted their daughter to play sports just like her brothers.

Clark calls her father "my rock and my person, definitely, about basketball and about sports, that's just kind of a love that we shared together."

But they have different personalities, she said. "As competitive and as fiery as I am, my dad isn't that way. He's just very chill, very relaxed. It was never like 'You have to do this' or 'You have to do that.' He was just a very supportive dad in whatever I wanted to do, so that's something I've been forever grateful for."

•

For generations, our culture had a name for girls like Caitlin Clark: Tomboy.

This wasn't necessarily a compliment. Sporty girls were once anomalies in their neighborhoods. While they ran off to play baseball with the boys, the other girls played with their Barbies or played "dress up" in their mother's closet. This happened for decades in America. Some parents were fine with it, perfectly comfortable having a tomboy in the house. Others, not so much. Some truly wondered if we as a society should be encouraging girls to play sports.

Caitlin Clark's timing was impeccable; she was a competitive girl at the moment the nation was most ready for it. She was born January 22, 2002, just two and a half years after one of the seminal moments not just in women's sports history, but all of American sports, the 1999 Women's World Cup soccer tournament.

On July 10, 1999, a beautiful, sun-splashed day in Southern California, the Rose Bowl was filled with 90,185 fans, with 40 million more watching on television, as the United States and China battled to a scoreless tie through regulation and two overtimes before the US won the World Cup final on penalty kicks. US hero Brandi Chastain and her teammates made the covers of *Time*, *Newsweek*, *People*, and *Sports Illustrated* in the following week, the first and only time that has happened with any news story.

The nation fell in love with what it had created 27 years after the signing of Title IX: strong female athletes, tall and broad-shouldered, aggressive and undaunted, dressed in baggy shorts and shirts, with tall socks and cleats. For decades, Americans had cheered for female athletes in tennis dresses, figure skating sequins, gymnastics leotards, and swimming suits. But the 1999 soccer team led by Mia Hamm, Briana Scurry, and Chastain, among others, didn't look anything like those heroines from other eras. It was raw athleticism that Americans fell for that summer of '99. It was the girl next door we'd all seen in our neighborhoods, coming back from a game with a grass-stained jersey and scuffed-up knees, now all grown up.

Less than three years later, along came Caitlin Clark. What does that mean? For a family like the Clarks, probably not all that much. The Clark kids were going to play sports no matter what, the sons and the daughter. But how the nation would view an utterly fearless, confident, and driven girl playing sports was changing. A level of acceptance existed that had not been there before.

Parents, especially fathers, were all in for their daughters' sports in a way that hadn't happened a generation or two earlier. The coaching was better. The opportunities were greater. The competition was fiercer. The skill was so much more advanced. Everyone was invested. Girls born at the beginning of the 21st century were getting the absolute best of Title IX.

•

When Clark was in the third grade, she listed her goals, in order, for a school project labeled "Future Dreams":

1. Be in the WNBA
2. To live in a huge mansion
3. To have three or four kids
4. To get married
5. To own a restaurant
6. To win the lottery
7. To be in a basketball movie
8. To be strong
9. To go on a basketball scholarship
10. To travel across the whole world
11. To meet Maya Moore
12. To have two Bernese Mountain dogs

The drive from the Clark home in West Des Moines, Iowa, to the Target Center in downtown Minneapolis is around 3 hours and 45 minutes, making the Minnesota Lynx the closest WNBA team to Caitlin as she grew up. It was there, in 2012, that 10-year-old Clark was able to check #11 off her list.

"It was my first WNBA game," Clark said. "They were playing the Seattle Storm. There was some sort of promotional thing going on where you were able to stay after the game and the team had some sort of Q and A, I can't remember exactly what it was, but Maya was a part of it. I don't think I was necessarily supposed to be there. My dad had called the ticket office. If you know my dad, he does everything last minute. So we drove up to Minnesota, got to the hotel, and then he decided to buy tickets to the game.

"And the person at the box office was like, yeah, do you want to come and watch court time? Like, where you can't really get in unless you have a special pass? So, I remember I was sitting courtside and got to watch all the players work out, and I took a picture with some of the players, so that was really cool for me."

That alone would have been made it a thrilling trip, but there was more. "After the game, I got to stay and listen to a Q and A. I didn't have a Sharpie, and obviously, I was at the age where I didn't have a phone, and I kind of just ran away from my dad because I wanted to meet the players. And I just ran up to [Moore], and I just gave her a hug. There's no documentation of that moment, but obviously, in my brain, that was one of the most pivotal moments of, probably, my entire basketball career. And obviously, as a young girl and loving sports, that meant the world to me. I didn't get an autograph. I didn't get a picture. I got a hug, which is probably a lot better than both of those."

•

This illustrated another advancement for Clark's generation of girls growing up playing sports. They had actual female sports role models, dozens of role models to pick from, to watch on TV, to read about in magazines, in books, in the newspaper, online. For generations of girls coming before Clark, there had been a handful of top tennis players, and Olympians, and the occasional golfer, but no major women's professional team sport stars playing locally day in and day out for a full season—because there were no major women's professional team sports. The role models for girls in the '60s, '70s, '80s, and even the '90s were in individual sports, they played sparingly, and they almost never came to your town.

For Clark, role models were plentiful. The list started with Moore, but it didn't end there. Clark had other favorites: Lindsay Whalen, Rebekkah Brunson, Seimone Augustus, and Sylvia Fowles, all of them playing for the Lynx. "I obviously loved that team," Clark said. The first player she met and also took a picture with was Augustus, who at that time held the WNBA rookie scoring record—one that would last until the kid in the photo came along and broke it in 2024. "I got my picture with her on my dad's little phone," Clark said. "It was maybe a BlackBerry back in the day or something like that. It hardly worked, but I vividly remember it. It was the first WNBA player I ever met."

Clark praised them all as players—and more. "They were really good, so they were easy to root for. They played the game the right way, but also all of them were really good people too."

She said that from the perspective of her parents, "Those are the type of people you want your young daughter to idolize . . . just the passion and the joy that you could always see [Moore] play with—she always had a smile, she was competitive, she was fiery, but she was just a solid basketball player. And then, obviously, a solid individual, and even though you have to know her on a personal level to be able to understand that, I think that's, like, the main reason why I loved her so much."

What Clark is to thousands of American girls now, Moore and Mia Hamm were to her. "I remember doing those projects in grade school, I would do it on Mia Hamm," she said on a New York Yankees broadcast. "I remember dressing up as her in, like, second grade. So, it's cool to kind of be in that position now."

Clark often credits her parents for her sense of perspective, which can come in handy now and then, or literally all the time. "I bet on myself and I always believed in myself," she told *Good Morning America*. "My parents always instilled confidence in me. They never told me I couldn't achieve something, but also, I worked really hard for it. . . . I earned it. I deserved it. Nothing was ever given to me."

•

Competition lurked everywhere for young Caitlin Clark. Halloween wasn't just a chance to dress in a costume, ring doorbells, tell a joke (those were the rules in her neighborhood), and score some candy. It was a contest to be played—and won.

"I was worried about beating everybody I was trick-or-treating with to the next house," Clark said. "I was worried about getting the full-size candy bars and being the first to knock on the door."

As she uttered those words, she smiled broadly. "I know that's super surprising."

The way she ran from house to house, it was a workout. "I was in a full sweat at trick or treat. I came home, I had to go straight to the shower before I counted my candy because all that mattered is that I got first. I got first every year at the amount of candy I had. I was the first to the door. I had the best costume. I just dominated trick or treat."

# CHAPTER TWO

# "If You Build It, She Will Come"

Millions of girls and women have played sports in America. A few have become superstars: Serena Williams, Simone Biles, and Katie Ledecky most recently come to mind. But each of those women, and others like them, were in the public eye for quite a few years and competed around the world, wearing the red, white, and blue of the United States in high-profile international events like the Olympic Games.

No female athlete has ever come on the scene so quickly, and dominated it so completely, while wearing her college colors, then the uniform of a WNBA team, as Caitlin Clark.

Why? Out of the millions, why her?

The answers are numerous, but they can begin to be found on the rolling plains of the American heartland, just west of the Mississippi River. In particular, the state of Iowa, with as rich a tradition of encouraging and welcoming young female athletes to play sports as any state in the land.

•

Caitlin Clark was sitting on the edge of her theater-style seat in the front row of the University of Iowa's women's basketball meeting room, tightly gripping the booklet that had just been handed to her. It was September 2022, the beginning of her junior year, the season she would become a household name across the nation. It also was just three months past the fiftieth anniversary of Title IX, the law that directed schools to give girls and women the chance to play sports.

There are 37 words in what is officially known as "Title IX of the Education Amendments of 1972":

> "No person in the United States shall, on the basis of sex, be excluded from participation in, be denied the benefits of, or be subjected to discrimination under any education program or activity receiving Federal financial assistance."

That's it. That's the whole thing. Every girl and woman you watch playing sports in your neighborhood, in your school system, in college, in the pros, in the Olympics, is there, playing that sport, because of those 37 words and the national mindset they created.

For years, Title IX was ignored by many, including high schools and colleges that most definitely were receiving federal financial assistance, which is basically every school, even private schools. Football coaches and athletic directors at our biggest athletic universities scoffed at it.

Women's teams began to spring up, but not without a fight. Some men were dragged kicking and screaming into this time of long-awaited opportunity for girls and women. One was legendary University of Michigan football coach Bo Schembechler, who wrote a letter to Michigan athletic director Don Canham on May 1, 1975, saying that a request by female athletes at the school to receive the same varsity "Block M" letter as male athletes would "minimize the value of the *M* in the eyes of not only our [football] players but the public who place such a high value on it."

Furthermore, Schembechler said if women did receive the same letter *M* as his football players, he would "petition to change the award for football, rather than give identical awards for football and women's sports."

Years later, I was interviewing Schembechler and asked him about it. He apologized.

"What was I thinking?" he said with a laugh.

What he was thinking was what most men were thinking when Title IX began, especially men in athletic departments at colleges around the country, particularly those steeped in football. They saw Title IX as a threat to their sports, as a way to diminish men's sports. They didn't see it for what it really was: the chance for this nation to give the other 50 percent of its population the opportunity to learn how to win, and, even more important, learn how to lose at a young age; to teach girls and women about teamwork, sportsmanship, leadership, and physical fitness.

According to a 2015 survey by EY—the accounting firm Ernst and Young—and ESPNW, 94 percent of women in the C-suites of American companies played sports as they were growing up. Yet, for generations, we were telling girls and women, "No, you cannot learn these life lessons."

What on earth were *we* thinking?

•

Title IX was the reason Clark and her teammates were in their meeting room for a special presentation on that September day in 2022. Amy Wilson, the NCAA's managing director of the office of inclusion, had been asked by Iowa coach Lisa Bluder to speak to her team about the law that made it possible for Clark and her teammates to play basketball at Iowa, to receive full scholarships and charter flights and top-notch coaching, and to have the wonderful lives they had as Division I female athletes in the 21st century.

Young women who play sports often know very little about Title IX, mostly because our schools don't teach them about it, but that wasn't going to be the case at Iowa. Bluder made sure of that. Wilson received her PhD at Iowa in 2013, working under Dr. Christine Grant, who became Iowa's first women's athletic director in 1973. Grant was a dear friend of both Bluder's and Wilson's, so it was natural for Bluder to call on Wilson to come back to Iowa City.

After Wilson handed out her report, titled *The State of Women in College Sports*, she spoke for 20 minutes. The way Clark and her teammates kept eye contact struck her.

"You know when you have a room and when you don't," Wilson said, remembering the moment. "I felt their intense interest." Wilson then answered questions from Bluder for another 10 minutes or so before the players adjourned for practice.

On her way out of the room, Clark approached Wilson. "I really learned a lot, thank you," she told her. They shook hands and Clark went out to the court.

"What athlete does that?" Wilson asked herself. She gives presentations on Title IX around the country, some more successful than others. This one had been a delight.

•

One hundred years ago, when very few American girls played sports, something extraordinary was happening in Iowa. Of course it was. Something magical always seems to be happening there. In the movies, brooding dreamer Ray Kinsella met long-gone baseball legends who had returned to play ball in his Dyersville cornfield in the iconic *Field of Dreams*.

"Is this heaven?" asks Shoeless Joe Jackson, back from the dead.

"No," Kinsella says, "it's Iowa."

When mythical Ray hears a voice telling him, "If you build it, he will come," it might as well have been the voice of the very real leaders of Iowa girls' basketball from decades ago.

They built it, and the girls came. "If you build it, *she* will come."

•

"The farm girl would get her chores done so she could go play basketball, and they'd have hoops in the hay lofts, and when the high school girls' team would make it to state, the town would shut down, and they would all be at the state basketball tournament. The winters in Iowa—it was girls' basketball that would get you through it."

The brand of basketball Caitlin Clark's college coach, Lisa Bluder, was describing doesn't exist today. But because it did exist as long as 100 years ago, and it existed in a state that has never had men's major-league professional sports—other than the brief run of the Waterloo Hawks in the National Basketball League and then the NBA from 1948 to 1950—a precedent was established. If our girls are playing basketball, those long-ago Iowans said, we'll support, respect, and adore them as we do our boys, perhaps even more.

Does this devotion to girls playing basketball sound familiar to anyone now? "The seeds were being planted for Caitlin Clark all the way back then," said Dr. Peg Burke, an Iowa professor and colleague of Christine Grant's for decades.

This was Iowa's 6x6 girls' basketball. Three girls on each team played offense on one half of the court and three played defense on the other half. The other team had the same configuration. No one could cross the half-court line, mostly because of fears at that time that girls didn't have the fitness and stamina to play full-court basketball. Maybe they'd never be able to have children if they ran the length of the court. Or perhaps they didn't want girls to perspire. Who knew? Only two dribbles were allowed before a player had to pass or shoot. Forwards were the only players allowed to shoot. Guards could play only defense.

The games often were offensive masterpieces, with teams regularly scoring over 100 points. In 1987, high school senior Jan Jensen, who would later go on to coach with Bluder at Iowa, then succeed her, averaged a stunning 66 points per game. It all was so popular that the state tournament drew thousands to Des Moines each year.

Bluder grew up in Marion, Iowa, outside Cedar Rapids, and played 6x6 basketball for Linn-Mar High School. She was a forward, meaning she played solely on offense. Her team at Linn-Mar in the mid- to late 1970s was "good, but not great," never making it into the 16-team state tournament. "It still burns me to this day," she said. "It does, it honestly does, it gets to me."

As with Indiana boys' basketball, celebrated in the movie *Hoosiers*, there was just one state girls' tournament back then, no matter the size of the school. And if the teams didn't make the tournament as players, they went as spectators. "Every year, every girls' basketball team would go to the state tournament because that's something you would dream about, being a part of it," Bluder said.

Brenda Frese, the University of Maryland head coach who led the Terrapins to the 2006 NCAA title, was nine years behind Bluder, growing up in Cedar Rapids. She played 6x6 through eighth grade before her school switched to 5x5 in the mid-1980s, nearly a decade ahead of the statewide decision to end 6x6 in 1993. "I remember the crowds that would go out and support the girls' game," Frese said. "You had half-court basketball, 6x6, it didn't have the speed and the entertainment value that the women's game has now, yet the fans in Iowa would still support it."

•

But let's get back to that rule that astounds us today: Girls weren't allowed to run full-court.

"This is so silly now," Bluder said, "but I do remember working so hard that you'd get to that half-court line and you'd bend over and catch your breath because you were so out of breath as the other team played. We'd just be standing there at the half-court line while the other side was on offense and defense, and I laugh now to think that we really got tired playing this game."

When Bluder was in high school, a survey was sent around asking about the possibility of switching to 5x5. The winds in women's sports were shifting, and Iowa was an outlier. The 6x6 game allowed girls to play either offense or defense, but not both. This wasn't exactly enticing to women's college coaches around the nation whose teams were playing the 5x5 game. As the level of competition rose and the stakes grew higher in the college game, it was the rare coach who would take a chance and recruit a girl who had played only 6x6 her entire life, never having run the length of the court or learned both offense and defense. If the goal was to continue their athletic careers in college, Iowa girls were playing the wrong game in high school.

The change to 5x5 happened after Bluder left high school, but because she was a forward, meaning she had been able to hone her shooting skills throughout her high school career, she received a half scholarship to play at the University of Northern Iowa.

But those girls across the state who were the guards, who only played defense? They usually weren't so lucky, because, as Bluder said, "They didn't know how to shoot the ball."

•

When Dr. Christine Grant settled behind her desk in her new office in Iowa City as the University of Iowa women's athletic director in 1973, she knew the fight for women's equality in sports wasn't going to be easy. She knew this because Title IX was so new, having just been signed by President Richard Nixon a year earlier. She also knew this because of where her office was located in Iowa's women's gymnasium.

In the kitchen.

Iowa's president at the time, Willard "Sandy" Boyd, had just elevated 12 women's club sports to varsity status. Grant called that move "astonishing" in an interview we did in 2012. "We had no place to put people for a brand-new varsity program, and they had to put me somewhere, so I ended up literally in the kitchen. I had a desk, but I also had a stove and a sink. Occasionally, one of the secretaries would call and say, 'Christine, would you put on my soup, please?' and I did."

Grant's budget for that first year was $3,000. "That was for everything," she said. "There were no coaches' salaries. We got time off from some of our other responsibilities to coach."

The now-varsity female athletes didn't have it so great either. "Literally, we had one set of jerseys in that first year, so athletes from different sports shared them. With 12 sports as diverse as gymnastics and basketball, it took a lot of creativity to get the necessities for all of our sports. We had a laundry, obviously, and it was used nonstop."

Of all the indignities this fledgling program faced, Grant said, the worst might have been that the Hawkeye women's basketball team had to play in a gym that was not regulation size. "Between the sideline and the wall, there was no space," said Grant, who served as women's athletic director at Iowa until 2000 and died in 2021 at 85. "But we had to play there because our women's team wasn't allowed into our main fieldhouse."

The University of Iowa ended up building another basketball arena in 1983, the one now known as Carver-Hawkeye Arena. The women's team was most definitely allowed to play there.

•

Even though Grant is gone, her spirit and message remain alive for the Hawkeye basketball players. Bluder, who coached at Iowa from 2000 to 2024, would ask Grant to come by to speak to her teams, as she would later ask Amy Wilson to do. "When Christine was healthy, I'd bring her in every two years," Bluder said, "and she'd give a lecture on gender equity and Title IX. And it was amazing to me because the players just don't know the history of our game. And then, when Christine wasn't feeling well, and then, obviously, when she passed, I talked about her a lot."

The great Billie Jean King, the tennis pioneer who beat Bobby Riggs in 1973's "Battle of the Sexes" and fought for equal pay for women in tennis decades before the issue became popular in other sports, has a word for this.

"You know what Billie Jean always says, right? Know your 'herstory,' and know who came before you, and honor those people," said US soccer standout Julie Foudy, who has worked with King on women's sports issues for a quarter century. "Title IX isn't taught in most schools, so I love that Lisa Bluder had these sessions with her players, including Caitlin. It's important that every young woman understands that we stand on the shoulders of the giants who came before us."

It sometimes was more than conversation for Bluder and her players. During Clark's first Final Four, in Dallas, on the morning before Iowa's game with No. 1 South Carolina, Bluder gathered her players together in a circle during the team's shootaround. This was normal operating procedure for Bluder, bringing the team together to sit on the floor. But this time, she had something special to pass around.

Grant was born in Scotland—her sport was field hockey—before making her way to Iowa.

"Somebody had given me one of her old Scottish V-neck sweaters, and so I passed it around that morning," Bluder said. "I talked about Dr. Grant . . . about her importance and how she'd be so proud of this team, and would have loved to have been there, and the team knew how much I had a love for Christine. And so, I think that meant a lot to them, too, just because they knew I loved her."

How much that meant to Bluder's players was on display a year and a half later, when Clark, participating in her final interview of the 2024 WNBA season at Gainbridge Fieldhouse in Indianapolis, was asked about how the grand tradition of support for girls' and women's basketball in Iowa helped prepare her for the massive attention she received during her rookie year with the Indiana Fever.

There was no mention of Title IX in the question, nor of Christine Grant. Yet, barely 36 hours removed from the end of an unprecedented and intense first season, Clark answered this way:

"I don't think people always realize the University of Iowa was one of the premier universities in Title IX. Dr. Grant was obviously somebody that was very close to my coach . . . and she wanted women to have as many opportunities as men, and if it wasn't for her, and if it wasn't for the way she fought for women's athletics, I'm not sure I would have had that opportunity at Iowa. And I'm not sure people would have showed up for the women's basketball program in the manner that they did every single night. People don't realize that the women's basketball program at Iowa had so many fans before I got there, and then they continued to rally around our teams and celebrate our teams, and they just love women's basketball and the way it was played and the people on the court, and I think a lot of that has definitely carried over to the WNBA. . . ."

The Title IX presentation, the Bluder conversations, Grant's sweater—someone clearly was paying attention.

# CHAPTER THREE

# Decisions, Decisions

Caitlin Clark almost didn't become the Caitlin Clark we know today. When she was in high school, she originally made a decision that could have changed everything: she was going to Notre Dame.

As her senior year at Dowling Catholic High School unfolded, Clark was committed to playing basketball in South Bend, Indiana. It made all the sense in the world. Coach Muffet McGraw's program was one of the nation's finest, strong on the court and in the classroom, both of which were important to Clark. Caitlin also is Catholic, which certainly made Notre Dame more appealing.

McGraw, who won NCAA titles at Notre Dame in 2001 and 2018, first saw Clark in person playing for All Iowa Attack at an AAU tournament when she was a high school sophomore.

"I loved the way she could pass," McGraw said. "I was looking for a point guard and I was like, 'Oh my God, she is a great passer. She's got great vision.'" McGraw didn't see Clark launching three-pointers as she does now, but the coach made a mental note when she saw one or two. "I remember thinking, 'I'm not sure if I'm going to want her to take that shot. That could be something that she's going to have to figure out in the offense.'"

But McGraw wasn't worried. In addition to the passes, she adored Clark's personality. "Just how much she wanted to win, her competitive spirit. I just liked her right away. I remember talking to her, thinking, 'I want to coach her.' I just could relate to her. I thought we had a pretty good connection, which doesn't always happen, because as I got older and kids got younger, I have nothing in common with them. But with her, it was different. I mean, she has just a great family, she had her values in the right place, we really had some great conversations early on the phone. So I always came away from my conversations with her thinking, 'Man, I really want her, I really want her to come here. I think she'd be great.'"

But something didn't feel quite right. Even after giving McGraw the good news, Clark hadn't yet gone public with word that she was, in fact, going to Notre Dame. McGraw noticed. How could a head coach not notice that? "It was interesting, because once she committed, it was still, I thought, kind of a soft commitment, because she didn't announce it publicly."

Clark also was still in touch with the Iowa coaches, McGraw said, which seemed a little strange to her considering Clark was planning to play for her, not them. McGraw happened to run into one of them at a funeral. "Why do you guys keep talking to Caitlin?" McGraw asked.

"She's calling us."

Reflecting on it much later, McGraw said, "That's when I knew, yeah, okay, we're done."

•

Clark had a phone call to make. She went to her bedroom. She was nervous. This wasn't going to be easy. She called McGraw and told her she had changed her mind. She was not coming to South Bend. It was November 2019. Caitlin Clark was going to be an Iowa Hawkeye.

"My memory of the call is thinking that she handled it well," McGraw said. "It wasn't a surprise at that point. I mean, she didn't want to leave Iowa."

Other suitors who never got as far as McGraw saw it clear as day.

"I thought I'd lose her to Notre Dame," said Northwestern coach Joe McKeown. "I tried to recruit her hard. Then I realized she ain't leaving Iowa."

"She definitely wasn't leaving Iowa," said Maryland coach Brenda Frese.

"We heard she was interested in staying close to home," said former Stanford coach Tara VanDerveer.

What was bad news for Notre Dame, and Northwestern, and Maryland, and Stanford, and many other schools, turned out to be wonderful news for women's basketball.

Why? Because had Caitlin Clark gone somewhere other than the University of Iowa, especially a top-ranked program like Notre Dame or the University of Connecticut, she might never have been the Caitlin Clark the nation has come to know. The green light to take over games and launch so many threes, the never-ending love of Iowa fans who always showed up for their local girl, the enormous platform of the mighty Big Ten Conference and the long reach of its Big Ten Network—all contributed to making Clark the omnipresent personality she became.

"It would have been great to have her at Notre Dame, and our fan base would have loved her," McGraw said. "But Iowa just made so much sense. She made a great decision, looking at how it turned out. It sounds terrible to say, because they went to two Final Fours with her, but we would have had better players around her and she would have had more help, so it would have been different. Maybe we would have won an NCAA championship. Who knows? I'm looking at it from my perspective. But I mean, Iowa? She could probably run for governor."

This could become a fun game of What If?

"If she went to UConn [where she was not recruited], unfortunately because they're such a powerhouse that pushes out talent literally every year, she might have fallen to just one of another of Geno's [Coach Geno Auriemma's] all-stars," said then–Washington Mystics associate head coach LaToya Sanders at the 2024 Povich Center panel on Clark at the University of Maryland.

ESPN senior writer Michael Voepel, who has reported on Clark for the length of her college and pro career, said Clark's allure today has everything to do with staying in Iowa. "I think she would have still been a great player had she gone somewhere else, but the legend wouldn't have been the same," Voepel said. "She's an Iowa kid playing for Iowa, and especially in today's world of constant transferring and everything else that takes college athletes a little bit away from what people want to idealistically believe they are, Caitlin was a throwback and that appealed to people.

"She also never would have become the all-time leading scorer at the blue-blood programs because that simply wouldn't have been allowed due to the system they play," he added. "But she didn't need a blue-blood program to become big. She went to a good program, no question, but a program that hadn't been to the Final Four since nine years before she was born. She bet on herself and she bet on herself in the one place that loved her the most and that she loved the most."

Said Frese: "Kudos to the kids that have that inner belief in themselves to take the harder path. That's what Caitlin did."

•

Dickson Jensen had a front-row seat for all of this. As he does for all his AAU players, he listed the pros and cons of the various schools Clark was considering, including Oregon, where Clark was shown around by Ducks star Sabrina Ionescu, who is four years older than Clark. "She loved that area," Jensen said, but she wasn't going to go to college there.

"It was about staying closer to home; the reality of it was closeness to family," Jensen said. "If Notre Dame would have been in Iowa City, and Iowa would have been in South Bend, Indiana, she would have gone to Notre Dame."

There was a time when Clark, like probably every girl basketball player in the country, wanted to be a UConn Husky, but Geno Auriemma's lack of interest in her is no mystery. Paige Bueckers, the No. 1

high school recruit in the nation, committed to UConn in April 2019. Clark was highly regarded, the No. 4 recruit in the nation, but at the time not quite as sought after as Bueckers. Interestingly, the two young women grew up less than a four-hour drive apart, Paige in the Minneapolis suburbs, Caitlin in the Des Moines suburbs. They're also almost exactly the same age, just three months apart: Bueckers born in October 2001, Clark in January 2002.

"Paige and Caitlin, are you really going to have them both?" Jensen asked.

Jensen is not completely sold on the idea Clark would not have been Clark at another school. "If she still goes to Notre Dame, good question, we'll never know, but I don't want to say Caitlin would not have been Caitlin. I think because she is so special, I would say I could put her in any environment and somehow that environment will flip and turn, and Caitlin will become Caitlin and do Caitlin things."

That said, there is no doubt, he says, that the marriage of Clark and Iowa was magical, running through his AAU club. In her four years at Iowa, several of her Hawkeye teammates also were Attack alums, including Hannah Stuelke, Kylie Feuerbach, and Sydney Affolter.

Jensen had conversations with all of them. He related how one went: "So, Hannah, you've got to know and appreciate and want to be Robin to her Batman. You're not going to be Batman. Caitlin is Batman."

The players understood. "Because they'd all played with me and kind of been in that environment, they were like, 'Well, of course, I want to do that. Caitlin is great. We love Caitlin. And, you know, I'm fine with that, and Caitlin gets me the ball.'"

Said Jensen, "Caitlin makes all those kids look better and so they were very comfortable with that, which allowed Caitlin to be Caitlin quicker."

The homegrown kids knew their roles because there was no secret about how Iowans viewed Clark. "This was kind of our joke," Jensen said. "Instead of saying, 'are you going to the Iowa game tonight,' most people would say, 'are you going to Caitlin's game tonight?'"

•

Jensen played a vital role in another area of Clark's development: her on-court behavior. Every college coach who recruited her saw it at one time or another: a flash of anger at a teammate or a referee, a flurry of complaints, an outburst on the court. She was such a talented athlete that they looked beyond it, but it was there.

"We started on that very early when she was playing with us," Jensen said, "and she also needed to be reminded a lot when she was in eighth and ninth grade because that was when she started to get out in front of coaches, and everybody started talking about it, and that could have spun one direction or the other direction."

He said these conversations happened after games, at practices, in hallways, sometimes with her parents, sometimes just with him. "We said, 'Caitlin, you know, you don't do this without your teammates. You don't do this without your coaches. You don't do this without your family. You don't do this without the referees. And you do this by respecting them. They're going to allow you to be Caitlin and if you don't get everybody else on board, it's going to be harder to be Caitlin.' And she knew what I meant. We were going to try to help her mature and be not only the basketball player that we see today, but the person that we all see and admire."

Kristin Meyer, Clark's high school coach at Dowling Catholic, also spent a fair share of time working with Clark on her on-court demeanor. "I would say probably, on average, two times a game I would sub her out for body-language-type things. There were certain times when things weren't acceptable, things I wouldn't accept from other players."

Meyer's message to Clark was simple: "If you're worried about the calls on the court, or your opponent, then you can't be focused on the next play. If you're worried that they didn't call a foul on your layup and you're complaining to the refs, then you're not running back on defense, or if you're throwing your hands up because your teammate wasn't ready for your no-look pass and turned the ball over, then you're not transitioning to defense—or what is that message you're giving to your teammate, who already is a little bit nervous because they know they're not at the same level?"

Meyer praised Clark, saying she is "one of the smartest people I know. She makes judgments quicker than almost anyone, on the court and off. . . . She knows the game so well, she expects things to be somewhat fair, so when someone fouls her, she expects there to be a call. Part of it, especially at the high school level, was she probably was fouled every possession, just for people to be able to stay close enough to her that she didn't score every time, and so the refs were in a tough spot at times because you call every single foul and then the game takes forever. So there were times that she was just frustrated, and it's okay, so how do we channel that into moving on to the next play?"

All of this, Meyer said, was part of the challenge and delight of coaching Caitlin Clark. "She just has a bold personality. She's going to play big. . . . It's just natural reactions, how she reacts is kind of like how she plays the game, just by feel and just in the moment. You don't want to make her into a statue."

•

It's almost impossible to imagine Caitlin Clark playing in empty arenas anywhere, especially in the women's basketball–crazed state of Iowa. But there she was, in her first game in college, November 25, 2020, at home against Northern Iowa, driving to the basket and shooting threes silhouetted against whole sections of seats without people in them, not a soul to be seen, in Iowa's Carver-Hawkeye Arena.

Clark was one of those unlucky kids who were members of the high school class of 2020. She and her peers got the worst of the COVID-19 pandemic, robbing her senior year of rite-of-passage events, including several all-star basketball games that were canceled. And when it was time to start playing for the Hawkeyes, very little was the way it was supposed to be. Clark looked up at the seats and saw cardboard cutouts filling some and nothing at all filling others. She and her teammates played in relative silence broken only by the squeaking of their shoes, the referees' whistles, the occasional shouted instructions of masked coaches, and a thin smattering of applause from the bench and school officials and family members who were allowed in. The announced attendance for her first game was 365. The place holds 14,998.

In that game, Clark scored 27 points, including 3 three-pointers, and had 8 rebounds, 4 assists, and 3 steals. She shot 58 percent from the field. Iowa beat Northern Iowa, 96–81.

"She is what we expected," Lisa Bluder said. "We'd been hoping for this day for a long time, that we would actually get to coach her, so it was fun to have that happen."

Clark was most definitely on her way. She scored 30 or more points in three of her first five games and had a triple-double within a month. When the season was over, Clark had had a stunning freshman year. She led the nation in points per game (26.6), assists (214), total points (799), and three-pointers made (116), winning all kinds of awards and honors, nationally and in the Big Ten, but not the various National Player of the Year awards (those went to fellow freshman Bueckers), nor even an Associated Press first-team All-America selection.

"Freshman year, I was, like, the media darling," Bueckers said in April 2024.

Clark's season ended with the two of them meeting in the NCAA Sweet Sixteen, where UConn defeated Iowa, 92–72. Clark had 21 points to Bueckers's 18, but Bueckers outrebounded Clark (9–3) and produced more assists (8–5) as the Huskies made their way to the Final Four. That would not be the last of their college rivalry.

•

There is a notion that Clark is so poised, it's almost too good to be true, that perhaps it's a sign that she is a product of constant professional media training. In that freshman year, in January 2021, Clark and Iowa were going to be on national TV for the first time on the Big Ten Network. Lisa Byington and Meghan McKeown were the announcers on the game, being played at Northwestern, where McKeown had played guard and her father, Joe, is the head coach.

"We were going to see Caitlin Clark for the first time, this freshman who's doing big things," McKeown said. "So, we obviously asked to talk to Caitlin before the game, and we get on a Zoom with her, and I tell you what, from start to finish, I was so impressed with how mature and poised she was as a freshman, just from being really personable to answering every question."

Because Clark played with speed and abandon even then, turnovers had become an issue, just as they still can be, so the broadcasters ended up asking the 18-year-old about her mistakes, which can be a touchy subject for a freshman.

Not Clark.

"She answered so well and was so thorough," McKeown said. "She said, 'Yeah, I know it's a problem,' and explained her process. For her to have that type of maturity kind of blew me out of the water, and even her presence on the Zoom call was impressive, which can be really hard when you're talking to someone for the first time and not picking up on social cues and whatnot as you do in person."

It turns out that Clark scored only eight points in that game, an Iowa loss, the only time she was held to single digits in her entire Iowa career, which spanned 139 games. During games like that, the COVID-19 year became a blessing in disguise for her. "I think it almost played to my advantage that I was getting to play in front of nobody," she said. "You don't have that added pressure of the environment and the crowd that you're trying to navigate as well as navigate the game."

•

Playing in front of nobody wasn't going to last long.

Clark's Iowa running mate and best friend Kate Martin calls it, simply, "the Michigan game." Others might know it from the omnipresent TV highlights as the game with the pink jerseys, which the Hawkeyes were wearing to highlight breast cancer awareness.

Whatever the case, it's the moment that awakened not the women's basketball world—they were already wide awake—but the sports nation as a whole to something unusual happening in the Big Ten.

It was February 6, 2022, in Ann Arbor, Michigan, Clark's sophomore year. Michigan, ranked sixth in the nation, had led No. 21 Iowa by as many as 25 points and was up by 16 points going into the fourth quarter. The Wolverines won by eight, 98–90.

Sounds like a rather routine loss for the Hawkeyes, doesn't it?

Clark scored 25 points in those 10 minutes.

Flying all over the court, throwing the ball into the air from practically anywhere, Clark made 8 of 10 shots in the quarter, including four-for-five from beyond the three-point arc, all four of which she launched while dancing near—or once even standing on—Michigan's large blue midcourt Block M logo. If people occasionally liberally apply the adjective "logo" to a Clark three-pointer, that was not the case this time.

Clark finished with 46 points. The highlights from the Big Ten Network broadcast spread quickly, from ESPN's *SportsCenter* to social media and back again.

"We had a bunch of people out due to COVID," Martin said in an interview for this book. "We only had seven players eligible that entire game, and so we were dog tired, but at the end of that game, Caitlin was just bringing us back into that game single-handedly. She was just coming down in transition, and literally, she hit probably five or six logo threes [during the entire game]. And that went a little viral and people were like, 'She's the real deal.'"

Spectators were coming back to games that season, and that mattered, Martin said. "She had a lot of buzz her freshman year, but nobody could come and see that in person [due to COVID]. You'd see it on

TV, but when you saw something like that in person, it was almost magical. Something that's just super cool that I hear a lot from my dad's friends or from my brother's friends or just a lot of men in general is, 'Yeah, you know, I never really watched women's basketball, but then I watched you guys, I watched the Iowa Hawkeyes, and I fell in love.'"

Clark's stunning show that February evening in Michigan, as wild as it was, didn't surprise Martin. "We'd scrimmage and she was doing that in those games. It happened in two different scrimmages, I vividly remember, where we were down, and she came back and hit, like, 4 threes in a row, and nobody could guard her, nobody could do anything about it, and we'd come back and win. And it was just insane."

Iowa had a strong regular season, clinching a share of the Big Ten title and then winning the conference tournament with hopes that the previous year's Sweet Sixteen run was just the beginning. But the season abruptly ended with a crushing upset loss at home in the second round of the NCAA Tournament, 64–62, to 10th-seeded Creighton. Rotating three different defenders on Clark, Creighton held her to 15 points on 21 percent shooting.

Nonetheless, individual awards cascaded in. Clark was named Big Ten Player of the Year, made AP first-team All-America as well as every other All-America list, and was a finalist for all the big national awards. She once again led the nation in points per game (27.0), this time also in assists per game (8.0), total points (863), triple-doubles (5), and 30-point games (11). She was the first Division I player to lead the nation in points per game and assists per game in the same season—and she was only halfway through her college career.

# CHAPTER FOUR

# "You Can't See Me"

How often does the heartland ever turn heads on the coasts? When does one of the nation's biggest cultural stories emanate from a college town far from the bright lights of our biggest cities? In 2023, with Clark at Iowa, that's exactly what happened.

This was the season Clark, now a junior, became the first women's player in Big Ten history to sweep the National Player of the Year awards while leading Iowa to its first Final Four since 1993. This was the season Clark lifted an entire team to not just the Final Four, but the NCAA title game. This was the season that the nation got a good look at Clark and her enticing style of play, both earnest and effortless, and decided it wanted more. Much more.

"It took someone very special like Caitlin to come around," Kate Martin said. "And I think, post-COVID, everybody started watching. We missed sports, right? They missed coming to events. And also in the social media era that we're in, you get information quick, right? It's just crazy how much you can see in such a short amount of time, like one thing happens and it's tweeted a million times, or it's got a million shares, whatever."

That was certainly the case with Clark's off-kilter, three-point buzzer-beater to defeat Indiana in late February. Iowa then won the Big Ten Tournament for a second consecutive year before beginning to work its way through the NCAA Tournament as a No. 2 seed. There was a nerve-racking game against Georgia where Brent Clark was caught on camera doubled over with anxiety in the final minutes, the picture of every dad watching a child during a big game.

Soon, there was an Elite Eight showdown between Iowa and Louisville, a fifth seed, for the Hawkeyes to finally make it back to the Final Four. And in that game, Clark outdid herself with a brilliant performance. She became the first player in NCAA Tournament history, male or female, to have a 40-point triple-double: 41 points with 12 assists and 10 rebounds to lead the Hawkeyes to a 97–83 victory.

"I dreamed of this moment as a little girl," Clark said, "to take a team to the Final Four and be in these moments and have confetti fall down on me."

But a certain moment of theatrics lingered long beyond the game. After sinking her sixth three-pointer, Clark was caught on camera waving her right hand in front of her face, mimicking the "You can't see me" gesture made famous by actor and professional wrestler John Cena. The presumption on social media was that Clark was taunting Hailey Van Lith, Louisville's star guard and a teammate of hers on USA Basketball's under-19 team at the 2019 World Cup.

As with practically anything Clark did, the video took on a life of its own. Cena himself got into the act, tweeting, "Even if they could see you . . . they couldn't guard you!"

Others who saw it included LSU's Angel Reese.

•

To reach the final, Iowa had to defeat defending national champion and top-ranked South Carolina in the Final Four. A tall order, to be sure, but Clark was now saving her best moments for her biggest moments. She scored 41 points again to carry Iowa to a 77–73 victory, while adding another controversial gesture that turned into a viral moment: dismissively waving off wide-open South Carolina freshman guard

Raven Johnson, daring her to shoot rather than guarding her. It worked. Johnson didn't attempt the three-pointer, passing to a teammate.

Earlier, LSU defeated Virginia Tech, so the stage was set for something that would have been unthinkable in women's basketball even months earlier: a true national rivalry between two female players, with people taking sides and millions thoroughly invested.

Caitlin vs. Angel, Clark vs. Reese.

•

Unbeknownst to the throngs of newcomers to women's basketball, Caitlin Clark and Angel Reese go back a long way. They played on different powerhouse teams in AAU basketball, then faced each other in the Big Ten when Reese was at Maryland for two years before transferring to LSU. They both have big personalities and big games, are eminently quotable, and are absolutely beloved by their fans.

That's what they have in common. Otherwise, Reese is three inches taller than Clark, 6'3" to 6'0", they play different positions, have different roles on the court, and don't guard each other. Of course, one is white, the other Black. And while both are stars, one is more visible during a game than the other, simply by nature of the position she plays and the way she dominates a game with the ball in her hands.

All eyes are on Clark, the point guard, as she brings the ball up the court, either alone or with a defender shadowing her. She is the quarterback. She creates the action—running, passing, shooting. That's why, for those who never spent much time watching basketball BCC (Before Caitlin Clark), she's so simple to follow. She's like Tiger Woods in that way, the singular athlete on your TV screen, easy to identify, doing spectacular things.

"It's the threes, it's the passing, it's her vision on the court," said former Stanford coach Tara VanDerveer. "I actually think she's a better passer than shooter, but the threes—it's not just the fact that she shoots threes, it's a long three-point shot, but she's not shooting it because time is running out; it's just her shot. Everything she does, she carries her team, it's just phenomenal."

Reese's role is different. She is an exceptionally mobile forward, an explosive force around the rim, a tireless rebounder, a defensive stalwart, a fearless competitor. She's at her best when she's fighting for position under the basket, grabbing rebounds and creating opportunities for her teammates and herself.

So, in many ways, they had little to do with one another on the afternoon of April 2, 2023, in the NCAA final—until events at the end of the game ensured they had everything to do with one another.

•

LSU had the game won. Its lead was insurmountable when, with less than a minute remaining, Reese proudly walked up to the vanquished Clark, waving her hand in her own face, mocking the gesture Clark had made in the Louisville game. Reese also pointed to her fourth finger, indicating where her NCAA championship ring would be going. In the game's final seconds, Reese followed Clark around the court, doing it again.

Clark kept walking and paid no attention, but this was a moment that was not going away, exacerbated by First Lady Dr. Jill Biden's unprecedented public call to invite both winner LSU and runner-up Iowa to the White House. It was a bad idea that was roundly criticized and quickly withdrawn. Clark herself said it shouldn't happen, one of dozens of instances when she said exactly the right thing at the right time. The winning team goes to the White House. The losing team does not.

Reese's gestures toward Clark immediately blew up on social media, naturally, so Clark was asked about them minutes after she left the court in her press conference.

"Honestly, I have no idea," she said. "I was just trying to get to the handshake line and shake hands and be grateful that my team was in that position. That's all you can do, is hold your head high, be proud of what you did, and all the credit in the world to LSU, they were tremendous. They deserve it. They had a tremendous season. Kim Mulkey coached them so, so well. She's one of the best basketball coaches of all time, and it shows. And she only said really kind things to me in the handshake line. So, I'm very grateful for that too . . . I was just trying to spend the last few moments on the court with, especially, the five people that I've started 93 games with and relishing every second of that."

Amid the LSU celebration and trophy ceremony, Reese's first public words about what she did were delivered courtside on the ESPN set.

"I was waiting, I tell you, I was waiting, I was waiting," she said. "Caitlin Clark is a hell of a player, for sure, but I don't take disrespect lightly, and she disrespected . . . South Carolina, they're still my SEC girls, too. Y'all not gonna disrespect them either. I wanted to pick her pocket, but I had a moment at the end of the game, and I was just in my bag, I was in my moment."

In her press conference, Reese went further.

"All year, I was critiqued about who I was," she said. "I don't fit the narrative. I don't fit in the box that y'all want me to be in. I'm too 'hood. I'm too ghetto. Y'all told me that all year. But when other people do it, y'all say nothing.

"So, this was for the girls that look like me, that's going to speak up on what they believe in. It's unapologetically you, and that's what I did it for tonight. It was bigger than me tonight. It was bigger than me. Twitter is going to go in a rage every time. And I mean, I'm happy. I feel like I've helped grow women's basketball this year."

Back and forth it went in those early-April days—and in many ways, it's still going back and forth today, now in the WNBA. Had this happened a generation ago, before social media, it would have been discussed for a while by fans, work colleagues, neighbors, and families—and that would have been that. The players would have mostly moved on.

But not now, not in today's world. No, this is a topic that has never left us.

Two days after the championship game, Clark was asked about it all on ESPN. "We're all competitive. We all show our emotions in a different way. Angel's a tremendous, tremendous player. I have nothing but respect for her. I love her game. The way she rebounds the ball, scores the ball, is absolutely incredible. I'm a big fan of her—even the entire LSU team, they played an amazing game. I don't think there should be any criticism for what she did."

Asked specifically by ESPN anchor Jeremy Schaap about the racial component in what transpired, Clark said: "I don't think Angel should be criticized at all. I'm just one that competes, and she competed. I think everybody knew there was going to be a little trash talk in the entire tournament. It's not just me and Angel."

Clark also defended bold, brash play. "I'm just lucky enough that I get to play this game and have emotion and wear it on my sleeve, and so does everybody else. . . . That should never be criticized because I believe that's what makes this game so fun. That's what draws people to this game. . . . That's how I'm going to continue to play. That's how every girl should continue to play."

Angel Reese and LSU won that day in Dallas, 102–85. Reese scored 15 points with 10 rebounds and was named the tournament's most outstanding player. Clark scored 30 points with 8 threes and 8 assists.

Other numbers surrounding the Final Four ended up being so much more important. The first of the two NCAA semifinals, the LSU–Virginia Tech game, was watched by 3.4 million viewers. The later game was Iowa vs. South Carolina. That attracted 5.5 million viewers, making it the most-watched women's semifinal in history. What's more, Clark's presence elevated that Iowa–South Carolina semifinal to a higher rating than the previous year's NCAA final. The 2022 title game, featuring two of the best-known women's programs in the country, South Carolina and UConn, was watched by 4.85 million, which was considered a terrific viewership number. It was the most-viewed women's national championship game since 2004. And then it was beaten by a semifinal a year later.

So, it was no surprise at all that viewership for the Iowa–LSU final—9.9 million—was more than double the previous year's number. Women's basketball, and women's sports, were in new, uncharted territory.

•

It was two months later, on June 12, 2023, that Hailey Van Lith was asked about Clark's "You can't see me" gesture by *Bleacher Report*'s Taylor Rooks. "Right after the game, I texted her and I was like, 'The media is dumb. I'm sorry. They just make stuff up,'" Van Lith told Rooks. "We were laughing about it because she did it to her strength coach, she didn't do it to anyone on our team, especially me. I didn't even see it in the game, I was probably dribbling the ball up the court after she just hit a three in our face. It's just funny how camera angles and perceptions are skewed. . . . We laughed about it after."

CHAPTER FIVE

# "You Break It, You Own It"

The only way for Caitlin Clark to not play in front of a sold-out home crowd during her historic senior year was for Iowa to host a basketball game in a football stadium.

The Hawkeyes decided to start the season on October 15, 2023, with an exhibition game against DePaul University at Kinnick Stadium—called Crossover at Kinnick—that drew 55,646. The stadium can hold 69,250 for football games. The basketball court was placed near one end zone, which meant a lot of people bought tickets knowing they would be far, far away from the action.

But they were part of history: the largest crowd ever in women's basketball. Clark wore long sleeves in 53-degree weather with winds of 15–20 miles per hour whipping across the court, yet still managed a 34-point triple-double as the Hawkeyes won a game that didn't count, 94–72.

"You stop and think," Coach Lisa Bluder said, "we had over 55,000 people there. We should have known then, right? We should have known then just what was going to happen."

•

Iowa sold out every other home game for Clark's senior year—all the rest were indoors in Carver-Hawkeye Arena. Most of their road games

43

were sellouts as well, with hundreds waiting in line for hours outside in the winter cold for a general admission seat to see the Iowa phenom. The Big Ten women's tournament also was sold out for the first time.

TV viewership, too, was going way up for Clark, as were her appeal and exposure due to the NCAA's 2021 ruling allowing athletes to profit from their name, image, and likeness (NIL). The national commercials started rolling out as her senior year began. By the time she completed college, she reportedly had at least 11 NIL deals worth more than $3 million, with State Farm and Gatorade leading the way. This meant TV viewers watching one of her games never stopped seeing her: When an Iowa game went to a time-out and Clark went to the bench, she didn't disappear from the screen. No, she often immediately appeared again in a State Farm commercial, in the same uniform she was wearing in the game.

Madison Avenue's decision to go all in like this for a college athlete who wasn't even going to turn 22 until January 22, 2024, could have been seen as a bit of a gamble, but not with Clark. In addition to her growing national following and her willingness to spend time before and after games being swallowed up by packs of girls and boys seeking autographs, she was embarking on an epic quest: She was trying to break the most prestigious record in college basketball, the Division I scoring record, which was held by a man.

Clark came into the 2023–24 season with 2,717 points. The late "Pistol Pete" Maravich, the beloved floppy-socked sharpshooter from LSU, scored 3,667 points from 1967 to 1970. "Ponytail Pete" was a nickname Clark acquired when she was younger.

Before reaching him, Clark had to reel in Kelsey Plum, who played at Washington from 2013 to 2017 and currently held the NCAA women's Division I record of 3,527 points, and Lynette Woodard, who held the AIAW (Association for Intercollegiate Athletics for Women) record of 3,649, set from 1977 to 1981 while she played at Kansas.

The march began when Clark scored 28 points in No. 3 Iowa's 102–46 victory over Fairleigh Dickinson on November 6. She scored

44 in a victory over No. 8 Virginia Tech three days later. Then 24, 24 again, 35, and 29—you get the idea. It was a lot of points. There was no doubt, provided she didn't get injured, that she was going to pass Plum, Woodard, and Maravich by season's end.

Her journey to break all the records was the story of her season, but logo-three theatrics played a strong supporting role. On January 2, 2024, with the score tied and the clock winding down to just a sliver of a split second, Clark launched a nearly 30-foot prayer of a shot from the beak in a game with Michigan State.

From the beak? Yes, from the beak of the profile of a hawk—the "Tigerhawk" Iowa Hawkeye design—that forms the logo at mid-court.

Of course it went in, a dart into the same basket as her last-second shot against Indiana the season before, but this time she ran the other way, across the court to fans at the other end of the arena, arms outstretched, holding her hand to her ear to "listen" to the cheers, happily clapping, absolutely delighted. Those were her 38th, 39th, and 40th points of the game. "When it left my hand," she said, "I knew it was going in."

She scored no fewer than 26 points—and usually reached well into the 30s—in the 10 games that followed before arriving back at Carver-Hawkeye on Thursday night, February 15, needing just 7 points against Michigan to tie and 8 to break Plum's NCAA women's record.

•

As she warmed up for the big night, Clark sauntered over to the Peacock announcing crew she knew well, Zora Stephenson and Meghan McKeown. "I kind of feel like it's the first day of school," Clark told them.

"There was so much buildup and pressure on that game," McKeown said later, "but I've never seen someone so calm considering the circumstances. She was laughing, she was loose, and she came over to us to talk. When she said it was like the first day of school, I thought that was such an interesting thing to say because it was a huge deal and she personally might have been like, 'Oh my gosh, I'm gonna have millions of people watching this.' But she acted like it was just another day. There was obviously an excitement to it, acknowledging that this was a big deal, but also not making it bigger than what it was."

It was no surprise, then, that Clark came into the game as if shot out of a cannon. Off the opening tip, just 10 seconds into the game, she drove for a layup. Six points to go to break the record.

A half minute later, a three-point jump shot. Three points to go.

"Oh, this is gonna happen quick," Stephenson said into her microphone.

Sure enough, a minute and a half later, Iowa guard Gabbie Marshall tossed the ball to Clark, sprinting down the court.

"How will she go for history?!" Stephenson exclaimed.

Just 2 minutes and 12 seconds into the game, on the run, Clark fired a logo three from 33 feet 6 inches, more than 11 feet beyond the three-point line, from a spot on the court that would soon be adorned with her number, 22, to commemorate the historic occasion.

"The most Caitlin Clark way to get a bucket," McKeown offered on the broadcast moments later.

Play went on for 30 seconds before Iowa got the ball back and Bluder could call a time-out for the celebration to begin. Clark was now the all-time NCAA Division I women's basketball scoring leader, with 3,528 points.

But she didn't stop there. She ended the first quarter with a stunning 23 points, and finished with a career-high 49 points, which is the Iowa women's single-game scoring record. Did she want this record, or what?

"You all knew I was going to shoot a logo three for the record," Clark said. "I don't know if you can really script it any better."

The whole evening was a party, for her and the Iowa fans, who pivoted from this game to thoughts of what was to come. This was

Clark's senior year, of course, but a fifth COVID year was possible, if she wanted to take it.

Who in Iowa didn't want her to take it? As she stood on the court for postgame interviews after Iowa's 106–89 victory, the crowd started a chant: "One more year! One more year!"

That night, Nike, one of her sponsors, posted a congratulatory message on X (formerly Twitter), advertising a new Caitlin Clark T-shirt: "You break it, you own it."

•

Next up, Woodard. Clark was 81 points shy of passing the Kansas trailblazer who set her record before the three-point line was instituted and before the NCAA took over women's athletics in 1982.

Just three games later, on February 28, Clark passed her.

The next day, Leap Day, Clark had something to say on social media:

While this season is far from over and we have a lot more goals to achieve, it will be my last one at Iowa. I am excited to be entering the 2024 WNBA Draft.

It is impossible to fully express my gratitude to everyone who has supported me during my time at Iowa—my teammates, who made the last four years the best; my coaches, trainers, and staff who always let me be me; Hawkeye fans who filled Carver every night; and everyone who came out to support us across the country, especially the young kids.

Most importantly, none of this would have been possible without my family and friends, who have been by my side through it all. Because of all of you, my dreams came true.

News alerts popped up on the phones of sports fans around the country. Why Clark made the decision when she did was even a topic of conversation: Iowa's senior day was coming in three days, March 3 against Ohio State, and it was believed she wanted to get the news out of the way so it didn't distract from the celebration of the other seniors. The last thing she wanted was "One more year!" chants echoing through Carver-Hawkeye Arena when her fellow seniors were being honored.

•

It was quite a cast of characters who gathered to watch Clark go for Pistol Pete's record in Iowa City that Sunday afternoon as No. 6 Iowa hosted No. 2 Ohio State in a really big Big Ten game.

ESPN and Clark sponsor State Farm planned a surprise for her before the game. As Clark stood on camera, Maya Moore popped out of the backstage shadows live on the *College GameDay* broadcast.

"Oh my gosh!" Clark squealed. The confident player we see on the court melted a little in that moment. "I feel like I'm fan-girling so hard. Thanks for being here," she said to Moore. "I still feel like I was this tall and freaking out. I ran across the court and gave you a hug." Nearly 12 years after 10-year-old Caitlin did that, the two were hugging again. "A full-circle moment," Moore said.

Senior day, which also was Clark's last regular-season home game, became the "hottest ticket in women's basketball history," according to *The Des Moines Register*, with prices higher than $400 per seat. It turned out that 100 years of girls' and women's basketball in the state had been building to this extraordinary crescendo.

Clark needed just 18 points to pass Maravich, who scored all his points before the advent of the three-point line and the shot clock, and in just three years of eligibility—but he also attempted nearly twice as many shots per game as Clark did.

How would she do it? Another logo three? Just a regular old three?

No. Clark achieved the record not with a bang, but with a relative whimper, sinking two free throws after a technical foul was called on Ohio State—one shot to tie Maravich, the second to pass him.

Bluder didn't think that was so bad. "Those free throws are important, and she's very, very good. Go back to fundamentals, everybody, right? I'm kind of glad it wasn't a logo three."

Clark scored 35 points in all as Iowa upset Ohio State, 93–83.

In addition to Moore, Woodard also was there, invited by Bluder and the Hawkeyes to receive a hero's welcome for what she accomplished so long ago. The Iowa crowd warmly embraced her with a standing ovation when she was introduced on the court during the game.

"Because of her, my records are being honored," Woodard said of Clark in an interview on Fox while sitting courtside. "Every walk of life, everybody knows Caitlin Clark and the University of Iowa and what she's done and they deserve it."

After the game, Clark spoke about the honor of being "in the same realm" as Maravich, Plum, and Woodard, adding, "Hopefully somebody comes after me and breaks my records and I can be there supporting them."

In sports, women's accomplishments usually aren't taken as seriously as men's, and certainly not when a woman is trying to break a man's record. Male sportswriters and broadcasters, in particular, aren't always big fans of giving women their due compared with men. But this time, when a woman broke a man's record, it became national news, with CNN, *PBS News Hour*, and NPR, among many others, on the story.

Sports fans, too, couldn't get enough of this. Average viewership for the game was 3.39 million, reaching a high of 4.42 million late in the second half, Fox Sports said. It was the most-watched regular-season women's game on any network since 3.88 million watched a UConn–Tennessee game in 1999, when there were far fewer channels and viewing options. The viewership beat all but one men's college game of the 2023–24 season to that point, and it surpassed the 3.01 million who watched the NBA's Boston Celtics–Golden State Warriors game on ABC, also on that day.

Why was this happening? Well, the record, obviously, but also because Clark was such a compelling personality.

"Caitlin is the whole package," ESPN commentator Rebecca Lobo told Michael Voepel. "She's playing the game in a way we haven't seen before by a woman. We've not seen someone take that many shots from quite that distance and hit them at such [a high percentage]. And she's like Steph Curry—he's charismatic and he's not a physical giant. So, every kid can visualize themselves as Caitlin Clark. It's not like, 'Well, to play like her I'd have to be 6'4" or 6'5".' Caitlin is 6'0", but you actually don't have to be that tall to try to do the things she does."

•

Clark and Iowa rolled on, winning the Big Ten Tournament for the third consecutive year, but high hopes for a return to the Final Four were tempered when the NCAA revealed its women's bracket. While Iowa was a No. 1 seed, it would have to run a murderer's row gauntlet to get to Cleveland, where the NCAA championship would be decided in April 2024.

If anyone thought the NCAA was going to give Clark and her teammates as easy path to the Final Four to maximize her impact on TV ratings, they were mistaken. Quite the opposite; it was as if the selection committee bent over backward to make the bracket supremely challenging for Iowa, setting up the Hawkeyes with early games against physical teams like West Virginia and Colorado, then putting them on a collision course for a national championship rematch with LSU in the Elite Eight—meaning one of the two teams wouldn't make it to the Final Four.

But first, there was the opening first-round game with Holy Cross in Iowa City. This wasn't supposed to be a problem—and turned out not to be one—as Iowa won, 91–65, but one wouldn't have known that from Clark's mood. Iowa got off to a slow start and led by only two points after the first quarter. Clark was fidgety. During one moment of deep frustration, she angrily bounced the ball off her head, and the cameras caught it.

Dickson Jensen, her AAU coach, was in the stands at the game. "Expectations were ridiculously high," he said. "They didn't want to lose at home. You're also dealing with a 22-year-old, she has emotions, you know? I mean, she has other things going on, moving to a new city, all those things that are outside of basketball continue to be in every one of these kids' minds as they play. And I think she wasn't as dialed in. You're playing Holy Cross, you're gonna win this game. She wasn't mentally prepared for the game, and that was a really good lesson for her to learn, that when things start to go a little sideways, you can't just flip a switch and get back."

Clark still scored 27 points with 10 assists, but she wasn't quite her usual self. The weight of the basketball world was on her shoulders. Actually, the weight of decades of women's sports history was on her shoulders, too. With all the interest in her, TV viewership for the Final Four was going to be off the charts for a women's sporting event.

But what if Clark and her teammates lost too early? What if they didn't reach the Final Four? What would it look like if Iowa and Clark weren't there? Sports TV executives shuddered at the thought.

They were there.

The Hawkeyes held on against West Virginia, 64–54, playing a nerve-racking second-round game at home for a third consecutive year, then beat Colorado by 21, then met their old friends the LSU Tigers in the regional final in Albany, New York, on Monday night, April 1.

A day before the game, Angel Reese said that being seen as Clark's enemy—being cast in the "villain role" by the media and public— hadn't been easy. "I think people just take it like we hate each other," she said. "Me and Caitlin Clark don't hate each other. I want everybody to understand that. It's just a super-competitive game."

In the rematch, Clark was unstoppable, scoring 41—there's that number again—with 12 assists to lift Iowa over LSU, 94–87. Even though it was an Elite Eight matchup, it drew over 2 million more viewers than the same teams' NCAA final a year earlier: 12.3 million, the largest audience to ever watch a women's college basketball game.

Clark took over the game with nine three-pointers, faraway jumpers over Hailey Van Lith, who now was with LSU, and Reese, and anyone else who tried in vain to swat one away.

"Oh my! From Schenectady!" ESPN's Ryan Ruocco exclaimed after one. After another: "She's possessed!" His sidekick, Lobo, chimed in: "The distance on these Caitlin Clark threes . . . it's just ridiculous."

Said LSU coach Kim Mulkey afterward: "She's just a generational player and she makes everybody around her better." When they met in the handshake line, Mulkey had nothing but praise for Clark: "Girl, you something else. Never seen anything like it."

She had one other message for her: "I sure am glad you're leaving."

●

The Final Four was set: Iowa vs. UConn, one last college battle between Caitlin Clark and Paige Bueckers, and No. 1 South Carolina against North Carolina State.

Geno Auriemma, who had called Bueckers "the best player in America" earlier in the tournament, changed his tune when he knew Clark was next on their schedule. "I don't need to be seeing her drop 50 on us. . . . Forget I ever said Paige is the best player in the country. . . . I don't know whoever said that I said that Paige is the best player in the country."

On Friday evening, April 5, Iowa defeated UConn, 71–69. Clark scored 21, Bueckers 17. UConn's defense swarmed Clark early in the game and she ended up having a poor shooting night from the three-point line, just 3-for-11, but Clark did have the last laugh, and not just because Iowa won.

Inbounding the ball under her basket with that two-point lead with 1.1 seconds to play, she threw the ball off Bueckers's backside to run some time off the clock after Bueckers had turned around to help on defense.

"I watch a lot of basketball," Clark said afterward. "I understand basketball. She had her back turned to me. The biggest thing at that point of the game is you just want the clock to go down. You don't want to give them the ball, but she had her back completely turned, so I was just trying to waste some clock. It just came to my brain, so I just went for it and it kinda worked."

That Clark moment of moxie took 0.3 seconds off the clock—a minuscule amount, perhaps, but worth every fraction of a second to a team trying desperately to finish off an opponent.

With 0.8 seconds left for the next inbounds pass, Clark found Martin, who wisely threw the ball high into the air to take care of the rest of the time, and the game was won.

•

In the NCAA final, Iowa was reunited with a familiar opponent—and the best team in the country: Dawn Staley's South Carolina Gamecocks. Clark did her best to make it a game, scoring 18 points in the first 10 minutes for a 27–20 Iowa lead, but South Carolina soon took command. The storyline for Iowa was similar to the previous year: a huge victory in the semifinal, then a tough and not particularly close loss in the final, this time an 87–75 defeat to the Gamecocks, with Clark scoring 30 overall for a grand career total of 3,951 points.

Clark left the floor and was back in her locker room with her teammates as the South Carolina celebration continued on the court. After the various speeches and interviews, Staley asked for the microphone. "I want to personally thank Caitlin Clark for lifting up our sport," she said. "She carried a heavy load for our sport, and it just is not gonna stop on the collegiate tour. But when she is the No. 1 pick in the WNBA Draft, she's gonna lift that league up as well. So, Caitlin Clark, if you're out there, you are one of the GOATs of our game, and we appreciate you."

She's also one of the greatest of all time in the halls of ABC and its partner ESPN. That NCAA final—which was played on a Sunday afternoon, not in prime time—drew 18.9 million viewers on ABC, peaking at 24.1 million. It was the most-watched women's basketball game ever, passing the previous most-watched game, the Iowa–UConn semifinal two days earlier, which attracted 14.2 million viewers.

To show the impact of Clark, the other semifinal between South Carolina and North Carolina State had half the audience: 7.2 million.

It was a sea of superlatives: The Iowa–South Carolina game was the most-watched sporting event of any kind in the United States since 2019, with the exception of some college and pro football games, the Women's World Cup in soccer, and some Olympic events, according to ESPN. It beat everything else: Tiger Woods's victory at the Masters, the World Series, you name it.

And, most significantly, it outdrew the 2024 men's NCAA final, played the following night, by four million viewers, the first time the women had ever attracted more viewers than the men.

•

For a second consecutive year, Clark won the Wooden and Naismith Awards and was again named the Associated Press Player of the Year. She also was selected, for the second year in a row, as Academic All-America Team Member of the Year, with a 3.64 GPA while majoring in marketing.

Clark's singular success throughout her college career was extraordinary, but she continually made a point to say she never did it alone, that it never was solely about her. The basketball world knew that Clark was a spectacular star, but it also knew she still was a product of Lisa Bluder's respected coaching system, with a team built around her, fueled by her, and carried to almost unimaginable heights by her.

Clark understood that the road to those two Final Fours was very much a two-way street. "I never want to stop being coached," she said during her senior year. "I never want to stop being told what's right, what's wrong, no matter how good I play, how bad I play. There's always things to learn, things to get better at."

•

Of all her statistics and records, perhaps the most intriguing, and important, is that Clark never missed a game in college. She also never missed an AAU game, Dickson Jensen said. And she missed only one game in high school, in November 2017, her sophomore year, due to a badly sprained ankle. "It about killed her to not get to play," Dowling Catholic High School coach Kristin Meyer said.

Clark has spoken about never wanting to disappoint fans who've traveled to see her. She occasionally suffers from migraines, but felt it was her responsibility to always show up and keep playing, come what may.

"Knock on wood over and over again," Jensen said.

In this way, the contrast with Bueckers is undeniable, sadly. Bueckers won the various National Player of the Year honors as a freshman, but since then has had to overcome not one but two serious knee injuries, missing significant playing time.

"Caitlin has never missed a practice," Jensen said. "She's never missed a game. She's certainly blessed with a body that is not injury-prone, and she takes care of her body. I mean, that girl just works her tail off, and I think that keeps her body healthy, I really do—and that's helping Caitlin be Caitlin.

"I mean, if we don't see Caitlin for a year when she was in college, Caitlin isn't Caitlin, right?"

CHAPTER SIX

# A League of Their Own

The phone call was placed a day after Caitlin Clark declared for the 2024 WNBA Draft.

"Do you know how big this is?" I asked a top WNBA official who wanted to remain anonymous in this book.

"Yeah, this is the biggest thing to happen to the W since Maya Moore came into the league."

That was a surprising answer.

Maya Moore is one of the most talented and beloved WNBA players of all time, a Hall of Famer and a tireless advocate for social justice, but Clark's extraordinary national popularity, as documented by record TV viewership, attendance figures, and media coverage, was so much bigger than the attention surrounding Moore when she came out of Connecticut with two NCAA titles. It's unfortunate that a vast swath of the sports nation didn't follow Moore as she led the Minnesota Lynx, Clark's favorite team, to four WNBA titles in a pro career that stretched from 2011 to 2018, but the reality was that the attention Moore received at the time wasn't even close to what Clark was getting.

I mentioned this. The official laughed nervously, as if what I had just said didn't seem real.

I followed up. Fans, TV viewership, media interest—it was all coming with Clark. They knew that, right?

"Uh . . . yes."

Could the WNBA truly not see, or perhaps not allow itself to believe, what was on the way? Was what Clark had done in college just an unfathomable thought for the WNBA? Did the league think it was all going to end with her college days? Or was the league just completely unprepared for the moment?

All sports and leagues miscalculate at times. Everyone makes mistakes. Sometimes the most obvious moments catch us by surprise. But that short exchange, it turns out, foretold so much of what would occur over the next seven months—not just in the WNBA, but in our national sports conversation.

The greatest thing to ever happen to the WNBA was on her way—not the greatest player, certainly not yet, maybe never, but the most impactful player in history, as judged by any number of measures, including ticket sales, TV ratings, jersey sales, social media hits, you name it. So there was no need to compare Clark with Moore, or anyone. This was an unprecedented moment in the relatively short history of the league.

Yet, what was I hearing in that WNBA official's voice? Not happiness. Not anticipation. Not excitement. No, it was something else entirely.

•

Within the ecosystem of America's male-dominated big-time sports, the WNBA had always been a league of low TV ratings, low attendance, low salaries—and high purpose. Born out of the success of the 1996 Atlanta Olympics—the "Women's Olympics"—the league began in 1997 as a brainchild of NBA commissioner David Stern. He believed it was time to give women's basketball players a true league of their own, one that had a chance to succeed if backed by NBA owners, some of whom agreed to use their arenas and all of whom publicly supported the NBA putting its weight, and even its name, behind the start-up league. Those NBA owners would be big brothers, if you will, to the WNBA's little sisters. These days, the NBA still owns 42 percent of the WNBA, and when NBA team owners' individual stakes are included, it rises to nearly 60 percent.

The WNBA wasn't the first try at this. "We had to do Nexus searches to look for all the old leagues because we didn't have the internet," said Val Ackerman, the first president of the WNBA, who served until 2005. "There were leagues that lasted a season or two. There were some that had a press conference and then vanished. One league was going to have lower rims and have the players wear short shorts. I mean, there were quite a few. We were using the number 15—there probably were 15 attempts to start women's pro basketball leagues in the '70s, after Title IX. We knew it was going to be really, really, really hard."

Trying to shoehorn any new women's professional league into the already-crowded American sports calendar was never going to be easy. In fact, another women's league, the American Basketball League, was competing with the WNBA at its inception, but it soon went away and the WNBA was on its own.

•

The early days of the WNBA were filled with unusual challenges. Lin Dunn, whose various stops in the women's game included successful coaching stints at the University of Miami and Purdue, was hired as the first coach and general manager of the new Seattle Storm WNBA expansion team in 1999. "We had no team. No logo. Nothing," she said.

They also didn't have enough fans. Needing to sell 1,500 more season tickets to reach the minimum required by the league, the Storm's marketing people came to Dunn with an idea:

"Dribble through the city of Seattle."

Dunn was in. "I thought the plan was I would dribble through the city for a mile and a half. I was in my early 50s. It's hilly in Seattle, but I could do that, no problem."

She arrived that morning ready to go. "We were starting off with a big to-do, with a public-address announcer and Seattle TV and the city's two newspapers, trying to publicize the team and get people to buy tickets, and the PA announcer says, 'We're just so excited that Coach Dunn has agreed to dribble through the city of Seattle for five and a half miles.'"

Five and a half miles?!

"I thought, 'What is he thinking—*one* and a half, right?' But they told me, no, it's five and a half."

Unable to back out then, Dunn set off, surrounded by 15 to 20 people—members of the media, Storm officials, and curious onlookers. "We go down First Avenue, and I'm dribbling with both hands, and I'm like, 'Okay, I can do it, I'll just take my time.' Then I start going up a hill, and about halfway up, everybody is dropping out. I've lost them all, except for one reporter who is still with me. And I'm thinking, 'Good God, if I could just get rid of her, I could call a taxi. I can dribble in the taxi and then I can say I did it.'"

Dunn turned toward the reporter. "How long are you gonna be around?"

"I need to be here the whole time," she replied, according to Dunn. "I've trained. I'm ready."

That's not what Dunn wanted to hear. "I got up that hill and kept going. It took me, I don't know how many hours, but I didn't do any more hills. I stayed level and did all five and a half miles. I kept telling myself, 'If you think this is hard, look at what we're trying to do here, building a team from scratch.'"

There were consequences, good and bad. "For a week afterward, I couldn't raise one of my arms. That was what hurt, and I had blisters, but we did it, we sold the tickets, we got the team."

Dunn would stay in Seattle for three years, building a playoff team around No. 1 draft pick Sue Bird before moving on to the Indiana Fever, where as coach, she took the team to the WNBA championship in 2012. She became the Fever's general manager in 2022.

Twenty-two years after she drafted Bird, she drafted Caitlin Clark.

•

As the WNBA carried on and franchises and players came and went, it often was described as "a Black, gay league." In the 2023 season, according to the most recent report on the WNBA by The Institute for Diversity and Ethics in Sport at the University of Central Florida, 63.8 percent of the league's players were African American or Black, while 19.1 percent were white. The number of players who identified as two or more races was 10.6 percent; Hispanic/Latina players constituted 1.4 percent; and Asian players, 1.4 percent. Players reporting their race as "unknown" totaled 3.5 percent.

Sexual identity wasn't part of the study, but a substantial portion of the league identifies as LGBTQ+. Commentator and writer Jemele Hill, speaking at the 2024 Association for Women in Sports Media conference, said the WNBA "often has been under attack because a third of the players in the WNBA are identified as being part of the LGBTQ+ community."

Because of the WNBA's diversity, it became a league of social activism, responding to tragic and controversial issues and events, a league for its time. On July 9, 2016, after two Black men—Philando Castile in a suburb of Saint Paul, Minnesota, and Alton Sterling in Baton Rouge, Louisiana—were fatally shot by police, and then five white Dallas police officers were fatally shot by a Black sniper, the four captains of the Minnesota Lynx held an unprecedented pregame press conference.

They were wearing black warm-up shirts with a message. On the front were the words "Change Starts with Us" and "Justice & Accountability." On the back were Castile's and Sterling's names, the Dallas police department shield, and the words "Black Lives Matter."

"In the wake of the tragedies that have continued to plague our society, we have decided it is important to take a stand and raise our voices," Rebekkah Brunson said. "Racial profiling is a problem. Senseless violence is a problem. The divide is way too big between our community and those who have vowed to protect and serve us."

Said Maya Moore: "This is a human issue and we need to speak up for change, together. If we take this time to see that this is a human issue and speak out together, we can greatly decrease fear and create change. Tonight we will be wearing shirts to honor and mourn the losses of precious American citizens and to plead for change in all of us."

Moore also spoke about the Dallas shooting, praising the city's efforts in "de-escalation training and other efforts that led to a noticeable drop in the number of shootings by officers in the last few years. . . . We do not in any way condone violence against the men and women who serve in our police force. Senseless violence and retaliation do not bring us peace." Moore and Brunson were flanked by Lindsay Whalen and Seimone Augustus—all four of them the favorite players of young Caitlin Clark.

The following day, New York Liberty players wore black warm-up shirts with #BlackLivesMatter and #Dallas5 on the front and, on the back, another hashtag followed by a blank space, a chilling symbol signifying a place for the name of a future victim. When players from other teams, including the Indiana Fever and Phoenix Mercury, wore similar black shirts during pregame warm-ups, the WNBA initially fined them for violating the league's uniform rules: $5,000 per team and $500 per player. But, within a few weeks, the league reconsidered and rescinded the fines.

It's important to place these acts of protest and awareness by WNBA players in the context of a larger 2016 sports timeline: They all occurred more than a month before San Francisco quarterback Colin Kaepernick's first protest during the national anthem. It was on August 14, 2016, during a preseason game, that Kaepernick remained seated on the bench during the anthem. He did it again on August 20. His protest was first noticed before the third game, August 26, when he was asked about it by members of the media. So, the WNBA players were weeks ahead of Kaepernick, but because there was so little national media coverage of their league, very few knew, or remember.

On September 22, 2017, while speaking during a US Senate campaign in Alabama, President Donald Trump said this about Kaepernick and other NFL players who kneeled in protest during the national anthem: "Wouldn't you love to see one of these NFL owners, when somebody disrespects our flag, say, 'Get that son of a bitch off the field right now. Out! He's fired. He's fired!'"

Game One of the 2017 WNBA Finals was two days later. The Los Angeles Sparks decided to protest Trump's words by staying in their locker room during the national anthem, while the Minnesota Lynx stood on the court with their arms linked. "We are a league that speaks for minorities," Sparks star Candace Parker told ESPN's Michael Voepel. "We represent women, African Americans, LGBT. We are doing this as a stance for all minorities. We just want to be equal, what everyone wants. That's why we're doing this."

•

The COVID-19 lockdown of 2020 brought all the WNBA players together in one place, their bubble in Bradenton, Florida, affectionately known as the "Wubble." There, the players continued their social activism, shining a light on racial injustice after the police killings of Breonna Taylor and George Floyd, and, in a remarkable move, they also worked to defeat a US senator, Georgia Republican Kelly Loeffler, who was co-owner of one of the league's teams, the Atlanta Dream. They did this after Loeffler denounced the league's plans to dedicate the season to the Black Lives Matter movement.

Later that summer, after the shooting of Jacob Blake in Kenosha, Wisconsin, the Milwaukee Bucks chose not to play their playoff game in the NBA bubble in Orlando, while the Washington Mystics and Dream met on the court in their bubble, took a knee, and also decided not to play—one of three games postponed that night. The Mystics wore T-shirts with bullet holes drawn on the back.

•

From February 17, 2022, to December 8, 2022, Phoenix Mercury All-Star Brittney Griner, a 6'9" center, was unjustly held in a Russian prison and ignominiously caged during courtroom proceedings. She was detained after less than a gram of hashish oil, illegal in Russia, was found in her luggage as she entered the country to play basketball during the WNBA off-season.

Griner was in Russia to supplement her WNBA income (about $220,000) with the much larger paydays—over $1 million—players can receive overseas. She is one of many WNBA players, stars and reserves, who travel overseas in the off-season—to China, Turkey, and Spain, among other nations.

During the agonizing months when Griner was imprisoned, on trial, and sentenced to nine years in jail, WNBA players worked diligently to make sure she wasn't forgotten. Her number, 42, was emblazoned on each team's court and worn by every player during the second half of the WNBA's July All-Star Game. Players used their social media accounts to call for Griner's release and often steered interviews away from the intended topic to discuss the unfairness of Griner's captivity.

The day Griner was released from her Russian jail cell in a prisoner exchange might have been the finest hour ever for any US professional sports league.

I wrote about it in my *USA Today* column on December 9, 2022.

> In the early days of Brittney Griner's imprisonment, as the nation learned that a top US women's basketball player had been detained in Russia on a drug charge, the conversation quickly focused on a comparison:
>
> If this were a male athlete, not a female athlete, people would care a lot more about this story. If, say, LeBron James or Tom Brady were being held hostage by Vladimir Putin,

well, they wouldn't be hostages anymore. They'd already be home because America would have demanded it, right away.

It was a valid point, not that either James or Brady ever would have been in the position of having to leave their country to make a good living playing their sport as Griner did.

So someone had to create a similar demand for Griner, to make sure she wasn't forgotten by reminding people how important she was. Griner's wife, Cherelle, would admirably shoulder much of that burden, but she wouldn't do it alone.

It turns out she had a veritable battalion by her side, a group of women ready to fight for their teammate, colleague and friend: tall, basketball-playing women armed with social media accounts, a national stage and the savvy to turn their arenas into a nightly reminder of just who was missing.

The WNBA players' efforts were a stunning success. "It was contagious," I wrote. "NBA players soon were saying her name, and as summer turned to fall, an athlete who should have been a household name for years finally became one. . . . A national conversation had been built all around her. The next step had to be a deal to get her home, and that is exactly what happened."

•

Griner received more publicity and coverage for being imprisoned in Russia than for her then-13 years as one of the biggest stars in women's basketball, both at Baylor and in the pros. That's the sad reality of being a WNBA player. By and large, the male-dominated mainstream sports media has ignored every single one of them for much of the past three decades.

News organizations with teams in their cities often put summer interns or new young hires on the WNBA, not seasoned pros. With relatively meager attendance and often minuscule TV ratings, the league wasn't important enough to those editors or their news organizations. It's telling that the Washington Mystics opened a 4,200-seat arena in 2019 rather than continuing to play in their old home, the 20,000-seat Capital One Arena. They thought that small venue was the perfect size for their fan base.

When those of us fighting for more coverage of women's sports would bring up the old "Which came first, the chicken or the egg?" dilemma—if there were more coverage, wouldn't that likely lead to more fans?—editors wouldn't disagree, but would lament staffing shortages or lack of money to have reporters travel with their local WNBA team. It was always something.

Understandably, those who covered the WNBA—many of them women, some Black, some quite young, some working for fledgling news organizations or websites—became protective of it. This was their beat, but it also was their world. Every writer covering a beat gets close to the athletes and coaches on it. The trick is not to get too close, because a journalist's responsibility is always to report for their readers and/or viewers and to ask tough and difficult questions when necessary. The closer you get, the harder that becomes.

Protecting the players is someone else's job. That's why there are team and agency public relations people. But when a league is small and often ignored, as the WNBA has been, there can be an inclination among some members of the media to want to fight for it, and even be reluctant to let outsiders in.

Into this world landed Caitlin Clark, a white, straight, 22-year-old woman who had not played a second in the WNBA, but already was a national phenomenon and about to become the face of the league. She would bring millions of new people to see her on TV and thousands more in person. Those new spectators and viewers would see more than Clark. They would see all of the players who had been ignored for so long but richly deserved their attention. TV ratings and attendance would rise, which means salaries would too. It appeared to be exactly what everyone in the WNBA had been waiting and hoping for.

"In 1997, we thought it would take a generation for the league to come into its own," said Val Ackerman, now the commissioner of the Big East Conference. "It was going to be a marathon, not a sprint. We thought that the league would benefit from the passage of time. Our hope was that societal currents would change in a progressive way, meaning in a way that was more respectful, tolerant, and embracing of women athletes. There were a lot of naysayers at that time who didn't think the league was going to make it, and might even have been rooting against us, but we did it anyway, with the hope that—we were not sure who or what it was going to be—but we thought there was going to be a point in the future where the spark would ignite."

The spark had most definitely ignited. To say people were conflicted about it would be a vast understatement.

# CHAPTER SEVEN

# "Reality Is Coming"

The ESPN simulcast of the 2024 NCAA Women's Final Four, with basketball stars–turned–commentators Diana Taurasi and Sue Bird, was going along as expected. It was edgy and funny and just what the network wanted. The longtime UConn pals and WNBA legends explained, analyzed, laughed, and even answered questions, including this one: Who would they take with the first pick in the draft if they were building a WNBA team: Caitlin Clark, or Paige Bueckers, who wasn't even entering the 2024 draft?

After Bird picked Clark—"the fan energy behind Caitlin is going to be a game changer for a WNBA franchise," she said, presciently—it was Taurasi's turn, and she was vintage Taurasi, brusque and unyielding:

"I'm taking Paige. Next question."

Bird followed up. "So, you get the No. 1 pick this year, you would take Paige over Caitlin?"

"Absolutely."

After Iowa defeated UConn in their national semifinal, Taurasi and Bird appeared on-screen with ESPN host Scott Van Pelt. When Van Pelt asked about what was in store for rookies like Clark and South Carolina's Kamilla Cardoso coming into the league, Taurasi was delighted to give them a proverbial swift kick to the shins.

"Look, SVP, reality is coming," Taurasi said, laughing, as Van Pelt giggled and clapped. At that moment, ESPN was displaying a graphic on the screen showing how Clark had outplayed Bueckers in their NCAA semifinal won by Iowa, scoring more points (21–17), with more assists (7–3) and more rebounds (9–4). Taurasi continued. "There's levels to this thing, and that's just life, we all went through it. . . . You look superhuman playing against 18-year-olds, but you're going to come with some grown women that have been playing professional basketball for a long time. . . ."

This is why Taurasi is on TV. She provokes. She makes you think. She is tough, brash, controversial, and a force to be reckoned with, always. The problem for Taurasi, if she even cared about this, was all the new eyeballs being brought to the game for the first time by Clark. Millions of new women's basketball fans didn't necessarily know much about Taurasi, which was too bad, but true. They certainly were getting an introduction now.

Taurasi, 41 at the time, was talking about a young woman nearly half her age who was thrilled to be following in her footsteps, a young woman who Taurasi's own team, the Phoenix Mercury, was going to use on social media to promote ticket sales in Taurasi's home arena— tickets that Taurasi herself apparently couldn't sell, no matter how magnificent her stellar career had been.

This is the point in the Caitlin Clark conversation where sports fans, especially male sports fans, might suggest that this is exactly the way the old guard treats rookies in men's sports, so why not in women's too? Isn't this a sign that women's sports have grown to the point that older players feel they can take a shot at younger players, as if that is some sort of goal or measure of advancement? Taurasi clearly thought so.

But let's ask a couple of questions: Are women's sports equal to men's sports in our society today in terms of salaries, sponsorships, media coverage, and attendance? Is the WNBA equal to the NBA in all those categories? The answer is of course not. Women's sports still have so much catching up to do, decades and decades of catching up.

So, along comes a woman who can help accelerate that timeline, draw those fans, raise those salaries—and Taurasi gives her the cold shoulder?

Asked twice through her agent if she wanted another chance to talk about Clark, Taurasi and the agent never replied.

But one person did have second thoughts about what transpired, and talked about them more than five months later, after the WNBA regular season ended in late September. "I think Diana Taurasi had it wrong," Van Pelt said on air. "I think [Clark] was the reality. I think Caitlin, they should call her 'The Reality' because she was coming and she's here in this league. She's been great."

•

The question should have been a layup for another former UConn star and WNBA superstar, Breanna Stewart, the day before the Final Four in Cleveland. Sports journalist Nicole Auerbach, broadcasting for Sirius XM, asked this: "Does Caitlin Clark need a championship to be considered one of the greats in women's college basketball history?" To be clear, the question wasn't whether Clark needed a championship to be the GOAT, the greatest of all time. It was merely: Was Clark "*one* of the greats"?

There can be dozens of those; the more, the merrier. One would certainly think that the person who had scored the most points in NCAA Division I basketball history, male or female, would be one of them.

Not Stewart.

"Yeah, she does [need a championship]," Stewart replied. "I think so. Because then you're gonna look ten years back and you're gonna see all the records she's broken, and the points and stuff like that, but anybody knows your goal when you play college basketball is to win a national championship. So you need one."

Needless to say, that created some news. Like Taurasi, the then-29-year-old Stewart seemed to want to minimize Clark, not wanting to acknowledge that this young woman, more than seven years her junior, was changing how the nation looks at her sport. Stewart instead brought to the conversation her roots as a former star at UConn, where she was fortunate to play on a roster full of future WNBA players who had teamed with her to win four consecutive NCAA titles. Clark, by contrast, had played on a roster full of future non-WNBA players, with the exception of Kate Martin.

A week after Stewart's initial comments, Stewart's agent, who is also Taurasi's agent, Lindsay Kagawa Colas, sent me a comment from Stewart: "Caitlin is a star and we are excited to have her in the WNBA. She is unquestionably great for what she has accomplished on and off the court."

•

There was a lot happening off the court at that Final Four. Even Lynette Woodard, whose AIAW all-time scoring record had been broken by Clark a month earlier, got into the act. "I am the hidden figure, but no longer now," Woodard said at a Women's Basketball Coaches Association event. "My record was hidden from everyone for 43 years—43 years. I'll just go ahead and get the elephant out of the room: I don't think my record has been broken because you can't duplicate what you're not duplicating. So, unless you come with a men's basketball and two-point shot, hey, you know. But just for you, so you can understand, so you can help me spread that word."

The Iowa Hawkeyes had invited Woodard to the Ohio State game so she could be recognized and metaphorically pass the torch from herself to Clark. A few weeks later, she apparently wanted the torch back. Of course, there was a social media reaction, and it wasn't good, so Woodard quickly tried to walk it all back. "No one respects Caitlin Clark's accomplishments more than I do," she wrote in a post. "My message was: A lot has changed, on and off the court, which makes it difficult to compare statistical accomplishments from different eras. Each is a snapshot in time."

Then, in bold, she added: "Caitlin holds the scoring record. I salute her and will be cheering for her throughout the rest of her career."

•

Then there was Sheryl Swoopes, a four-time WNBA champion, three-time MVP, and six-time All-Star who led Texas Tech to the 1993 NCAA title. On a podcast with former NBA player Gilbert Arenas during the college season, Swoopes made one incorrect statement after another when she was asked about Clark breaking the women's NCAA Division I career scoring record.

Among her comments, Swoopes said Clark was set to become the all-time leading scorer because she had already taken an extra season due to the COVID-19 pandemic. "If Kelsey Plum set that record in four years, well, Caitlin should've broken that record in four years," Swoopes said. "But because there's a COVID year, and then there's another year, you know what I mean? So she's already had an extra year to break that record. So, is it truly a broken record? I don't know. I don't think so. But yeah, that'll go in the record books as Caitlin Clark is the all-time whatever it is, I don't even know what the number is, but that's the way it will be. And I don't think it should be."

There was a problem with Swoopes's analysis: It was all wrong. Clark didn't take a COVID year. She played four years, just like Plum. She broke the record in four years.

Swoopes also said that Clark "right now probably takes about 40 shots a game," when Clark averaged 20 per game in her college career, with 22.7 per game her senior year. And Swoopes insinuated that Clark was 25 years old. "So people say, 'Dang, like he or she is killing them,' but you have a 25-year-old playing against a 20-year-old, like, you *should* be killing them because you've been doing it a lot longer than they have."

Clark wasn't 25. She turned 22 on January 22, 2024. She will turn 25 on January 22, 2027.

Swoopes declined to comment for this book through her agent, Gina Paradiso.

•

Coaches also got into the act. Over a couple of months, two very big names who understand the economics of women's basketball as well as anyone went public with their thoughts about Clark. Had there been a welcoming committee for Clark as she entered the WNBA, they would not have been on it.

Cheryl Reeve was more than the coach of the Minnesota Lynx, a team that would play Clark three times during the WNBA season. She also was the 2024 US Olympic women's basketball coach.

On May 3, as Reeve was preparing for the Olympics and Clark was still officially in the selection pool for her team, Reeve posted on X about the first preseason game for her Lynx. Specifically, she was telling her followers where and how to keep track of the game, since, unlike the first preseason game of the Indiana Fever, Clark's new team, it wasn't being televised.

In her posts, Reeve chose an interesting person to focus on: She appeared to place blame for the decision to televise one game over the other, or one game rather than both, on a rookie who had nothing to do with it. Reeve first reposted a WNBA tweet promoting Indiana's upcoming game with Dallas, adding this message on top of it: "ALSO in action tonight—@minnesotalynx vs @chicagosky 7 pm CST. Though fans won't be able to watch, #Lynx fans can go to the Lynx app to follow along via play by play. Or if you are in market, come to the game . . . as we start the season off right."

Reeve then added two hashtags to her post: "#12teams" (the number of WNBA teams) and "#theWismorethanoneplayer"—that is, the WNBA is more than one player.

Someone else on X, under that post, asked, "Is there a reason why it's not being shown?" A second person wrote, "Because they only care about Caitlin."

Reeve appeared to agree with that unknown person when she added this comment: "That part."

Then there was the man who didn't recruit Clark, UConn's Geno Auriemma. On June 6, he appeared on sportscaster Dan Patrick's radio show and unloaded on Clark and her fans. "The delusional fan base that follows her disrespected the WNBA players by saying she's going to go in that league and tear it apart. There were actually odds . . . she's third or fourth in betting odds on being MVP of the WNBA. These people are so disrespectful and so unknowledgeable and so stupid that it gives women's basketball a bad name. . . . So the kid was set up for failure right from the beginning. . . .

"Diana said it best, this kid's in for a rude awakening. And they all jumped over her, but they didn't read the whole thing that she said, but nobody's printing, you know, Diana Taurasi was right. This kid's on the wrong team. She's got the wrong skill set to handle the physicality of that league. . . . She's not quick enough to get away from the physicality, so there's a lot of learning curve, like Diana said, and when she gets it, she has elite skills that are going to really help her, but she needs to be on a better team, and she needs to be more experienced, and that will come. But for these ridiculous fans who had her slotted as the next Diana now, they're out of their mind."

As sports predictions go, that turned out to be as bad as it gets.

•

Observing all this from afar was Dr. Harry Edwards, the legendary sociologist and civil rights leader whose work at San Jose State organizing the Olympic Project for Human Rights inspired the famous Black Power salute by US medalists Tommie Smith and John Carlos at the 1968 Mexico City Olympic Games. Edwards, a PhD and professor emeritus at Cal-Berkeley, made the empowerment of Black athletes a major part of his life's work. Fighting cancer at his home in Fremont, California, he was one of the millions of Americans enthralled by the play of Caitlin Clark. "This," he said, "is a great basketball player."

I've interviewed Edwards for numerous stories and columns, and he and I have appeared on panels together discussing racial issues in sports. I wanted to hear what he thought of the reception Clark was receiving when her career turned from the NCAA to the WNBA, so I asked him about it in August 2024.

He said it bluntly: "The league failed the players. The WNBA not only missed an opportunity to prepare its players for this moment, they set the traps along the path that the league was going to travel." He said the WNBA needed to understand and prepare for the "disappointment and anger" some Black players, in particular, would be experiencing due to Clark's ballyhooed arrival.

"This was predictable," he said. "It's human nature for people not to be happy for you when you're new and successful, especially if it's in an arena where they have toiled all their lives and not come close to the kind of reward or applause that [Clark] is receiving."

As someone who has counseled players and leagues for decades, Edwards said that the WNBA should have established "a series of seminars" in the preseason for every team in the league.

"There are people out there who could have gone in and given those talks to each franchise, experts and specialists from a sports sociological perspective with the understanding and grasp of the situation, and told each team: 'Hey, we have Caitlin Clark coming in and the media has grabbed ahold of this, the public has grabbed ahold of this, but let me tell you something, you sitting right here in this room, you set the stage for this. You in this room, many people may never have seen you play a basketball game despite being in the league for five years or whatever. That's reality. But this is true: You are the wind beneath the wings of Caitlin Clark, you made this possible because you are the WNBA. Take pride in that, lift her up, lift all the rookies up—Angel Reese, all of them—because as they soar, so do we all.'

"Then they would at least have been aware," Edwards continued.

"You wouldn't have had this wall of negativity toward Caitlin Clark. This is something new we are talking about in the WNBA, a white Steph Curry. The league needed to do a better job in preparing those people who have built the league to take advantage of the tsunami of popularity that is raising all of the boats and sweeping them in directions that they never would have gone before."

•

Briana Scurry was the goalkeeper for the 1999 US women's soccer team whose lunging save of a Chinese penalty kick during the Women's World Cup final in the Rose Bowl set the stage for Brandi Chastain's winning kick. She also was the first Black superstar on the most famous women's team on earth.

"Caitlin Clark's presence, while polarizing for some people, is really a watershed moment for the league, and I just hope that all these amazing Black players are taking full advantage of the fact that the spotlight is on what they're doing now," Scurry said in a January 2025 interview. "I understand there's a lot of frustration and there's some anger because the league has been around for 27 years before she came. But my goodness, it's having this moment right now. And please, please, please, as players in the league, do not let this opportunity pass you by to get yours."

Scurry also endorsed Edwards's idea for programming to prepare the players for this unprecedented time. "That would have been absolutely brilliant to have something like that. Even if the players didn't themselves want to see things holistically, they would have at least been able to see someone talking about it and saying, 'Okay, I may be angry about all this and feeling like we've been here this whole time; however, I can find this silver lining in here.' But because the WNBA unfortunately didn't do that, the players didn't even understand how big that tsunami was that was coming for them, in a good way. And they were just woefully unprepared for it."

# CHAPTER EIGHT

# Hello, Indianapolis

Waiting in the wings just off camera at 30 Rockefeller Plaza, just past midnight and into a new day, Sunday, April 14, Caitlin Clark was poised to put an exclamation point on a whirlwind week. After playing in the NCAA championship game in Cleveland, Clark had quite a travel itinerary. She flew back to the University of Iowa with her teammates, drove to West Des Moines for a home-cooked meal, then drove back to Iowa City for the team's campus celebration—where it was announced that her No. 22 jersey would be retired. From there, she flew to Los Angeles to receive the Wooden Award, then traveled to New York for the WNBA Draft, where she was going to be the No. 1 pick of the Indiana Fever.

But first, she was suddenly appearing at the desk of *Saturday Night Live*'s *Weekend Update* as a surprise guest.

Clark later said she had been incredibly nervous. A three-pointer to win a game was nothing compared to this. "I was terrified. . . . My heart was about to explode out of my chest." Nonetheless, wearing a sporty black Nike letter jacket, she deftly bantered with cohost Michael Che, teasing him for his sexist jokes at the expense of female athletes—"You make a lot of jokes about women's sports, don't you, Michael?"—before delivering a classy homage to the women who had come before her.

"Thanks to all the great players like Sheryl Swoopes, Lisa Leslie, Cynthia Cooper, the great Dawn Staley, and my basketball hero, Maya Moore," Clark said. "These are the women that kicked down the door so I could walk inside. So, I want to thank them tonight for laying the foundation."

That she led off with Swoopes was telling, considering the flurry of falsehoods the WNBA legend had showered upon Clark during the college season. It was also notable that every woman she named was Black. This was a rare cross-cultural moment for the league: a young white star delivering praise on a popular non-sports network TV show for the Black players who formed the foundation of the women's game.

•

A year and a half earlier, the vast majority of Americans had no idea who Clark was. Her rise had been swift and it had been organic—bottom-up, not top-down—driven by her play and her fans. In a world of comparisons, one stood out: Clark had become the individualized version of the 1999 US Women's World Cup team. Interest in that team was fueled by moms and dads and soccer-playing daughters unexpectedly filling US football stadiums—a minivan revolution, if you will—driving newspaper coverage and TV ratings in such an unexpected way, unlike any previous American women's sports story.

Twenty-five years later, here we were again. But there was a significant difference. After the US won the World Cup on July 10, 1999, that team largely went away for 14 months, only to reappear in September 2000 at the Summer Olympic Games in Australia, where the Americans won the silver medal. There were honors and magazine covers and some exhibition games, to be sure, but there was no major competition and no professional soccer league—not yet. That wasn't coming until 2001.

After Iowa lost the 2024 NCAA final, Clark went away too—for eight days, from the NCAA championship game on April 7 until the

WNBA Draft on April 15. Her popularity never waned because she never really left.

•

If the sports universe had a grand plan to advance women's sports as quickly as possible, and could place Caitlin Clark in the perfect spot for that to happen, it would have put her exactly where she ended up: Indianapolis, Indiana.

Not New York, Los Angeles, or Chicago, but Indy, a city in a state known for its enduring love of the game of basketball: high school, college, pro, boys and girls, men and women. A city that houses the NCAA and Olympic national governing bodies and, over the years, has not only hosted but enthusiastically supported major international and Olympic-style events, including multiple US Olympic trials and Men's and Women's Final Fours, the 1987 Pan American Games, the 1991 World Artistic Gymnastics Championships, and the 2012 Super Bowl.

A Midwestern city that is not small, but not too big—meaning that supporting an arriving athlete like Clark wouldn't just be a sports endeavor, but also a matter of civic pride. There was absolutely no way she would get lost in the shuffle in a city of 876,000, and even a metropolitan area of 2.1 million. Significantly, Indy was also located in the heart of Big Ten country and already familiar with Clark. Local sports fans had watched her on the Big Ten Network and Clark had played games at Indiana University and Purdue, so women's basketball fans had already seen her in person. No introduction was needed.

Indianapolis also had another big advantage: It was instantly ready for Clark and her massive fan base because it was a city with arguably the best relationship between its NBA and WNBA teams, linked under Pacers Sports & Entertainment by longtime owner Herb Simon. The Fever had immediate access to the full force of the company's ticketing, marketing, merchandising, and social media operations. Billboards were up. Clark merchandise was ordered, ready and plentiful. And the social media following Clark had developed at Iowa was not going to be ignored. Three years earlier, the Pacers and Fever had twelve staffers working on their digital team. Now they had 23, a team spokesperson said.

"Right time, right place, right moment with Caitlin," said Hall of Famer Tamika Catchings, who led the Fever to the 2012 WNBA title in her 15 seasons with the team. She was the Fever general manager from 2020 to 2022 and still lives in the city, owning a trio of tea cafés called Tea's Me.

This also was a place where thousands of free tickets were scooped up by fans for a WNBA Draft watch party on a school night in April to witness an event in which everyone already knew the result.

•

While Clark was walking the WNBA's "orange carpet" at the Brooklyn Academy of Music in the early evening of April 15, Indianapolis sports fans were lining up 700 miles away in the glistening lobby of Gainbridge Fieldhouse to watch the draft on the arena's big screen. A crowd of at least 8,000 filled much of the lower bowl and reached into the second deck. It was a bigger gathering than what the Fever usually drew for their games.

In New York, the No. 1 draft pick wore Prada. In Indy, her fans already were wearing her No. 22 Fever jersey.

Deep inside Gainbridge, Fever general manager Lin Dunn, a gregarious soul who'd had to muzzle herself for months on the topic of drafting Clark, was in the team's draft "war room" about to unmuzzle herself. She put in the call to the WNBA and made it official: The Fever were selecting Clark. Moments later, Commissioner Cathy Engelbert walked to the lectern in Brooklyn and made the announcement to hundreds in the auditorium and a historic audience of more than two million watching on ESPN: "With the first pick in the 2024 WNBA Draft, the Indiana Fever select Caitlin Clark, University of Iowa."

In New York, Clark stood up and circled a table hugging her brothers, her father, and her mother. In Indianapolis, veteran Fever point guard Erica Wheeler exploded from her courtside seat in Gainbridge. Giddy with anticipation at the news she knew was coming, Wheeler had placed one hand on the knee of Lexie Hull and the other on the knee of Maya Caldwell, both Fever teammates at the time, and waited to hear Engelbert's words.

Wheeler—known as "EW" to her teammates—leaped for joy with Hull and Caldwell, then pulled a red Fever No. 22 jersey over her head and ran around the court as the fans stood and roared. "Let's go!" Wheeler shouted to every corner of the arena.

Her happiness was predictable, but also admirable, for as she danced, she knew she was celebrating the moment that she had lost her starting job. Clark was going to be the starting point guard for the Fever, guaranteed. Wheeler would be her backup, a difficult role, but one she understood, and even relished. "You know when you go to a different school," said the 33-year-old Wheeler, "the first day of school, you don't know anybody, and you find that one person that says hi to you that becomes your best friend."

Wheeler, who is Black, became that person for Clark.

·

The party went on for some time in Gainbridge. Fever head coach Christie Sides said she could hear the reverberations from the crowd in the draft room, so she popped onto the court to join the celebration. When Dunn spoke to the assembled media, she saw a women's sports landscape that was changing in front of her eyes. "She's already had an impact and we hadn't even drafted her, so let's see what's going to happen now that we drafted her."

Within an hour, nearly every size of Clark's Fever jersey was sold out. Ticket sales for Fever games, home and away, were booming. Even before Clark was drafted, the WNBA defending champion Las

Vegas Aces announced they were moving their July 2 home game with Indiana to a bigger arena. Also before Clark was selected, the WNBA announced that 36 of the Fever's 40 games would be shown on national television, more than any other team in the league.

That decision looked prescient when the TV numbers came in for the 2024 draft. It attracted its largest viewership ever, 2.45 million, which was a million more viewers than had ever watched a WNBA game to that point on ESPN. And it was more than four times larger than the previous year's draft. If any cynics or doubters had questions about whether Clark's popularity would transfer from college to the pros, they were immediately answered.

•

Two days later, walking a red carpet between rows of cheering Pacers and Fever employees inside Gainbridge, wearing a black dress with a white jacket slung over her shoulders, Caitlin Clark arrived at her first job out of college.

"I can't think of a better place to start my career, a place that loves basketball, supports women's basketball," Clark said at her opening press conference on April 17. As she always does, she leaned into her Midwestern roots, explaining how being relatively close to home, in a city and state that reminded her of her own, was where she wanted to be. "To be able to come here and stay in the Midwest—it's only five hours from Iowa City, seven hours from where I grew up—you really can't script it any better."

It also didn't hurt that her boyfriend, former Iowa men's basketball player Connor McCaffery, had settled in Indianapolis, too, working for the Pacers before he would become an assistant coach for the in-town Butler University men's basketball program later in the year. Clark happened to mention him in her press conference as well.

But for all the joy in Gainbridge that day, there was a troubling moment that served as a harbinger for the season ahead, when Clark would be dragged into raging debates on various societal issues, often while just minding her own business.

Called upon for the second question of the press conference, *Indianapolis Star* columnist Gregg Doyel made a heart shape with his fingers to Clark, who is known for making the gesture to family members at her games. That was followed by this exchange:

Clark: "You like that?"
Doyel: "I like that you're here; I like that you're here."
Clark: "Yeah, I do that at my family after every game, so it's pretty cool."
Doyel: "Okay, well, start doing it to me and we'll get along just fine."

Later in the press conference, Doyel had a question for Sides. "You just were given the keys to *that*. What are you gonna do with it?"

Negative reaction to Doyel's inappropriate comments rippled through the USA Today Network, of which the *Star* is a part, as well as through the Fever organization. The *Star* suspended Doyel for two weeks, according to reporting by longtime Indianapolis sports columnist Bob Kravitz, and he was prohibited from covering the Fever and Clark for the entire season.

•

Clark was in the headlines that week for another reason: the amount of money she was making in the WNBA. She signed a four-year deal with the Fever worth $338,056. Her base salary was $76,535 for her rookie season. As a comparison, the four-year deal signed by the top male basketball player selected in the 2024 NBA Draft, Atlanta's Zaccharie Risacher, was $57 million. His base salary was $12.57 million for his rookie season.

Even though Clark was making millions with her various endorsements, including her eight-year, $28 million Nike shoe deal, the paltry size of her WNBA contract drew instant and much-needed attention to the pay disparity in the women's game, with the promise that her immense popularity could lead to higher salaries for all soon enough.

•

As Clark's first preseason game, scheduled for May 3, approached in Dallas, the WNBA was insisting that all its players, including Clark, would be flying on commercial flights, just as the fledgling league always had. Progress was being made on private charter flights: Commissioner Cathy Engelbert had recently announced an increase in the number of back-to-back-game charter flights, one day to the next. And the charter program the league had in place for the playoffs would continue. But otherwise, WNBA spokesman Ron Howard said, things would be the same as they had been for the players, including going through security and walking through the concourse to the gate like other passengers. The only difference between the average commercial passenger and WNBA players was that all teams would be traveling with security on every trip.

This was going to be an adjustment for players like Clark and the other rookies who had flown on private charters throughout their college careers. It also created a troubling security risk for Clark and all the players. The WNBA had had a taste of that trouble, of what could happen, just a year earlier, in June 2023. Only six months after being released from her captivity in Russia, flying commercial per WNBA policy no matter how famous and visible she now was, Brittney Griner was accosted in the concourse at Dallas Fort Worth International Airport by a right-wing YouTube personality who yelled at her and tussled with Phoenix Mercury security. Things got so heated that the man was tackled and law enforcement was called. The league reacted by allowing Griner to fly privately the rest of the season.

Now it was a new season, and Clark was heading to Dallas Fort Worth.

•

Early in the evening of Thursday, May 2, two videos started to appear on social media. Wearing Fever sweats and carrying a backpack, Clark walked purposefully through baggage claim with her teammates, flanked by two members of the Fever security team. In the background of each video was a man filming her with his phone, meaning the men shooting the videos of Clark were also capturing each other in their sights.

In those videos, Clark and her teammates were being treated like objects, there for the public's viewing. All these tall, recognizable young women, many of them Black, on display in an unsecured area? It was a discomforting American tableau. One could easily imagine someone recognizing Clark and rushing toward her. Texas, of course, allows people to carry guns in public; when she was walking by the baggage carousels, Clark was no longer inside airport security.

How had the WNBA, and the NBA, not realized how significant a problem this was? Why were they mandating that Clark, and every other recognizable player, rookie or veteran, had to travel with and among members of the public? Was this another example of the WNBA's lack of preparation for Clark's fame and popularity? Did the NBA not see it either? The NFL would never allow Patrick Mahomes to walk through baggage claim while flying to a game. The NBA would never allow LeBron James to do what the Fever had to do. Was it a case of sexism, of not thinking as much about the safety and well-being of female athletes as they would about male athletes? Did the powers that be not force the issue because they didn't want to look like they were giving special treatment to Clark after not delivering league-wide charters for Griner?

There were financial issues as well. The cost of the charters was about $25 million a year, Engelbert said. But a new TV rights deal was coming, and after the soaring viewership for Clark during the previous two college seasons, there was reason to hope that, with Clark now a pro, the financial future of the league was going to become much brighter.

This was an important issue that I thought might be worthy of a column, so I emailed a top NBA official to ask just those questions not long after I saw the videos. This person, whose name will remain anonymous at their request, asked to speak to me the next day.

We talked for 45 minutes on Friday, May 3. I believe it's important to have frank discussions with top sports officials, hear them out, run my ideas by them, see what I can learn. As we spoke, I was fairly certain I would be writing a column criticizing the two leagues for failing to start private charter service for all players in the WNBA this year of all years. But my source also said there might be more information on Monday, May 6. I was willing to wait a couple of days.

We did talk on Monday, and on that call, I was informed, much to my surprise, that the WNBA was going to begin charter flights for all 12 of its teams as soon as possible for the 2024 season—and I could break the news the next day.

My post went out on X at 1 p.m. Eastern on Tuesday, May 7: "Breaking: I'm hearing the WNBA is in discussions to begin charter travel for all 12 of its teams as soon as this regular season. Why now? The explosion of interest in the league, business growth and anticipated future revenue from the next media deal."

In other words, Caitlin Clark.

The news boomeranged around WNBA locker rooms. Some players were looking at their phones, seeing the post and calling their agents. A couple of those agents called me.

"What's going on?" one asked.

"Is it true?" asked another.

"It's true," I replied.

Within minutes, Engelbert was in a previously planned meeting in a league conference room in New York with about a dozen sports editors from around the country. Because they saw my post while in their meeting, they asked Engelbert about it and she immediately confirmed the news.

Stories were quickly written and published online. The facts were as I had reported them. All 12 teams would begin charter travel "as soon as we logistically can get planes in places," Engelbert was quoted as saying in *USA Today*. "We intend to fund a full-time charter for this season. We're going to as soon as we can get it up and running. Maybe it's a couple weeks, maybe it's a month. . . . We are really excited for the prospects here."

The Fever had been planning to fly commercial to their first regular-season game, on May 14 against the Connecticut Sun in Uncasville, Connecticut—not an easy place to get to. Their travels would have taken them from Indianapolis to Atlanta, followed by a two-hour layover at Hartsfield–Jackson Atlanta International Airport, then a connecting flight to Hartford. A Fever official was understandably concerned about how Clark and her teammates would be able to avoid the public in the bustling Atlanta airport. "What's going to happen in those two hours in Atlanta?" the official said. "That was going to be very interesting."

It was no longer a concern. With Clark lounging in her headphones in a window seat in the first row of a Delta charter, the Fever simply took a flight from Indianapolis to Hartford. They celebrated their inaugural private flight with a video that went viral.

However, not everyone was entirely pleased that Clark was on a charter when others still were not. "It's tough that the season is starting today and we're still trying to figure out those kinks," Connecticut Sun guard DiJonai Carrington, the team's players association representative, told CBS Sports. "But some teams haven't figured it out. I don't know. It's just—not happy about it, especially as a member of the players union."

Months later, the haphazard way it happened—on a Friday, there were no charters; on a Tuesday, there were—was still a topic fraught with controversy. "They were begging for charter flights," ESPN's Stephen A. Smith said on air in December 2024. "[Clark] arrives there, and two weeks later, they got charter flights. She automatically and instantaneously improved the conditions. . . . Clearly, things are on an upward-trending trajectory, it's improving and she has everything to do with it."

*Washington Post* columnist and University of Maryland journalism professor Kevin Blackistone saw it differently in a January 2025 interview: "Brittney Griner comes back from being locked up in a gulag, and the WNBA players plead for extra security because they know this is going to be an issue. And what happens? Brittney Griner is verbally assaulted in an airport. So now arrives Caitlin Clark and almost overnight, everything is resolved. So I understand the resentment of a large number of the women who play professional basketball to the arrival of Caitlin Clark. I don't perceive anything from them about disliking Caitlin Clark personally, or even as a rookie player in the WNBA, but I do understand that they resent the fact that everyone and everything seems to be catering to her, her needs, when they've been screaming for these needs to be addressed for years and no one seemed to be listening to them."

# CHAPTER NINE

# "Give 'Em Time"

Twenty minutes had gone by in the professional career of Caitlin Clark. Twenty difficult minutes. The horn had just sounded; the first half was over. It almost was a relief. *Whew, what was that?*

Double-teamed, pickpocketed, and guarded the length of the floor by the Connecticut Sun on Tuesday evening, May 14, Clark collected two fouls so quickly that she had to go to the bench for five minutes of the first quarter. Sitting on the sidelines was no way to begin your first day at the office, Clark knew. She was held scoreless in that first quarter.

She finally made her first basket in the WNBA with 5:24 remaining in the first half, a play that was vintage Clark: stealing the ball, faking out a defender as she hesitated for a moment as if she might shoot a three-pointer, then blowing by that Sun veteran, DeWanna Bonner, for a layup. Clark finished the half with seven points.

But that defense she was facing, led by DiJonai Carrington—it was withering. The Sun were a veteran, unrelenting, defensive powerhouse of a team that had made the semifinals of the 2023 WNBA playoffs. The young Fever players had no such résumé. Indiana, and Clark, were overmatched from the get-go.

The Sun were all over Clark, treating her like the raw new kid who'd just arrived—but also like a feared superstar who could beat them if they gave her the chance. They forced her into five turnovers in those first two quarters. They smothered her when she got the ball. They picked off her passes. Nothing was more embarrassing for Clark than when, two minutes before halftime, Carrington met her at half-court, poked the ball away from Clark as she dribbled, scooped up the bouncing ball herself, and laid it in for a 15-point Sun lead.

When the first half mercifully ended for Clark with the Fever trailing by 10, someone grabbed her left arm and wanted to walk with her to the locker room. Walk, and talk.

•

Center Aliyah Boston, who won a national title at South Carolina one year and then lost to Clark and Iowa in the Final Four the next, knew exactly what Clark was going through. Boston had been the first pick of the 2023 draft. The Indiana Fever were so bad, they drafted first in 2023, then again in 2024. Boston one year, Clark the next. As the two joined their teammates leaving the court at the Mohegan Sun Arena, Boston linked her right arm in Clark's left arm and accompanied her through the tunnel to the locker room, delivering a 15-second pep talk.

What was happening on the court was hardly surprising. The Fever knew this was going to be hard. They'd practiced together for little more than two weeks. "We started training camp on April 28," Coach Christie Sides said. "Five days later, we're playing our first preseason game. Four practices later, we're playing our second preseason game. Five days later, the season starts. We barely had time to get to know each other."

Boston and Clark, however, were familiar with one another, having forged a friendship from their time playing together as members of the gold medal–winning US team at the 2019 FIBA Under-19 Women's Basketball World Cup in Thailand. So it made sense that Boston was the one walking with Clark, urging her to hang in there and stay calm, but also to never stop being aggressive. "Be you," she told Clark.

Clark leaned in and listened, then, as they were steps away from the locker room, she opened her left palm toward Boston, who gave it a light slap, a quick low-five. Superstar teammates, they were in this together. "That calming moment," said Tamika Catchings, looking back on it. "That was Aliyah looking out for Caitlin right away."

Of all the opportunities Clark was dreaming of as the Fever season began, the most exciting was working with the talented 6'5" Boston. "My point guard eyes just light up at that," Clark said. "As a point guard, my biggest job is I'm just feeding Aliyah the ball every single day. I'm going to be in there and be like, 'Go make a layup.' She's going to make my life easy."

But, as the season was just beginning, there were times when the two of them were making things up as they went along, Clark said. "Me and Aliyah are just trying to learn on the fly, get to know each other on the fly." Nothing about this was going to be easy.

•

The newness of it all was notable. After ESPN began its broadcast with a montage of highlights from the previous season, the opening video then went to black before displaying an image of Clark in silhouette. Various voices heralded the moment: "A new level of excitement is here . . . the Caitlin Clark Effect. . . . When eyes are on Caitlin, eyes are on the league. . . . She's the show." Some of Clark's greatest college hits were shown for the umpteenth time, ending with one nice touch, a video of Clark in an Iowa uniform morphing into a Fever uniform.

ESPN announcers Ryan Ruocco and Rebecca Lobo, who had broadcast many of Clark's college games, were aware that it was not just Clark who was making an adjustment to the WNBA. "To all of those fans that have followed her here to the WNBA, welcome, this league is ready for you," Lobo said in a tone that turned out to be more hopeful than true. Meanwhile, Ruocco offered a light primer for new viewers, noting that WNBA players were allowed six fouls in a game, not five as in college.

Hundreds of Clark fans showed up to the Fever road game in No. 22 T-shirts and jerseys, both the Iowa and Indiana variety. ESPN's Holly Rowe reported that a father paid $6,000 for courtside seats for himself and his two daughters. Christie Sides, looking back a few months later, said that she would never forget the wall of Fever fans as she, Clark, and teammate Victaria Saxton exited an elevator in the Mohegan Sun Casino complex on their way to the arena.

"That's when I knew," Sides said. "Steve, Caitlin's security guy, was standing there and he said, 'Just want to give you a heads-up, there are a lot of people here.' And I mean there were people my parents' age and people my age, men, women, it didn't matter. There were people crying just seeing her. People were screaming, taking videos, taking pictures. I'd never witnessed that before, and when I got to the bus, Lin Dunn and I were sitting there, and I was like, 'Lin, it was like what you'd see in a movie with Elvis or the Beatles.' I have coached in this league for 14 years and I'd never seen anything like that, ever."

During the game, the Sun staff had a little fun with a few of those new fans, showing them on the scoreboard video screen with a graphic saying that they had been on the Indiana bandwagon "since 2024." However, while they teased the new Clark-enthused fans, they also were very happy to have them. For the first time since the franchise's first game, which was in 2003, the Sun sold out their home opener with a crowd of 8,910. That new Clark bandwagon already was reaping dividends for opposing teams.

On that opening night in the small arena built in the middle of the massive Mohegan Sun complex in Connecticut, in a game that drew 2.1 million viewers, making it the most-watched WNBA game since 2001, Clark ended up scoring a team-high 20 points, including four of her signature three-pointers, in the Fever's 92–71 loss. No one scored more than Clark that night; Bonner also ended up with 20 points to lead her team.

But that was not the story that emanated from the game. No, the most momentous season in WNBA history began with a new national obsession: Caitlin Clark's turnovers. She had five more in the second half for 10 total. One game into Clark's pro career and one look at social media told the story: Clark was flailing. You might as well subtract an *l*. She was failing. People on the internet had a good chuckle at Clark's expense. She had her first double-double, they said: points and turnovers. Obviously, that's not what anyone thinks of when they credit a player with a double-double. For Clark, that's almost always points and assists.

The 10 turnovers were the most ever by a rookie in her debut in WNBA history, 2 more than the great Cynthia Cooper had in 1997. It was a disjointed and chaotic performance by Clark at times, but it also provided a window into her mindset: she was not timid, she was not backing down, she had brought her full confidence from Iowa right to the WNBA. Then she ran into a brick wall, devised by Sun head coach Stephanie White, who also is a TV analyst and knew Clark well from calling some of her college games.

It wasn't difficult to imagine that once Clark figured out how to adjust to the speed, length, and height of her opponents, and she and her teammates got to know each other better on and off the court, this just might work out well for her.

But it wasn't working yet. Clark had a difficult first game. She knew it. Everyone knew it. The story was simple and easy to digest for the casual fan, as well as for those rooting for her to fail:

"Caitlin Clark struggles in WNBA debut," said NBC News. "Reality check," said *The Athletic*.

"For Caitlin Clark, an ugly stat sheet, a blowout loss and a WNBA lesson," read the headline in *The Washington Post* above a column by Candace Buckner.

. . . those expecting Clark to just pick up where she left off in college aren't accounting for all of the great players she will now face in the WNBA. She's playing against grown women who will force her to throw bad passes out of double-team traps. They're not going to stand there and allow Clark to be the conductor of a beautiful basketball symphony as she did for Iowa, pounding the rock while probing the defense. Instead, these career women will force her into discomfort and some very un-Caitlin-like moments.

This accurate snapshot of that challenging first game touched on something that actually was quite complimentary for Clark. Connecticut's defense was so concerned about her, so respectful of her, that it not only picked her up defensively the full length of the floor, it "blitzed" her, sending a second defender racing over to smother her, trap her, and make it difficult, if not impossible, for her to pass the ball. Hence all the turnovers.

Who does that to a rookie in her first game if she's not an immediate concern? "It was a total compliment to Caitlin, right from the start," said Debbie Antonelli, the longtime basketball announcer who is the color commentator on Fever games. "What the defense in that game was saying is 'We want to win this game, Caitlin is our focus, we want to make things challenging for her, we don't want to let her do what she wants, we want to take away her vision, we want to be real physical with her.' It's kind of incredible to think that was the scouting report from day one with a rookie, but that's how important she was already."

The Sun became the first defense to be obsessed with stopping Clark, but they were hardly the last. Statistics quickly proved that Clark, having just shown up, was receiving the toughest defense in the league. "Connecticut came in and punched us in the mouth tonight," Sides said. "We'll be in the gym tomorrow, watching a lot of video, trying to figure out how not to turn the ball over 25 times [the team's total]."

Clark didn't shy away from criticism, including her own. "I didn't have the greatest start," she said. "Just a lot to learn from. It's the first one. There's going to be good ones, there's going to be bad ones. . . . Some uncharacteristic stuff: I pick up the ball and travel, I dribble off my foot. Those are situations where you're just giving the other team the ball. I thought it took me a little while to settle into the game."

But she wasn't going to dwell on it. "I don't think you can beat yourself up too much about one game."

This was typical Clark, her Iowa teammate Kate Martin said. "She's not the type of person that's ever gonna let other people worry about her or make excuses for her."

And those 10 Clark turnovers? That never happened again. She would have 9 in an overtime victory against Atlanta in September, but averaged 5.6 per game for the entire season, certainly not low, but nowhere near the trouble some wanted it to be—and a sign of just how much success a high-risk/high-reward Caitlin Clark–led offense was going to have.

•

Next up for Clark and the Fever was New York, New York. Literally. The young Fever were playing the formidable New York Liberty twice within 48 hours in a murderer's row schedule that the WNBA said had been planned months before and couldn't be changed—but that made victories for Clark a distant dream, threatening to kill interest in the golden goose before she even got started.

Spoiler alert: It did not kill interest.

The first game of the two was Indiana's home opener. A sellout crowd of 17,274 on a Thursday night during the school year showed up at Gainbridge Fieldhouse. The press conferences were packed as well. Sides took it all in from behind the microphone: "There's never been this many people in this interview room."

In front of all those reporters, Clark was able to somehow set aside the intense pressure she was under after her less-than-stellar perfor-mance two days earlier and uncork an all-world statement on respecting fans and playing every game: "People are sacrificing a lot to spend money to get here, spend resources to get here or travel or pay for their young daughter, their young son, to come and watch us and support us, or buy our jerseys or buy whatever merchandise it is. I understand it because I was that young girl. That's what my parents did too. They were working parents. They would take time off to try to help me do something that I love to do or enjoy [doing]. . . . So, I'm very aware of it, and that's why I didn't miss a single game in college. I knew people were coming and wanting to support and watch me. For me, it was never an option to not play a game if I felt a little beat-up, if I felt a little under the weather. People get so excited to come to these games and are spending a lot of their time and money. I think first of all, [what's important is] just being aware of it and enjoying that and trying to make time for as many people as you can, but also, give it everything you've got. These people are coming for a show, and not everything's gonna be perfect, but just try to play with the same joy and fun that you always have."

Clark's performance in the interview room went unmatched on the court. The game was an even bigger blowout than the one two days earlier, with the Liberty, the WNBA Finals runner-up the previous season, defeating the Fever, 102–66, behind Breanna Stewart's 31 points. Clark notched just one three-pointer and only nine points total, but she did have seven rebounds and six assists—and just three turnovers.

One of them was a beautiful pass to forward Katie Lou Samuelson, a five-year veteran in her first season with the Fever, that Samuelson couldn't handle, with the ball skidding out of bounds. Clark put her hands on her head briefly. That pass should have connected. She clearly was still trying to get used to her teammates, and vice versa, but with so few practices, they still barely knew each other. The WNBA was rushing everything along, giving the Fever the worst of it, forcing them to play nine games in 17 days in May to make room for a monthlong break in July and August for the 2024 Paris Olympic Games. No other WNBA team had to do that. Now that the season had begun, there would be no more full practices for the Fever in the month of May, only games, one after another.

Headlines blared trouble, and those who didn't like Clark lived it up on social media, but people who knew basketball knew exactly what was happening. Catchings is not alone in saying point guard is the toughest position on the court to master, especially for a rookie, and with everything being new for the Fever, and Clark, it was logical that they wouldn't click right away.

"She has been so comfortable with her college teammates, so now Caitlin and her new teammates are trying to figure out how to play together," Catchings said. "It's the adjustment of coming into a totally different system, totally different coach and coaching staff. The only thing that is consistent is basketball. She knows how to play the game of basketball. A lot of the turnovers are adjusting to playing with her teammates and they are adjusting to her. . . . Everybody [commenting from the outside] is like, 'These players aren't as good as her Iowa teammates.' No, you have to learn them, and they need to learn you. It takes a little bit of time with new teammates."

As the Liberty game ended, Clark was sitting on the bench, looking at the floor, her hands holding the sides of her face. She was not happy. "People are playing her hard, people are playing her aggressively," Samuelson said. "We can do a better job of trying to help her get some space and help her get some freedom. But we trust her and we want to keep figuring out how to work with her in the best way. Teams are really, really, really hounding her full-court, 94 feet, so we've got to do some stuff as a unit to just flow better with that."

Clark readily admits she's a perfectionist, so all of this was difficult. "I want to be really good for our organization, for my teammates. . . . I've come into this league, and I'm trying to learn as much as I can. I'm 22 years old, and there's a lot of expectations on my shoulders."

The bad news was another game was coming. The good news was another game was coming, another chance for Clark and the Fever to begin figuring things out.

•

It took only four days: from Tuesday night, May 14, to Saturday afternoon, May 18. That quickly in her professional career, Clark showed the WNBA just how bright her future—and its—could be. It happened, fittingly, in the first basketball game she ever played in New York. There to witness it, and hug her or high-five her before or afterward, were tennis legend Billie Jean King, the WNBA's Sue Bird, golfer Michelle Wie West, actor and Clark fan Jason Sudeikis, and the *Today* show crew, among others.

In her first two games, Clark averaged 14.5 points per game and 30 percent shooting. On Saturday afternoon, she scored 22 points on better than 50 percent shooting (9-for-17), with 4 threes in 10 attempts. She also had 8 assists after having had just 9 total in the first 2 games.

In the first four minutes, Clark was a buzzsaw. She had 3 assists, a layup, and a long three. In the first seven minutes of the game, she scored 10 points, making four of her first five shots. She scored or assisted on 17 of the Fever's 22 points in the first quarter. "I came out and just played harder, and I think that's really just my biggest focus going forward. Just come out, have fun, compete, and play hard," said Clark, who credited a phone call with her father between the two New York games for the advice.

She looked much more comfortable on the court. When two Liberty players, Stewart and Betnijah Laney-Hamilton, attached themselves to her on a backcourt inbounds play halfway through the first quarter, Clark broke into a big smile as if to say, "Come on, guys." Three games in, the double-teaming defense had turned from a curse to a humorous nuisance, to be handled with a smile and a shrug.

Clark likes to say she is a kid at heart, and that was never more apparent than a couple of minutes later, when she was jumping on her tiptoes at the top of the key, throwing her head back, arms pinwheeling, smiling. Oh, what could have been. A beautiful arc of a three-point shot dropped in for what would have given her 13 points in the first seven and a half minutes of the game—but the referee's whistle on a foul a split second earlier negated all of that. Still, there was nothing about this that was work. This was fun.

Later, frustration set back in. It was late in the third quarter, and the Fever were losing by 17 points. (They would come back to narrow the margin and lose by 11 points, 91–80—still a defeat, but much closer than two days earlier.) Indiana veteran 6'4" forward Temi Fagbenle, already a favorite target of Clark's for the way she runs the floor, dropped a long Clark pass that looked to be a certain two points, although replays showed the ball was thrown slightly behind Fagbenle. A few plays later, the Liberty called a time-out.

In the huddle, Sides was mic'd up for television as she spoke with her team. As Clark got up and began to walk back onto the court, she wasn't happy. She had always demanded a lot from herself, and her teammates. Knowing that, Sides tried to reassure her young star. "Just give 'em time. Give 'em time."

"Her frustration was never directed at any player," Sides said a few months later in an interview. "She's a new point guard, a ball-dominant point guard, and there's a timing piece, getting to know each other, understand each other, understand people's speed and movements, and that's something that takes time. She's a fighter, a competitor, and that's exactly what I meant in that moment, it's going to take time, all of this is going to take time. With the turnovers early, I would tell her, that's a timing thing. We're getting killed at that point, playing Connecticut and then New York twice, and everything was about just trying to hold the ship together and just trying to find wins."

While the Fever fell to 0-3, Clark's play already was part of WNBA history. She became just the fourth player ever to score at least 50 points, with at least 15 assists, in her first three career games, joining Candace Parker, Nikki McCray, and the person sitting courtside, Sue Bird.

Considering the kind of defense she was facing, that was nothing short of remarkable. "Everybody's all over me," Clark said. "They're hounding me 94 feet, I'm getting trapped on every ball screen, getting blocked on every stagger screen. So I think it's just a learning process. I'm going to continue to learn from game to game, but I thought tonight was better."

•

Game Four of Clark's very new pro career came with a scare. With five and a half minutes to go in the first half of a tie game, 34–34, in Indianapolis against Connecticut (they were already playing Connecticut again), Clark, on defense, turned awkwardly and landed flat-footed on top of her left foot, turning her ankle. She crumpled to the floor by the free throw line, writhing in agony.

Silence enveloped sold-out Gainbridge Fieldhouse. "Oh no," Ryan Ruocco said on air, speaking for just about every basketball fan in America. "That is the last thing that anybody wants to see . . . Caitlin Clark limping towards the Indiana bench. . . . There are millions of people waiting to exhale."

One of them was Sides. "When she didn't get up, I knew it was serious."

Erica Wheeler tried to help Clark gingerly walk off the court, but Clark didn't want any assistance, something that Sides noticed and appreciated. "She's tough, she didn't want anybody to help her off the court. I love that about her. I love that that's what she's about." When Clark reached the bench, she slapped a chair and then limped to the locker room.

Watching the game in Iowa was her All Iowa Attack AAU coach Dickson Jensen. "People might have been saying she could be down a long time. And I'm like, 'Oh, no, she'll be right back.'"

He was right. It quickly became clear that she wasn't really hurt, she just needed the trainer to give her ankle an industrial-strength taping.

Clark returned at the start of the second half and was no worse for the wear. She finished with 17 points, 5 assists, and just 5 turnovers, which was half of what she had six days earlier against the same team. She and the Fever played very well, keeping the game close before losing, 88–84.

But that's not what people, even some of her teammates, remember about the game. No, they recall what arguably was Clark's most exhilarating three-point shot of the season.

With 7:23 left in the game, and the Fever trailing by one, Aliyah Boston stuffed DeWanna Bonner's attempt at a layup, grabbed the ball, and fired it to Wheeler, who was off to the races. Someone was running stride for stride with Wheeler, just about two steps behind. It was Clark. She was trailing the play on Wheeler's right, and Wheeler knew she was there as they crossed half-court.

Wheeler sneaked a side-eye look at Clark, then slipped a deft bounce pass back to her, knowing Clark would be there to collect it. Clark grabbed the ball, took a step, set her feet, and unloaded from the Gainbridge Fieldhouse logo, a whopping 33 feet from the basket. Her shot was a beauty, a dart on target from her fingertips to inside the rim in a blur to put the Fever ahead, 70–68. A sellout crowd that was already buzzing about Boston's block on the other end of the court erupted as Clark yelled and jumped and pumped her fists: "Let's go!"

Clark was loving the moment as much as the fans as she skipped back on defense. Wheeler was ecstatic, hopping up and down. They were in their own world, kids on the playground who had just devised the greatest play they could imagine—and pulled it off. If fans were ever going to leap to their feet over a shot that wasn't a last-second game winner, this was the one. Hundreds of arms raised, pumping, cheering. People jumping, screaming, refusing to stop celebrating, refusing to sit down. So many in their No. 22 jerseys and T-shirts looking like they had just seen the greatest thing in sports. "That was one of the loudest reactions I have ever heard in a game," Wheeler said months later.

The choreography between Wheeler and Clark, the way Wheeler so perfectly dropped the ball back for her, as if something so spontaneous could possibly have been planned, setting up this moment that was about to happen—it was a masterpiece. "A big shot, gave us some momentum, got the crowd going," Clark said.

That it was Wheeler who made the play happen was fitting because all she wanted to do at the start of the young season was to be there for Clark.

"For me as a big sister, I'm going to take the first step, to just let her know, 'We're here, we got you. Whatever you need from me as your vet, even in the same position, I got you.' . . . She's one of the biggest players in the world right now and she don't act like that. She's just like, 'Help me, in any way you can,' in a sweet way, there's no ego at all, she's not selfish. . . . She wants to learn, she wants to be a family, and I'm like a big sister to her."

•

Back on defense, Clark waved an arm as she often does, beckoning the crowd to stay standing, and they obliged, in full-throated delight, for several minutes. The Fever twice went up by four points over the next three minutes, but Connecticut always had an answer and pulled out the victory. It was a big-league, men's sports–style playoff atmosphere inside Gainbridge, in May, in a winless team's fourth game of the WNBA season. As majestic a sports moment as it was, it also was a harbinger. Months later, Wheeler said that's when she knew something really different was happening with this team for which she had been a cornerstone from 2016 to 2019, and again starting in 2023. It was as if by dropping off that pass to Clark, she was announcing what was coming—both in the moment, and over the next four months. And for that matter, for the foreseeable future in the WNBA.

"Yo, we are about to get this every night!"

•

The next day, in New York City, a photo of Clark dribbling in her dark blue Fever uniform appeared, much larger than life, on a billboard in Times Square: "Welcome to Wilson CAITLIN CLARK." The venerable sporting goods company had just announced that Clark had signed a multiyear partnership, which included her own signature basketball collection. She became just the second athlete to develop such a collection with Wilson, after Michael Jordan. The company announced three different white-and-gold Clark-branded basketballs featuring laser engravings of some of her best-known moments at Iowa. The basketballs had names: "Threes Up," "Record Breaker," and "Crowd Maestro."

Her Times Square billboard was just another sign of how things were changing for Clark. She was asked when she arrived in Indianapolis for training camp a few weeks earlier a simple question: When did she accept that her life would never be the same? "After my junior year of basketball in college," she said, acknowledging, "I probably still don't really go about my life in the way that I probably should. I still try to do normal things and live as a normal person."

The Fever had assigned her a bodyguard. "Steve follows me around. Don't mess with Steve!" she said, laughing. "But no, I'm still 22 years old and trying to navigate life and enjoy everything that life has to offer and still have fun. That's one of the things that has gotten me to this point. I've had a lot of fun playing basketball, and that's exactly who I am off the court too. Very easygoing, and I like to have fun. I like to be around people, so I try to do that as much as I can, honestly."

•

Clark and the 0-4 Fever packed their bags and headed west for three more games—in four days. This unyielding schedule was hardly conducive to winning games; the team had no time for real practices. "Our shootarounds are our practices," Clark said. This was no way for any professional sports league to treat any team, much less to showcase its prized possession. But to the great credit of Sides and the Fever, and Clark, they not only persevered, they finally won.

They came close in Seattle on May 22. The largest crowd in the 25-year history of the Storm, 18,343, which also was the biggest WNBA crowd since 2018, came to see Clark. Reporter Roberta Rodrigues, who covers the Storm, posted a video on X of Clark signing autographs, writing, "I have been covering women's basketball for 16 years. I've been to the largest ball events in the USA, in Brazil and in Europe. Yet, I have NEVER, EVER seen anything like that. Not with Sue Bird, nor Brittney Griner, nor Taurasi. Caitlin Clark is the WBB unicorn. I'm astonished."

Clark scored 21 points with 7 assists and 7 rebounds, and just 3 turnovers, as the Fever had a chance to tie or win the game in the final seconds, but Clark couldn't handle an inbounds pass thrown slightly behind her, and the Fever threat was extinguished, 85–83.

That day, *USA Today* women's basketball writer Lindsay Schnell published her first WNBA rookie power rankings of the season. She didn't place Clark first. Or second. Or third. She ranked her fourth behind Cameron Brink of Los Angeles, Julie Vanloo of Washington, and Chicago's Angel Reese.

She put Vanloo, a 31-year-old Belgian who had played overseas for years, ahead of Clark even though Clark averaged 17 points per game to Vanloo's 8. Vanloo had one more assist per game than Clark, but was behind her in rebounds and virtually tied in field goal percentage. Also, Clark had made 12 three-pointers to Vanloo's 7. Minutiae, for sure, but Schnell was dishing out some tough love for the new arrival.

"Clark might be graded tougher than anyone else," Schnell wrote, "but that's life as the No. 1 overall pick and most heralded rookie to ever come into the league. Clark has had an up-and-down first week, hitting some big shots but also throwing the ball away way too much (26 total turnovers). Physical play has bothered her when she's on offense, and on defense she's still learning how to not foul. She looks more comfortable every game, but hasn't managed to lead the Fever to a win yet."

"Every single night, the opponent's game plan is structured around Caitlin Clark," said Tamika Catchings, who was named the WNBA

Defensive Player of the Year five times when she played for the Fever. "They're guarding her at the half-court line because of the fact she makes the logo threes. They're face-guarding her, they are picking her up on the free throw line on the defensive end. Every single night she's going to get single-teamed, double-teamed, triple-teamed, quadruple-teamed. That is a huge compliment."

•

It was on to Los Angeles, where Clark came as close to a Hollywood ending as she would create all season. After five consecutive losses, the Fever finally won a game. Two epic Clark three-pointers near the end sealed the deal. She slapped palms with actor Ashton Kutcher, sitting courtside, to celebrate the first one. It was that kind of night in front of a Sparks-record crowd of 19,103, as the team moved the game to Crypto.com Arena, formerly Staples Center, to take full advantage of Clark's presence.

A look at the columns of numbers on the box score would tell you almost none of this. Clark scored only 11 points, missing her first 7 three-point attempts. But she made her last 2, and long after the game was over, months later, she said that was one of the highlights she will most cherish about her rookie year. She also ended up with 10 rebounds for her first WNBA double-double, with 8 assists, just 2 assists shy of a triple-double in only her sixth game as a pro.

With two and a half minutes remaining in the game, the Fever were leading the Sparks by three when Clark finally splashed a three-pointer, a massive 33-footer to put Indiana up, 72–66. Many in the crowd stood and roared as if it were a home game. Clark stuck out her tongue and danced back on defense. "Oh my goodness, it never gets old," ION TV analyst Mary Murphy gushed.

As for the split-second celebration with Kutcher, who was sitting courtside with his wife, actress Mila Kunis, and their children, Clark said, "That's a fellow Hawkeye, somebody that's been very supportive of me over the course of my college career. He was encouraging me the whole game."

With 40 seconds left and LA having climbed back to within two points, Clark drained another bomb, this one a step-back 29-footer for a 76–71 lead. Spectators roared again. Clark celebrated again, this time with a shrug. It wasn't a buzzer-beater—the Fever went on to win, 78–73—but it was the next best thing.

Afterward, Clark's tone was the same as it had been for all the other games. Win or lose, she was calm, measured, and in it for the long haul. "I thought I honestly played a really good game," she said in her TV interview. "Some nights, you know the shot's going to fall, some nights it's not. I stayed in it, found my teammates that were open, rebounded the ball well, was active on defense, and then made some big shots when we needed it. Honestly, just proud of myself."

•

At this early stage of the season, understanding the public's fascination with her, Clark was speaking with reporters three times every game day: during the late-morning or noontime shootaround, before the game, and after the game. Some professional athletes talk to reporters three times *a week*, some talk only once a week, some very briefly, some not at all. Not Clark. She constantly made herself available to the media. She had plenty of practice at it, having received all that national attention at Iowa.

What's more, Clark rarely gives short answers to questions; she looks reporters in the eye and spends significant time with her answers even if she is receiving some of the same questions over and over again. But even for someone who enjoys the back-and-forth as much as Clark does, and was pleased to have won her first game as a pro, it was getting to be too much, she said in her press conference after the victory in Los Angeles. "I feel like I talk to the media more than I get to talk to my own family, which is really kind of sad in a way, and it's a lot for somebody that's 22 years old."

•

The Fever's reward for winning? Heading to Las Vegas for a game the next day against the defending WNBA champions. It was the dreaded "back-to-back" game, and it did not go well for Clark or the Fever. After leading by four points in the first quarter, they were overwhelmed by A'ja Wilson and the Aces, 99–80. While it was Indiana's seventh game, five of which were played on the road, it was just the fourth for Vegas, all of them at home, highlighting the quirky imbalance of the 2024 WNBA schedule.

Clark, once again picked up on defense from end to end, scored her fewest points as a pro to date, just eight. She was outscored by her best friend and Iowa teammate Kate Martin, the Aces rookie, who ended up with 12 points, something that did not go unnoticed on social media. Martin and Clark were texting or talking every day as rookies, Martin said. Of Clark's early losses, she said, "That was a pretty hard time; she had won one game, and that's not familiar territory for her."

As serious as all this sounds, Clark and Martin's pregame reunion lit up the internet when they leaped into each other's arms. It was the first time they had been together since leaving for their respective teams after the WNBA Draft. Said Martin: "It was weird . . . seeing her in a different jersey than me."

•

The Fever went home for two more games, and two more losses, to end the month of May with a dreadful 1-8 record. "You could see the exhaustion on our faces," Clark said. They fell to the Sparks by 6 and the Storm by 15. The defensive pressure on Clark was inexorable; ESPN's

Michael Voepel reported that Clark had been blitzed on ball screens 57 times after nine games, more than any other WNBA *team*, let alone any other player. She was blitzed 18 times in just the Seattle game, more than twice what any other player had faced in a game all season.

Despite that, Clark scored 20 against Seattle and reached a new season high with 30 points against LA—where her opponents' obsession with her was on full display when the Sparks' Aari McDonald made a free throw, then dashed away from the line to face-guard Clark, forgetting that she had a second free throw coming. "I don't think she'd realized that she got another free throw," Clark said when asked about the weird moment, adding, "A kind person, honestly."

Looking back on that trying month of May, Sides said the Fever "were teetering. It was just so hard and unprecedented." It was especially challenging for her, a 47-year-old career assistant coach who had been hired by Lin Dunn in November 2022 to take over a team that had hit rock bottom earlier that year, winning only five games. Under Sides's leadership, the Fever immediately improved to 13-27 in 2023. As the 2024 season unfolded, Sides often described herself as "a second-year head coach in the second year of a rebuild." In other words, expectations normally wouldn't have been high—until Clark's arrival, an event that Sides called "the atomic bomb."

"The world we live in today wants results now, they want us to be good now," Sides said. "I kept saying to the team, 'Stay with the process. Stay with what we know is going to be a great product later.' It's going to be hard early. The challenge was keeping it from going sideways."

The Fever were working through something that had never happened before in the league, or in women's team sports—or all of women's sports, for that matter: this sudden explosion of interest from millions of new fans who were there for one reason, for just one person, Caitlin Clark. As some Clark fans on social media called out her teammates for not catching her passes, and demanded foul calls benefiting Clark from referees who didn't make them, they were acting like fans of any big-time sport in the internet age. Think of kickers who miss last-second field goals, players who make a crucial error in a baseball game, goalies who allow a late goal in hockey. It happens throughout sports, but this kind of fan intensity was new to the WNBA.

Sports fans love a player—in this case, Clark—and want her to do well. They cheer for her. They're unconditionally on her side. They're protective of her. Rough fouls and collisions make them worry about her as if she were a member of the family. They might not be right, but that doesn't matter to them.

On the other side of the conversation, those who weren't so enamored of Clark thought her supporters were going overboard. It's a physical league, they said. Everyone gets hit hard, especially rookies being "welcomed" to the league. Some of them also went after the Fever rookie as being overhyped, a disappointment, a complainer, you name it.

●

All of this was set against the backdrop of race in the WNBA. In mid-May, Las Vegas Aces star A'ja Wilson spoke to the Associated Press about the racial element in Clark's popularity. "I think it's a huge thing. I think a lot of people may say it's not about Black and white, but to me, it is. It really is, because you can be top notch at what you are as a Black woman, but yet maybe that's something that people don't want to see.

"They don't see it as marketable, so it doesn't matter how hard I work. It doesn't matter what we all do as Black women; we're still going to be swept underneath the rug. That's why it boils my blood when people say it's not about race because it is."

●

Sides herself suffered the social media wrath of many Clark fans anytime she took her star player out of a game or called a play that didn't work, or even a play that didn't involve Clark. Because Sides knew what it was like to be targeted, she dealt with the ramifications for her players immediately, including encouraging them to log off their social media accounts.

Aliyah Boston was one who took that advice, lamenting the "couch coaches . . . that have never stepped on the floor that just continue to tell you how you should be playing basketball . . . like we're messing up whatever bets or whatever they have going on. Personally, I'd rather not know, because obviously I did try to get those rebounds, I just didn't. And so I just logged off. It's been better for me. I've been able to really talk to God a lot, I've been in my Bible a lot more, and it's been a blessing."

Clark said she stayed away for a while as well, calling it "the healthiest thing" she could do. "I feel like I have a pretty good skill of blocking everything out. Being in this position, you better have that skill or else it's gonna break you at some point. I've surrounded myself with really good people, whether it's my coaches [or] teammates, whether it was in college, whether it's here, and I think also my family, they've been a huge support, and they see all this stuff, too, and that definitely has to be hard on them. You have to remember, we're regular people with feelings. My parents have feelings. It can definitely be hard at times, but, you know, I would never change it for the world."

The Fever players, almost all in their 20s, "are social media people, this is their generation," Sides said. "For them to be so affected by it, that was our first conversation in our team meeting: Just keep the noise out. We did what we had to do to make sure we don't let the outside noise in."

That was all well and good, but some developments were beyond their control as May turned to June and the Chicago Sky were coming to town.

# CHAPTER TEN

# Hip Check

It was early in the afternoon on Saturday, June 1, when Chennedy Carter hip-checked Caitlin Clark into one of the biggest national sports conversations of the year.

This was the most anticipated game of the young WNBA season: Caitlin vs. Angel, the Fever vs. the Sky, in once-again sold-out Gainbridge Fieldhouse. The matchup averaged more than one and a half million viewers on ESPN, which was a 346 percent increase over the 2023 WNBA regular-season average on the network.

But on this day, the Caitlin–Angel rivalry wouldn't be the story. No, another Chicago player stepped into the spotlight to take on Clark.

It started innocuously with an 18-foot pull-up jumper with 15.8 seconds remaining in the third quarter and Indiana leading, 53–49. After Carter, a four-year veteran wearing the light blue of the Sky, hit that shot, Aliyah Boston grabbed the ball and took a step under the basket to inbound to Clark. Carter was lurking, as a defender might. Clark was waiting for Boston to pass the ball to her to begin their trip down the court on offense. There had been some pushing between Clark and Carter on a previous play, and words had been exchanged the last time down the floor—not that any of that was particularly unusual or portended the plot twist that was about to occur.

Carter took four quick steps toward Clark, who wasn't looking at her, then blindsided her with a fierce cheap shot to Clark's left side, knocking her to the floor. Dozens of Fever fans near the play jumped to their feet, pointing, waving, yelling. Boston calmly walked to Clark and helped her up with both hands as Clark shot a couple of glances at the official who watched it all happen right at his feet.

He called a common foul—an away-from-the-play infraction—but he and his fellow referees, remarkably, never reviewed the play on the video monitor, which means they didn't even consider upgrading Carter's hit to a flagrant foul, which means their inaction created a vacuum that was filled the rest of the afternoon and evening by every single fan, pundit, and media personality who had an opinion on the hip check and what it all meant.

Had the referees called the flagrant foul right then, the WNBA would have correctly been judged to have punished Carter in the moment. That wouldn't have ended all conversation—not with Carter being Black and Clark white in this WNBA season in our polarized society—but it would have shown that the league took what Carter did to Clark seriously, immediately. But the league didn't do that, because its officials didn't do that—opening up more chatter and dialogue on how Clark was being treated in this, her 10th game as a pro.

"I had a huge problem, because they were there and saw it," Sides said. "Just make the right call right there. You saw it, make the right call; you're right there on the out-of-bounds line."

"From the league standpoint, you have to protect your players," said Catchings, who attended the game. "The cheap shot, I don't agree with that, especially that's where injuries happen. . . . That's not a basketball play. The fact that the referees didn't take the time within the game to go and look at it, I was really surprised. I was really surprised that they didn't look at it and that they just kept it moving. . . . As a whole, we all have a responsibility to make sure that things like that don't happen, for anybody to get hit like that."

As Clark began to walk toward the Indiana free throw line for one shot, Erica Wheeler came to her side, helping to steer her away from Carter and the other Chicago players who were wandering about. Wheeler's help then, and Boston's assistance when Clark was down on the court, highlighted the fact that other Fever players did not immediately rush to Clark's aid. This soon became one of several subplots surrounding the incident. Why didn't they have Clark's back? Some wondered if there was a racial divide in the Indiana locker room, even though both Boston and Wheeler are Black. Most of these questions were being asked on social media or various sports talk shows for the next several days by men who believed a confrontation of some sort was in order.

Christie Sides believed the opposite, that this was not the issue that sportscasters and fans wanted it to be. Carter's hit on Clark happened so quickly, and so far from their bench at the other end of the court, that it caught everyone off guard. Sides said she didn't even see it happen. "We're all watching the team come down the floor toward us and our bench. It's an inbounds play at the other end of the floor. We're all looking the other way and then this kind of comes out of the blue."

The Fever also felt there was no need for any kind of retaliation that likely would have resulted in technical fouls or ejections. Boston, who was right there, was already in foul trouble in a close game, so why potentially lose her? They knew Clark would get a free throw, and likely make it. They also knew the league would review the incident.

Catchings said something else was at play. Everything was still so new for the Fever. Their relative unfamiliarity with each other also might be the reason why the "enforcer" that social media so desperately wanted Indiana to produce to protect Clark had yet to materialize. "I'm on the outside looking in," Catchings said, "but I would just say this: There have been very few practices and they are still trying to learn with each other and they are still trying to learn how to play for each other, so when you talk about an enforcer, you enforce because you're a team and you know and understand how to protect each other.

None of this happens without a team effort. I think they're still trying to get to that point."

But Sides said she had seen evidence that they definitely were at that point during a home loss to Seattle two days earlier. After Clark nailed a long three over Seattle defender Victoria Vivians, the two glared at one another as they walked back down the court, yammered a bit, and then bumped into each other. As the official blew his whistle and gave each a technical foul (Clark's third of the young season), Boston rushed over to Clark and pushed her away, while Fever forward NaLyssa Smith ran interference and made sure everyone remained separated. Sides came onto the court and grabbed Clark's wrist, walking her to the sideline for a moment.

"They all just surrounded her," Sides said of her team. "Caitlin and Vivians were coming down the floor, there was a little scuffle, and they kind of got into it. Then Aliyah and NaLyssa went to her to help. That is exactly what it should look like. And it de-escalated really quick, and we moved on."

Not having an enforcer worked out quite well for the Fever on this day. By calmly making the free throw, Clark gave Indiana a point that would become very important in a game it desperately wanted, and needed, to win.

•

As ESPN televised Carter's hit on Clark, the camera captured something else in the background. The moment Carter plowed into Clark, Angel Reese, who was on the bench at the time, immediately and enthusiastically stood up and clapped. When the third quarter ended, Reese came off the bench to greet Carter with a big smile, wrapping her right arm around Carter, then hugging her.

"From Angel's standpoint, same as Caitlin, all eyes are watching you," Catchings said. "Angel has got to be herself, but there's got to be a maturity level from all of our rookies. As you grow in this game and as you become more mature, you understand what is acceptable and what's not acceptable. And you learn from the mistakes that you make. Angel hopefully has the right people around her that are like, 'Hey, you know what, not cool right there.' And how do you adjust and how do you learn from the situation?"

Through a spokeswoman, Reese declined several requests to comment for this book.

Meanwhile, how was Clark handling it? As soon as the quarter ended, she spoke to one of the officials for a few seconds, then immediately walked to ESPN reporter Angel Gray for a prearranged interview during the break. It had not even been two minutes since Carter had slammed into her. What would Clark say? How would she handle it?

Gray asked Clark if she had received "any type of understanding from the officials."

Clark spoke calmly. "Yeah, that's just not a basketball play, but you know, gotta play through it. That's what basketball's about at this level." She then moved right along, talking about the Fever being "really physical," even though they'd missed some "bunnies around the rim." She was hoping that "those fall in the fourth," and said she was "really proud" of the team's defense. After a few more observations about the game that had nothing to do with Carter's hit, Clark smiled and thanked Gray, then hurried back to the team huddle.

Clark's critics often wonder how this 22-year-old rookie so adeptly handles every question thrown her way in this suddenly very public life she is leading. They figure she must be the product of intense media training, prepped to the very instant before she comes out and answers questions. That theory had just been thoroughly disproved. This was one of the season's most telling moments, for the league and for Clark. She had just been blindsided by an opponent. Now, with a microphone in her face and a national audience listening to her every word, she could have blasted Carter, the officials, the league. She had a myriad of conversational options at her disposal. Yet all she did was say, "That's just not a basketball play," and that she had to "play through it."

How lucky was the WNBA that this woman, with millions of people following her, hanging on everything she said, handled herself in this manner at such a fraught moment?

"It just shows who she is and how she was raised, and the character that she has," Kate Martin said. "She would never say a bad word about anybody, and she would never make excuses for herself. And that's what makes her great, and that's something that I love about her. It doesn't matter if it's a flagrant foul or whatever, you know she's gonna hop right back up and continue to do her thing and never let anything stop her."

•

Back to basketball. Indiana built a slight lead into the fourth quarter, helped by one of those magical Clark moments: she lofted a lengthy, soft pass to Wheeler, who then tossed the ball to Kelsey Mitchell, already in flight, for a scintillating layup followed by a free throw when she was fouled. Indiana was ahead, 64–57. Things were a bit rough-and-tumble as well, as Reese tossed Clark to the floor as they were tussling under the basket in the final minutes. No foul was called, they glared at each other, and play continued.

But the final theatrics were all Indiana's. The Fever held a one-point lead and possession of the ball with 6.6 seconds remaining. They needed to safely inbound the ball and kill those final seconds, and they had a grand plan to do it. As Katie Lou Samuelson took possession out of bounds, Wheeler sneaked down the court, away from the Indiana basket toward Chicago's, in the backcourt, not where anyone expected her to be, least of all the Sky. No one followed her. She was alone. There were no defenders.

Samuelson, of course, saw this and passed the ball to Wheeler, allowing valuable seconds to tick off the clock before Chicago's defense perked up and raced toward her. Wheeler then tossed the ball to Clark, who was all alone in the frontcourt with a tad more than two seconds left. This was a masterful game of keep-away by the Fever.

With one second left, Clark heaved the ball high into the air, mimicking Kate Martin's shrewd move in the Final Four against UConn two months earlier. What a fitting ending this was—no one could foul her when she didn't have the ball—and time was expiring as the ball dropped back to earth. The capacity crowd roared wildly as the ball went up and the horn sounded, then came back down, bouncing harmlessly near the players as they celebrated.

Clark is often praised for her "high basketball IQ." Normally, she deflects the compliment and pivots to talk about her teammates. Not this time. "It's just a genius basketball play," she said. "I don't get why more people don't do that. There's, like, three seconds on the clock. Why wouldn't you just launch it into the air? They can't foul you. The clock's still running. They can't get the ball. Like, I don't get why more people don't do that. It's just smart." Then she grinned. "I almost hit the scoreboard, or the jumbotron, so I don't know if the facilities people would have been too happy, but it felt good."

It turned out that the free throw Clark received, and made, after Carter's third-quarter cheap shot ended up being the difference in the game. Indiana won, 71–70, earning its second win in its 10th game, while Chicago fell to 3-4.

•

When the players left the court, they filed into their locker rooms, then to their respective interview rooms that were less than a minute's walk down the hall from one another. Among the reporters who beelined to the Chicago Sky press conference room were Annie Costabile, the *Chicago Sun-Times'* Sky beat writer, and Matthew Byrne, fresh out of Indiana University, covering the Fever for the website *ClutchPoints*.

Costabile was the first to ask about Carter's body check of Clark.

"Chennedy, just wanted to give you an opportunity to talk about that moment between you and Caitlin, what was that play, what was said, and kind of what led to . . ."

Carter: "Next question."

Other questions about other topics were asked, then, three minutes later, Byrne tried again: "Chennedy, on the play before bumping into Caitlin, it seemed like she turned to you a little bit after the Fever scored."

"I ain't answering no Caitlin Clark questions."

Byrne was undeterred. "Did she say anything to you?"

"I don't know what she said."

Byrne: "What did you say to her?"

Carter: "I didn't say anything."

Sitting at the interview table with Carter, Chicago head coach Teresa Weatherspoon interjected. "That's enough," she said. "We're good. She's good."

Angel Reese was requested by the media, but refused to show up to be interviewed and was later fined $1,000 by a league that is salivating for more media coverage and attention for its players. WNBA media rules require teams to make two players and the head coach available after a maximum 10-minute cooling-off period. Every other healthy player is required to be made available if they are requested by a credentialed member of the media, as Reese was.

Over in the Fever press conference, Clark showed up as usual and answered questions about the incident. "Yeah, I wasn't expecting it. But I think it's just, like, just respond, calm down, let your play do the talking. It is what it is. It's a physical game, go make the free throw and then execute on offense, and I feel like that's what we did."

A day before, she said that she felt like she was "getting hammered," and, in fact, Christie Sides had just been called for a technical two days earlier in large part because of the Fever's concern over how Clark was being treated and what they believed was a lack of foul calls. Clark said she "appreciated" Sides's action. "I feel like I'm just at the point where you accept it and don't retaliate, like, you know, just let them hit you, be what it is," Clark said. "I think at this point, I know I'm going to take a couple hard shots a game, and that's what it is. I'm trying not to let it bother me. And just stay in the game is what's important, because usually it's the second person that gets caught if you retaliate. So, just trying to stay in the game and focus on my team and focus on what's important."

"I'm just really proud of her not reacting," Sides said in her press conference after the Chicago game. "That was a moment. She's a competitor, and she kept her cool, and that's exactly what she needed to do in that moment. It was a tight game. She handled it amazingly." Sides also said she continued to be concerned about physical plays against Clark that weren't being called as fouls or, in this case, as a flagrant foul. "Trying not to get fined," Sides said cautiously, "we're just going to keep sending these possessions to the league and these plays, and hopefully they'll start taking a better look at some of the things that we see happening, or we think is happening. It's tough, you know, to keep getting hammered the way she does, and to not get rewarded with free throws or just a foul call. She's continuing to fight through that, and I'm really, really proud of her for doing that."

General Manager Lin Dunn went further on X. "There's a difference between tough defense and unnecessary—targeting actions! It needs to stop! The league needs to 'cleanup' the crap! That's NOT who this league is!!"

•

The next morning, Sunday, June 2, Carter's foul was upgraded to a Flagrant 1, but she wasn't suspended or fined. Carter had also been busy on Threads, going after Clark, this time with words. Under a social media post with a video of Carter's back-and-forth with Byrne, she posted:

> & that's that on that cause beside three point shooting what does she bring to the table man 😂.

At that moment, Clark was ranked 4th in the WNBA in assists per game, 18th in points per game, and was tied for 2nd in three-pointers. She was leading all rookies in points and assists per game, and in the second half of the Chicago game, she became just the second player in WNBA history (Sabrina Ionescu was the first) to record at least 150 points, 50 rebounds, and 50 assists in their first 10 career games. And, of course, she was drawing unprecedented attention to the league, which benefited all the players.

On Monday, June 3, back in Chicago, Carter finally spoke with the media about her hit on Clark, with Reese by her side. "I'm a competitor," Carter said, "and I'm going to compete no matter who you are, and no matter who's in front of me. So, that's just what it was. Heat-of-the-moment play. We're getting at it. We're going back and forth. It's basketball. It's all hoops. . . . I don't have any regrets for anything, I'm going to compete. . . . No, I don't have any regrets."

Weatherspoon said that she talked to Carter about the hip check and offered a different perspective in a statement. "Physical play, intensity, and a competitive spirit are hallmarks of Chicago Sky basketball. Chennedy got caught up in the heat of the moment in an effort to win the game. She and I have discussed what happened and that it was not appropriate, nor is it what we do or who we are. Chennedy understands that there are better ways to handle situations on the court, and she will learn from this, as we all will."

Reese also had comments for the assembled reporters. "I'll take the bad guy role," she said. "And I'll continue to take that on and be that for my teammates. I know I'll go down in history. I'll look back in 20 years and the reason why we are watching women's basketball is not just because of one person. It's because of me too."

The conversation about the hit on Clark carried on for days in the sports media, and outside of it. In its daily newsletter *The Pulse* on June 2, *The Athletic* posted video of Carter's body check of Clark, with these notes: "Two things: Well, friends, that is getting hammered. It was Chicago's Chennedy Carter delivering the stiff foul. (There are

NFL safeties nodding in approval.) And look closer: Jumping off the bench like a WWE tag team partner is Clark's longtime rival and fellow top rookie, Angel Reese."

Radio host and author Mitch Albom included a segment on the Carter hit on his show on WJR in Detroit, while CNN anchor Jake Tapper did the same on *The Lead*. Over the CNN chyron—"Foul on WNBA's Caitlin Clark stirs debate about race, privilege"—Tapper said, "Because it's her, because it's Caitlin Clark, it gets a lot of media coverage." He ended the segment saying no matter what side people were on, "I think it's exciting that we're talking about the WNBA."

ESPN senior writer Mina Kimes summed it up as well as anyone could on the *Pablo Torre Finds Out* podcast: "Everybody's looking at this one incident and then using it to paint a broad brush in whatever direction they want to go with. You say Caitlin Clark gets the benefit of her identity from a marketing promotion standpoint. There are people who say, by leading with that, you're discounting her skills as a basketball player. If you don't acknowledge it, people correctly will say, 'Well, you're ignoring something that is just fundamentally true.' I guess my point is, everybody is right. . . . It seems perfectly calibrated to piss off everybody because there are so many things that are true at once."

•

Nearly a week after the incident, on Friday, June 7, after the Fever's shootaround at Capital One Arena in Washington, Aliyah Boston said of Carter's hit, "It's a tough league, everyone just wants to prove that this is their league in a sense."

Then Clark walked over to the gathering of a dozen members of the media, where I asked her how much attention she was paying to the controversy and conversation about what happened in the Sky game.

"I'm not [currently] on social media, so I don't see a lot of it, but you would be surprised, I still have my TV on in my house, and I'm watching sports, you're still aware of it, and you still see it. But other than that, my focus is basketball. Sometimes it stinks how much the conversation is outside of basketball and not the product on the floor and the amazing players that are on the floor and how good they are for their teams, and how great this season has been for women's basketball, going from college basketball to now the WNBA. Some of the crowds are unprecedented and had never been seen before. The viewership's amazing.

"But I try to block it out. I don't have social media on my phone, I don't go on it. I don't see a lot of it. But . . . everybody's gonna have their opinion, everybody's entitled to their own opinion. That's just what it is. And I think you just got to be focused on what's in your locker room, what's in your organization, how your teammates feel, how your coaches feel. And for me, that's my focus, but also I have a job to do at the same time. . . .

"I just love playing basketball. This is what I'm here for. I'm not here for all the other stuff. That's not what my teammates are here for either. And that goes for the rest of the teams in the league as well. Like, they want to play basketball. That's what they've been doing their entire lives, and they are really good at it."

Later, in a pregame press conference, Clark was asked if Carter owed her a public apology. "No. Basketball's competitive. I get it. Sometimes your emotions get the best of you. It happened to me multiple times throughout the course of my career. People are competitive. It is what it is. . . . That's just not where my focus is. That's not what I think about on a day-to-day basis. I think about my team. I think about ways that I can get better. It's just basketball at the end of the day. There are no grudges."

Without being asked about it, Clark praised Carter's play. "She's having a tremendous season. She's played great basketball in my eyes, probably in first place for Sixth Player of the Year. She's been great off the bench for them. I think she had, what, 25 here [in the Chicago Sky–Washington Mystics game] last night and really helped them win the game."

•

Concerned about the message that was being sent by the Carter hit, Billie Jean King told a story in my *USA Today* column about what she did at the 1971 US Open to quell the veteran players' jealousy toward 16-year-old sensation Chris Evert. "She's the reason we had all those people watching us," King recalled. "I told them, 'Chris is fantastic for our sport. Look at the crowds. You could not get in the place. She's the next superstar. She's going to put more money in our pockets. . . . That means everyone has to be more hospitable. When you're on the court against her, you gotta play tough as always, but no cheap shots. It's our job to make sure she is treated fairly.'"

In that June 4 interview, King had a message for the WNBA: "As great as the WNBA has been, with amazing stars like Maya Moore, Sheryl Swoopes, Candace Parker, Diana Taurasi, A'ja Wilson, and Breanna Stewart, among others, this year is a turning point, and it's because of Caitlin. Breaking the college records, everyone wearing the No. 22 jerseys. Things are going good for the WNBA, for women's sports . . . with all these sellouts and all this interest, and we've got to keep that going now. Whether you like it or not, Caitlin is the reason for so much of this interest. She's a superstar. When she does well, everyone does better. The league is going to do better. The veterans were the building blocks, and now Caitlin and this rookie class have this incredible platform to take the league to an entirely new place."

King said the extraordinary attention being paid to the WNBA makes this opportunity especially crucial. "This generation is so important for the WNBA, you have to set an example. Children are watching. How do you want to be remembered? This generation has a chance to set this league on fire. Don't blow it with animosity. Do not blow it. Just play ball. Play hard, but no cheap shots."

Evert praised King's 1971 actions in a post on X. "Yes, there was jealousy towards me . . . It didn't feel good. I was just a teenager.

BJK stood up for me. ♥ I hope women's basketball follows suit. @CaitlinClark22 is making the sport better."

•

On Sunday, June 2, the Fever announced that they had already surpassed their entire 2023 home attendance of 81,336 in just their fifth 2024 home game, with 82,857 and counting. On Monday, June 3, the WNBA announced that Clark was the league's Rookie of the Month for May, with 17.6 points per game, 6.6 assists per game, and 5.1 rebounds per game. After all the conversation and analysis, the concern and criticism, Clark was right where she was expected to be.

# CHAPTER ELEVEN

# Olympic Snub

On the evening of Friday, June 7, the Washington Mystics moved their game with Indiana from their 4,200-seat arena to Capital One Arena, all so more people could see Caitlin Clark. Clark obliged by scoring 30 points, with a rookie record–tying 7 three-pointers, including at least one in which she was sideways when she let go of the ball. "As a shooter," she said, "once you see one and two go in, the basket just looks bigger and bigger."

The largest WNBA crowd in 17 years came to see her: 20,333. It was more than double the attendance the Chicago Sky and Angel Reese drew the night before in the same arena, announced at an even 10,000. The Fever won, 85–83, for their third victory of the young season.

Clark's play was only getting better despite a bizarre injury suffered five days earlier in a dreadful loss at New York. She ruptured her eardrum while running into the Liberty's Jonquel Jones on a screen, played only 29 minutes of the game, shot 1-for-10, and scored only 3 points in a 104–68 defeat. But now, other than tugging on her ear on occasion as she answered questions, she said she was fine.

In the postgame press conference, reporters fired almost all of their questions at Clark while seven-year veteran Kelsey Mitchell, who was the second-leading scorer with 16 points, sat quietly beside her. When Fever public relations director Ryan Stevens announced, "Last one, third row on the left," Clark interjected: "For Kelsey." Clark put her arm around Mitchell's chair and smiled at her. The kid wanted the vet to have the last word.

The question, ironically enough, was about the massive sellout crowd that had come to see the Fever play the Mystics because of Clark. Mitchell handled it like the pro she is. "I'm playing alongside this kid," she said, "so it makes everything a little bit more dramatic. People are coming out to see this person."

When Mitchell was finished, both women pushed back from the table and stood to leave the room. Clark dashed up a staircase, beaming, having played her best game of the young season. Top of mind for her, and everyone around her, was a decision that was believed to be coming within days. It was USA Basketball's announcement of the 2024 US Olympic women's team, already a much-discussed and anticipated topic.

In an April interview, four-time US Olympic gold medalist Lisa Leslie delivered a strong statement in support of Clark in a story by ESPN's Ramona Shelburne. "She better be on the Olympic team," Leslie said. "We should not leave the country without her. She's a bona fide baller. There's no doubt she's already one of the best players in the world." However, when US Olympic coach Cheryl Reeve was asked about Clark at the Team USA media summit, also in April, Reeve answered ominously, "I've never been in the trenches with her."

As this chatter was going on, the committee selecting the team was watching Clark's games—and this one had been a beauty. Would that portend good things for Clark's chances? She could only hope.

•

Later that evening, while Clark was sitting in the back of the team bus on the way to the airport, her phone rang.

There was news. It was not good.

USA Basketball had decided not to pick her for the 2024 US Olympic women's basketball team. The national governing body for women's basketball (and men's), the organization tasked with growing the game in America, was passing over the person who could grow the game like no one else. The powers that be in the women's game did not want Caitlin Clark on their team.

No matter how well she was playing, and no matter how convinced most basketball experts were that she was not only getting better daily, but also playing very well in the moment, and no matter how much USA Basketball indicated Clark was being given a shot to make the team, she never had a chance.

•

I had been at that Fever game and in that Clark press conference. When I arrived home at 11:45 p.m., a text message had just come in. It was from a source within the Olympic basketball world, a person I had been in touch with since February, which was when I began reporting within the women's basketball community about the Olympic team selection process.

Because I was gearing up to cover my 21st consecutive Olympic Games, winter and summer, in Paris, the women's basketball selection process was one of many topics I was staying on top of. And with Clark in the mix, it was a very hot topic. Other than Simone Biles and Katie Ledecky, no American athlete would be a bigger star and story at the Paris Games—if she ended up going.

I spoke with numerous women's basketball sources over the winter and into the spring, and the first thing I heard from many of them was that five-time Olympic gold medalist Diana Taurasi, oft-injured and about to turn 42, was going to be given a farewell present by USA Basketball. She would be put on one more Olympic team, the 2024 team headed to Paris, and, they hoped, earn an Olympic basketball–record sixth gold medal, whether she actually deserved to be on the team or not.

This meant 11 spots, not 12, were open and available. Taurasi was a lock unless she was totally injured and couldn't play. And, frankly, she would be going even if she was a little injured and could only play sparingly.

To say this wasn't the way an Olympic selection process should be run is an enormous understatement. Guaranteeing a place for a 42-year-old athlete on an Olympic team in any sport is very unusual, especially an athlete like Taurasi who was nursing injuries as the Olympics approached, sitting out four WNBA games in July—and whose statistics were worse than Clark's.

•

The text message was simple: "I've got the list of the names of the Olympic team."

I called my source, who offered to read it to me. "Here goes, but before I start, Caitlin Clark's name is not on this list."

I broke the news in a series of posts on X, which included: "I'm hearing that Caitlin Clark, the best-known women's basketball player & most popular athlete in the country, is not going to be selected for the US Olympic women's basketball team."

Also: "I've covered the great US Olympic WBB team since 1984. It never gets anywhere near the coverage it deserves. Sadly, it's an afterthought. With Clark's popularity, it would have been one of the biggest stories in Paris, reaching girls worldwide. Without her, none of that happens."

•

Hours earlier, at the Fever–Mystics game, two sources, both longtime US basketball veterans with decades of experience in the women's game and knowledge of the Olympic selection process, told me information that made no sense at the time.

When I asked what they were hearing about Clark and the Olympic team, each person, separately and independent of the other, answered the same way. They both shook their heads about Clark's chances of being on the team, saying they weren't optimistic about them. And the reason they weren't optimistic was startling: They both said they were hearing concerns from the USA Basketball Women's National Team Committee about how Clark's millions of fans would react to what would likely be limited playing time on a stacked roster if they put her on the team.

The first time I heard this, I laughed. I thought my source was joking. What serious organization makes decisions based on such a thing? Concern about how fans will react has absolutely no place in US Olympic team selections.

I didn't laugh the second time I heard it. Apparently, the leadership in US women's basketball was so worried about people's reactions to Clark's playing time—so concerned about critical posts on X and Facebook and the like—that they didn't want to deal with any of it. And how do you not deal with it? By excluding Clark from the team.

Geno Auriemma had called Clark's fan base "delusional" just a day earlier, which was a window into how real the tension was between the old guard of the women's game and this multimillion-dollar, once-in-a-generation superstar. It also was just another example of how unprepared the women's basketball establishment was to handle the unprecedented attention and adoration Clark was receiving.

Further confirmation came later, when one of the six women's national team committee members spoke to me on background, meaning they could be quoted anonymously. When I asked if this was real—this concern being voiced by the two sources, who also didn't want their names used, about the reaction of Clark's fans and how the committee was worried about it—the committee member replied quickly: "Of course." When I later told one of the members of USA

Basketball's board of directors about my reporting, the board member, also speaking on background, said disgustedly, "This would never, ever happen on the men's committee."

On Saturday, I wrote a column for *USA Today*, which read in part:

> You can love Caitlin Clark. You can hate Caitlin Clark. You can love her Iowa roots. You can hate her Iowa roots. You can like her because she's white, or dislike her because she's white. Same goes for being straight. You can love the media's fascination with her, or hate it. You can love the historic TV ratings and sell-out crowds, or hate them. You can love her interviews, or hate them.
>
> But there's one thing that we all know to be true:
>
> With Caitlin Clark on the 2024 US Olympic women's basketball team, players who have been largely ignored by the sports media at every Summer Olympic Games that I've covered, which is every one since 1984, would have finally received the spotlight they deserve from a national and global audience. . . .
>
> With Clark continuing to set records for TV ratings and attendance in her first eye-popping month in the WNBA as she did in NCAA basketball, it would have been inevitable: she would catapult US women's basketball to a place it so richly has deserved but has never attained—coverage from broadcasters and news organizations not just in the US but around the world, headlines every day, and most important, vastly increased respect from a still male-dominated international sports media that has for decades focused almost exclusively on the US men's basketball team rather than the women, who are so good they haven't lost since 1992.
>
> But following Clark would have meant following much more than Clark. She would have introduced all those Olympic viewers and readers—many of whom are not big sports

fans and have never watched a women's Olympic basketball game—to the entire US team.

You've never watched Breanna Stewart on one of her two previous Olympic teams? You would have been watching her this summer because America's interest and even obsession with Clark would have brought you there. Same goes for Brittney Griner, assuming she's healthy.

But Clark isn't coming to Paris, unless someone withdraws or is injured. Clark won't be there to bring the casual sports fan who fell in love with her at Iowa and now knows the difference between ION and Prime to finally and rightfully watch Diana Taurasi and Jackie Young at the Olympics.

She won't be there, so all those fans won't be there, because they're never there. And one could only have imagined the global appeal of Clark once writers and reporters from around the world dropped in and watched a few logo 3s fall from the sky and a few hundred more autographs be recorded for posterity. Perhaps little girls in Europe and Africa would have been just as entranced as girls in America are. That's not happening anymore, and it's all on USA Basketball, whose mission statement fascinatingly includes "promoting, growing and elevating the game at all levels." (Seems to be Caitlin Clark's job description these days.)

Because this great opportunity to publicize international women's basketball has been missed, the vast majority of broadcasters and reporters will be able to focus as they always have on the swimmers and gymnasts and runners, and leave the US women's basketball team alone.

I've watched all this happen in real time. I've covered at least five of the US women's gold-medal basketball games at the Olympics, plus countless other women's basketball stories at the five other Summer Games I've attended. When I've looked around and seen a half-empty press tribune and

wondered why, the answer I received from my peers always
was that the Americans are just too good for their own good.
People already know they're going to win. And they're right.

Later in the column, I made the case that Clark was already playing
well enough to be put on the team.

There seems to be a notion out there that Clark didn't deserve
to be put on the team on merit. That's ridiculous. First of
all, the decision is subjective, so you can make a case for just
about anyone and everyone.

But how about some statistics? Clark is 13th in the WNBA
in points per game. (Taurasi is 15th.) Clark is fourth in assists
per game. (Sabrina Ionescu, 8th; Kelsey Plum, 11th; and Jewell
Loyd, 14th, all are on the list for the Olympic team.) Clark is
second in 3-pointers made, two ahead of Taurasi. . . .

Clark has done all of this while facing the fiercest defensive pressure statistically in the league. No one has received
the kind of attention she has as a rookie. She is not the best
player in the league, but she's clearly the most important.

Never given a real chance to try out—USA Basketball
preposterously scheduled her tryout during the Women's
Final Four, when she was leading Iowa to the national title
game for a second consecutive season—Clark now has been
told by the US national governing body of basketball one
simple word: No.

No, Caitlin Clark, we don't want you on our Olympic
team.

I've seen some bad team and athlete selection decisions in
the 40 years I've covered the Olympics, but this is the worst
by far. Then again, we probably shouldn't be surprised. As
we've known for years, the last amateurs left in the Olympic
Games are the people running them.

•

By Monday morning, the exclusion of Clark from the Olympic team had developed into quite the national story. Those who thought Clark wasn't yet good enough to make the team despite what the statistics said—and the need for three-point shooting in the international game—didn't appear to mind at all that, in addition to Taurasi, another guard, Chelsea Gray, was put on the team despite not having played a minute that season due to a foot injury.

There were others who praised the decision to snub Clark by saying the Olympic break would do her good. There was little doubt about that; Clark had been playing basketball at the highest level nonstop since October 2023, with just those eight days off from the end of the NCAA season to the WNBA Draft. So, of course, a respite would allow her to rest and recharge. But wasn't it up to Clark, not the national governing body, to decide if she wanted to take a break?

Some focused their argument specifically on the fact that USA Basketball should never put a player on a team simply to send TV ratings and merchandise sales skyrocketing. But very few of those people spent any time discussing what the Caitlin Clark Effect would actually have meant for women's basketball in Paris and around the world.

Let's do that right here. Global growth is the goal of all sports. It's why the NFL plays in Europe. It's why the NHL shut down during several Winter Olympics—and will do so again in 2026—so its players can be showcased at those Games. Any other national governing body would have been delighted to have an opportunity to reach previously unreachable fans—especially women and girls—across the globe with an attention magnet like Clark. She could have been to women's international basketball what the 1992 Dream Team was to men's international basketball. And women's basketball, always an afterthought to the men's game, desperately needed that kind of a boost.

The interest in Clark was that intense. Journalists from England and Brazil, among other nations, told me they had been hoping to cover her games at the Olympics. A sports radio host in New Zealand told me his "mum" was shocked by Clark's exclusion from the US team.

Some analysts and commentators who scoffed at what might have been were men who had never covered a women's basketball game in their lives—at the Olympics, in college, anywhere—and, in most cases, didn't want to. I know this because, over the years, they've told me that. They didn't respect the women's game and consistently avoided covering it at the Olympics.

Despite all their victories and medals, the US women's basketball players are often largely ignored by the sports media at the Olympic Games. The gymnasts and swimmers and runners and, of course, the US women's soccer team get so much more attention. It's a crowded couple of weeks, with dozens of medals being handed out every day, so the competition for headlines, and top billing on NBC, is always intense. Because the women's basketball team is so good, editors often send reporters elsewhere on the jam-packed Olympic schedule. That's a terrible reason to not report on a team, and we, of course, know that race is always a part of this conversation with a majority of players on the US team being Black, but the fact remains that US sports journalists don't cover this team as they should.

There's also the obvious point that team selections are, by definition, not scientific. It's always a biased process when selections aren't based on times or a specific list of criteria and statistics—especially when a college player is selected, as Christian Laettner was on the men's side and Rebecca Lobo, Taurasi, and Stewart were on the women's.

USA Basketball turned all of those collegians into Olympians but left the greatest scorer in major college history, women's or men's, at home. There's no other way to say this: Given multiple reasons and opportunities to pick Clark, USA Basketball didn't just decide not to do it, it actually recoiled at the notion.

•

During an interview session after practice on Sunday, June 9, Clark was asked about the Olympic team decision. "I'm excited for the girls that are on the team," she said. "I know it's the most competitive team in the world, and I knew it could've gone either way—me being on the team, me not being on the team. I'm excited for them, I'm going to be rooting them on to win gold.

"Honestly, no disappointment," she added. "I think it just gives you something to work for. It's a dream; hopefully one day I can be there. I think it's just a little more motivation, you remember that, and hopefully, when four years comes back around I can be there."

Fever coach Christie Sides said during her availability with the media that Sunday that she and Clark texted right after she got the call on the bus. "She texted me to let me know. I just tried to keep her spirits up. The thing she said was, 'Hey, Coach, they woke a monster,' which I thought was awesome."

Although Clark took the high road, as usual, in her public comments, Sides said later in an interview that the Olympic decision was "such a disappointing moment for her. Being an Olympian is a huge dream of hers, and when she realized it wasn't going to happen, it just lit a fire under her."

As the team landed in Indianapolis and got off the plane, Sides said she and Clark "were walking and talking about the decision. She could have gone to practice that night, I mean, that's where she was, that's the competitor she is. She didn't really say much more after that."

Sides was criticized by some of Clark's fans on social media for revealing the content of her text exchange with Clark. "I didn't even think what I said was wrong. I was just taking up for a player. That was our private conversation, which to me was just raw and true. So, I didn't think anything about it, but I know now that I never should have said anything."

•

In the days that followed the snub, USA Basketball's answers about Clark were all over the map. The one member of the committee, speaking anonymously, focused on Clark not having been at her try-out at the national team training camp—even though the camp was scheduled during the weekend of the Women's Final Four in Cleveland, when Clark and her Iowa Hawkeyes were playing.

"Had she come to a training camp, we would know how she would fit. But she's never been to a training camp."

The committee, of course, was aware the camp was scheduled when Clark could not attend. "So, we're basing it all on how she's made this transition from college to the pros," the committee member said. "Some of it's great, some of it's not so great."

But when women's committee chair Jen Rizzotti met with the media on Zoom after the official team announcement, she said of Clark, "She's had a tremendous start to the WNBA season so far."

In addition to Rizzotti, the former UConn standout who was now president of the Connecticut Sun, the committee included South Carolina coach Dawn Staley, WNBA executive Bethany Donaphin, Atlanta Dream general manager Dan Padover, former Minnesota Lynx All-Star Seimone Augustus, and Old Dominion head coach and former WNBA All-Star DeLisha Milton-Jones. All members of the committee declined to be interviewed on the record for this book through USA Basketball spokesman Michael Terry.

The committee's choices for the Olympic team had to be approved by the USA Basketball board of directors, chaired by (ret.) General Martin Dempsey. When asked via email to comment for this book, Dempsey wrote, "I'm content about the process we followed in selecting our 2024 Women's Olympic Team."

•

Irony arrived with the official announcement of the team. Proving the point about the magnitude of Clark's appeal, the Associated Press promoted a story on the announcement of the US Olympic team on X with a photo of . . . Caitlin Clark. And the top of *USA Today*'s sports mobile app featured three stories on the Olympic team selection news—all with Clark's name in the headline. Editors making decisions on how to get people interested in stories about the naming of the US Olympic women's team chose to use the name and photo of someone who was not on the team.

•

Clark did have another option to get to Paris: the US women's 3x3 team. Even though she had never played on a national 3x3 team (she had experience on US under-16 and under-19 5x5 teams), USA Basketball offered her a spot on the 3x3 team well before June, knowing there was a qualifying event for her to play in to become eligible for the Olympics, according to two sources with knowledge of those conversations.

The 3x3 tournament was held in a temporary stadium at Place de la Concorde, where the guillotine was located during the French Revolution. Music blared and a DJ-style announcer talked incessantly. The atmosphere was light and fun, but there was no mistaking this relatively new addition to the Olympic Games for the venerable 5x5 game.

Nonetheless, USA Basketball was asking: Was this a possibility? Did Clark want to go to Paris on this US team?

The answer from Clark and her team was simple: No. She did not want to play 3x3 basketball at the Olympics.

•

Two weeks after Clark was left off the Olympic team, an interesting voice wanted to be heard on the subject: the man running the next Summer Olympics. Casey Wasserman, president of the 2028 Los Angeles Olympic Organizing Committee, who also owns a sports marketing and management company that represents Taurasi and Stewart, among others, showed up at the US Olympic swimming trials in Indianapolis on Saturday, June 22. Wasserman had just finished answering several questions from a dozen journalists when he playfully said, "No questions about Caitlin Clark?"

"Okay, what about Caitlin Clark being left off the Olympic team?"

"I think it's a missed opportunity because she's clearly a generational talent at a time when the world was ready for it," Wasserman said. "There have been incredible talents in the world; shame on all of us, the world wasn't in a place to embrace that. Take Diana [Taurasi] or Breanna Stewart, or some of our [Wasserman] clients who are going to be on the team. They are dominant at a level that's never been seen before, but the world wasn't ready to fill a building like Caitlin Clark did for whatever, the Final Four. . . . It would have been an opportunity to elevate the women's team, but I understand the other side of it, which is it's an independent process and it's hard to get in the way of telling [the committee] what to do."

•

On July 14, right before the WNBA shut down for the All-Star Game and the Olympics, Clark and the Fever traveled to Minnesota's Target Center to play Olympic coach Cheryl Reeve's Lynx for the first time in 2024. The place was sold out, thanks to Clark and her fans, many coming from next-door Iowa. When she played in the Big Ten championship there, Clark was so beloved by the fans that the Target Center had an unofficial nickname: "Carver North" (Iowa's home arena of course being Carver-Hawkeye Arena).

Before the game, Reeve was asked about facing "a lot of people cheering" for the road team.

"I don't give two shits," she said with a straight face.

Reporter: How about one?

"Not even one shit," she said, cracking a sly smile.

In that game, Clark scored 17 points with 6 assists as Indiana upset Minnesota, which was playing without injured star Napheesa Collier. Final score: 81–74. In the last seconds, when the game was won and

Clark was walking to the line to shoot, and make, two final free throws, she triumphantly applauded as the fans rose to their feet. She gave one big wave of her left arm. The cheers from the capacity crowd of 18,978 were deafening.

After the game, Reeve appeared to give . . . well, she cared a little bit more. Asked what the WNBA can do to encourage similar environments at more games, Reeve said, "I don't know that I quite understand the question, in that everybody knows that the reason why our teams around the league are having sellouts are because Caitlin Clark and the Indiana Fever are coming to town."

•

Rizzotti, the chair of USA Basketball's women's committee, was optimistic that the interest in Clark would die down as the Paris Games approached. "I would hope," she said on her Zoom press conference on June 11, "that the journey that this team is about to take and the unprecedented amount of success that they've had is story enough for people to want to follow it and to market it and to pay attention to these extraordinary 12 women that are going to be representing us this summer in Paris."

One member of the selection committee, Dawn Staley, did not get the memo. On July 28, on the NBC set during the Olympics, host Mike Tirico asked Staley for her "read" on the Clark situation now that some time had passed since she was left off the team.

"As a committee member," Staley said, "you're charged with putting together the best team of players, the best talent. Caitlin is just a rookie in the WNBA. Wasn't playing bad, but wasn't playing like she's playing now."

Of course, Clark had been playing well enough before the team was announced for Rizzotti to call her play "tremendous."

Then Staley pulled the pin out of the metaphorical hand grenade and heaved it into Reeve's Team USA huddle. "If we had to do it all over again," she said, "the way that she's playing, she would be in really high consideration of making the team because she is playing head and shoulders above a lot of people. Shooting the ball extremely well, I mean, she is an elite passer, she's just got a great basketball IQ, and she's a little more seasoned in the pro game than she was two months ago."

The question remained: How did all those skilled basketball minds on the committee miss how good Clark already was—and how well she would be playing by the Olympic break?

The answer was becoming clearer by the day: Because they wanted to.

# CHAPTER TWELVE

# "Great Job, Sister"

With the Olympic decision behind her, Caitlin Clark was back on the court at Gainbridge Fieldhouse. Basketballs were bouncing, her teammates were nearby, and she was being challenged in a way she had never quite been before. She wasn't facing a smothering defense or a superior team. No game had yet begun.

In two interview sessions across five hours on the afternoon of Thursday, June 13, Clark was asked four questions by two journalists. It was the most intense questioning of her young WNBA career, a continuation of the cultural conversation surrounding Clark's ascendance in the league, coming less than two weeks after Chennedy Carter's flagrant foul on Clark.

At the team's shootaround, Jim Trotter, a columnist for *The Athletic*, asked three questions of Clark: "It seems no matter what you do or what is done to you, it becomes a topic nationally, and a lot of times it becomes divisive. I wonder, from your standpoint, how you feel about people using your name in whatever culture wars or whatever wars they're fighting. How do you feel about that?"

"It's not something I can control," Clark said. "So, you know, I don't put too much thought and time into thinking about things like that. And to be honest, I don't see a lot of it. Like I said, basketball's my job, everything on the outside, I can't control that, so I'm not going to spend time thinking about that. You know, people can talk about what they want to talk about, create conversations about whatever it is, but I think for myself, I'm just here to play basketball. . . ."

Trotter: "How much do you think that it's impacted your ability to cultivate relationships within the league?"

Clark: "Everybody in the league understands, one, we're excited about all this attention we're getting . . . appreciative of it. I think the league has been great for a really long time. But my focus is on my teammates. They've been amazing. I don't think it's impacted me making relationships on my team. I'm not obviously talking to people on other teams on a daily basis. I have so much to focus on here, and getting my teammates to trust me and do all that is my main focus, same with our coaching staff, same with this organization."

Trotter: "But I understand your focus, but I'm just curious, though, are you bothered because folks would attempt to weaponize your name in whatever fight they're fighting?"

Clark: "No, I don't see it. That's not where my focus is. Again, my focus is here and on basketball. And that's where it needs to be and that's where it has been, and I'm just trying to get better on a daily basis."

Everything Clark says and does finds its way to social media as swiftly as possible, and so it was with the video of the Trotter–Clark Q and A, hitting the internet right around lunchtime. Connecticut's DiJonai Carrington—who relished her rivalry with Clark, having just mocked her on the court after being called for a foul on Clark in the Sun's 89–72 victory three days earlier—saw the interview and had something to say about it at 4:51 p.m. on X.

"Dawg. How one can not be bothered by their name being used to justify racism, bigotry, misogyny, xenophobia, homophobia & the intersectionalities of them all is nuts. We all see the sh*t. We all have a platform. We all have a voice & they all hold weight. Silence is a luxury."

•

In the early evening, Clark was back on the court and surrounded by reporters again. James Boyd, *The Athletic*'s Indianapolis beat writer, who, like Trotter, is Black, said he wanted to be very specific in his questioning of Clark. "I know you mentioned that you want to focus straight on basketball. Definitely respect that. But just asking you directly, when people use your name for racism, misogyny, whatever, what is your response to that specifically?"

"I think it's disappointing," Clark said in a video Boyd posted on X not long after the interview. "I think everybody in our world deserves the same amount of respect. The women in our league deserve the same amount of respect, so people should not be using my name to push those agendas. It's disappointing. It's not acceptable. But yeah, I mean, this league is the league I grew up admiring and wanting to be a part of. Like, some of the women in this league were my biggest idols and role models growing up, and helped me want to achieve this moment right here that I get to play in every single night. So, just treating every single woman in this league with the same amount of respect, I think, is just a basic human thing that everybody should do, just be a kind person and treat them how you would want to be treated."

Trotter wrote a column for *The Athletic* that day. In it, he said that Clark "backtracked" over the course of the afternoon, "but the damage had already been done," citing Carrington for speaking out against Clark's initial comments. Trotter said Clark's comments "were troubling because they lacked awareness and empathy toward Black peers who do not have the privilege of distancing themselves from the isms they are regularly confronted with. Carrington likened her silence to luxury. I see it as complicity."

Trotter added that it was "important that Clark revisited her comments" later. "It may have taken her time to express those sentiments, but that should not overshadow that she ultimately got to the right place. It was a positive step for her and the league."

•

Once again, there were many opinions on the questions to Clark, and how she answered them. As longtime sports columnist Mike Wise said in an interview, "She is the biggest racial wishbone we've ever seen, being pulled every which way."

The analysis was predictable in this polarized world of ours. Some wanted Clark to initiate a racial conversation, not wait to be asked about it. UConn's Paige Bueckers did this onstage at the 2021 ESPY Awards: "With the light that I have now as a white woman who leads a Black-led sport and celebrated here, I want to show a light on Black women. They don't get the media coverage that they deserve. They've given so much to the sport, the community, and society as a whole, and their value is undeniable."

Others thought Clark did just fine. "We're all different," Fever great Tamika Catchings said. "We all have different beliefs. . . . So, now you have Caitlin, who comes into this, and she doesn't care about the fight over all these issues. She wants to play. She wants to win. She's inclusive. You can tell by the way she is. She's kind of oblivious at times, and probably not purposely—she's young, she's just like that kid when you experience things for the first time, just like bouncing around, but that's what people love about her. And she's done a great job of handling herself in her interviews, done a great job."

•

Later that week, 15 days after Sky–Fever I, along came Sky–Fever II. Clark looked so comfortable—Iowa comfortable—playing all but three minutes and scoring a game-high 23 points with 9 assists and 8 rebounds, while Angel Reese had 13 rebounds and 11 points on her way to breaking the league record for most consecutive double-doubles with 15 and winning WNBA Rookie of the Month for June. Clark also continued to set historic league milestones, becoming the fastest player in WNBA history to reach 200 points, 75 rebounds, and 75 assists.

Rookie of the Year chatter was developing around both players, but that wasn't what connected them at noon on Sunday, Father's Day, June 16, before the usual packed house at Gainbridge and the usual record-breaking TV audience—2.25 million on CBS, the most-watched WNBA game on any network in 23 years.

Near the end of the third quarter, Reese clobbered Clark in the head as she was driving to the basket. The foul was ruled a Flagrant 1 right then and there—there was no overnight wait this time—and Clark, steady-eddy at the line, made both free throws to give the Fever a three-point lead on their way to a 91–83 win. Asked what was going through her mind after her encounter with Reese, Clark said, "What's going through my mind is I need to make these two free throws. That's all I'm thinking about."

For her part, Reese offered a few choice words about the officiating. "It was a basketball play. I can't control the refs. They affected the game, obviously, a lot today. I'm always going for the ball. Y'all are going to play that clip 20 times before Monday."

More like 20 times before dinner, and probably 200 times before Monday.

•

A bizarre "worlds collide" postscript occurred at the end of the Reese foul on Clark. As the ball flew out of bounds, it nearly hit a spectator sitting courtside under the basket: Olympic swimming legend Katie Ledecky's uncle, New York Islanders owner Jon Ledecky, in town for the US Olympic swimming trials five blocks away at Lucas Oil Stadium. Katie's brother Michael swatted the ball away from his uncle's head. Of course, social media took note.

Several days later, the Fever visited the Olympic trials in the Indianapolis Colts' stadium and were introduced to the crowd, with Clark receiving a predictably loud ovation. As they left the pool deck, Clark raced toward the pool's edge, pretended to jump in, and playfully stuck her index finger in the water. She then ran toward Kelsey Mitchell and jabbed her teammate's arm with her wet finger, laughing all the way.

"Up for a quick swim, @CaitlinClark22??" USA Swimming's social media team posted on X, with the video of Clark's antics. That post of a basketball player sticking her finger in the water received 630,000 views, the most of any of the dozens of posts USA Swimming put out, either about the competition or any individual athlete, during the nine-day meet. Only a post introducing the 2024 Olympic swimming team received more—a lot more, 11 million views.

•

Three days later, against Washington, the Fever won their fourth consecutive home game for the first time since 2015, which was during the Catchings era, when Aliyah Boston was a freshman in high school and Clark was in the eighth grade. Now 5-2 in June, 6-10 overall, Indiana was making a move up the standings and would qualify for the playoffs if the season ended right then. The bad memories of those first 9 games in 17 days, and 11 in 20 days, 6 of which were against the league's top three teams, were receding quickly.

"The youngest, least experienced team in the league," Christie Sides said about her squad. "That schedule was tough, with no practice time. Now they're feeling what it should have felt like at the beginning for them."

Clark's high-wire act was a nightly show. For instance, with the game tied nearing halftime, Clark nailed her first three-pointer, a dagger from 29 feet. In Washington's subsequent possession, she stole an errant Mystics pass and drove to the basket for an easy layup. It was five Clark points in 14 seconds—and a lead that Indiana never relinquished.

There still was interest in her turnovers—six this time. When she was asked about them in her press conference, Clark dutifully started going through each one when Boston, who played beautifully, scoring 22 points, interrupted from the seat next to her.

"You look at Caitlin and you look at the way she passes the ball, and so sometimes things are going to happen that way, and that's okay because we're not going to let her hang her head, we're not going to hang our head off of any missed passes," Boston said. "We're still continuing to jell together, and we know that she's a great passer, so she thinks she can get that ball there, she's going to throw it, and if I miss it, then we're good, we're all right, we're good."

•

The Fever hit the road for five consecutive games, the fourth of which was in Phoenix, the much-anticipated first game between "The GOAT" and "The ROOK," as the Mercury called it on social media, giving Clark equal billing with the legendary Diana Taurasi. The Mercury had been promoting the June 30 contest since early April. As the game approached, Taurasi was asked about facing Clark for the first time.

"Yeah, it'll be fun," she said blankly. Then she turned her head away from the camera. Taurasi being Taurasi, that was it. One second and she was done with Clark.

Clark, on the other hand, spoke about Taurasi for a minute and a half, including words like this: "That's somebody I grew up idolizing and looking up to and wanting to be like one day. Obviously, she's one of the greatest players our game has ever seen, greatest scorer our game has ever seen, so for me, I'm excited. That's fun. It's kind of like a dream come true."

The Fever didn't exactly come into the game on a roll. They had lost two in a row, including their first loss to the Sky in Chicago, and their star wasn't feeling good. Clark occasionally dealt with migraines, and she had one that day.

The players' greetings right before the tip were notable. Taurasi walked toward Clark and gave her a semi-warm quick little hug as

Clark smiled broadly. Moments later, Clark put out her hand as Brittney Griner approached, but Griner leaned in and wrapped her in a
welcoming one-arm embrace.

Enough with the pleasantries; the Fever got off to a terrible start
against the Mercury and their three Olympians, Taurasi, Griner, and
Kahleah Copper—falling behind, 17–4; trailing by 11 at halftime; and
being down by as many as 15 points in the second half. But, behind
the ailing Clark, the Fever stormed back and won, 88–82, as Clark fell
one rebound short of what would have been the first triple-double by
a WNBA rookie. She had 15 points; Taurasi had 19. But Clark had 12
assists to Taurasi's 3, and 9 rebounds to Taurasi's 3. Her most impressive
statistic was this: despite the migraine, she played 39 out of 40 minutes.
It was the Fever's first victory all season over a team with a winning
record. After starting the year 1-8 in May, the Fever were 7-4 in June.

Almost everyone was now acknowledging the ascendance of Clark—
even, stunningly, Taurasi. "It's amazing what Caitlin's been able to do
in her short career so far," Taurasi said after the game. "The one thing
that I really love about her, she loves the game. You can tell she's put
the work in. . . . It's been a lot of pressure, a lot of things thrown at
her, and she keeps showing up and keeps getting better every single
game. So her future is super bright, and being a veteran and being in
this league for a long, long time, [I see that as] pretty cool."

When she was asked right after the game about playing and beating Taurasi, Clark lowered a towel she was using to wipe her face and
flashed a very big grin. "I'm just happy we won," she said on ESPN. "It
was cool to play against [Taurasi] and obviously a really great game. . . .
This crowd was absolutely incredible."

After the interview, as she began her walk across the court toward
the children waiting for autographs, then the locker room, at least nine
cameras followed Clark every step of the way. Fans weren't leaving; a
standing ovation was ongoing; cheers were rising. This was an away
game? Yes, but no. Caitlin Clark has no away games. She had become
the hometown hero, even in other people's hometowns.

•

It was now July, and Clark and the Fever were on a march that was both exhilarating and melancholy. They would play six more games before the Olympic break, winning three and losing three. They won games they would have lost early in the season and lost games they now were good enough to win. They beat Phoenix again, and Minnesota on the road, but lost to Washington at home and Dallas on the road. They needed the monthlong break that was coming, but there was a part of them that didn't want to shut it all down now because things were going so much better than they had at the beginning of the season. They had room to breathe between games—three or even four days on occasion—and serious practice time to strengthen their burgeoning camaraderie.

It was no surprise that Clark's talent was now taking off, and the Fever with her. They achieved their biggest victory of the season to date as Clark became the first WNBA rookie ever to record a triple-double, with 19 points, 13 assists, and 12 rebounds in an 83–78 upset win over the league-leading New York Liberty at home on July 6.

Asked about that milestone, the first ever for a Fever player, Clark focused not on herself, or her passes, but on what happened to them after they left her hands. "Obviously, 13 assists, that means my teammates made 13 shots off my passes, so that goes to them."

"She's so humble, isn't she?" said Boston, who was sitting beside Clark. "Let me tell you, that's pretty cool, Caitlin. Great job, sister."

The passes kept clicking. Clark dished out a stunning 19 assists—a new WNBA single-game record—at Dallas on July 17 in the Fever's final game before the Olympic break. This wasn't a rookie record; it was the most assists anyone had ever accumulated in one game in the 27-year history of the WNBA. "I just try to set my teammates up for success," Clark said afterward. "You can tell our chemistry is really coming along and we're playing a lot better."

In a five-game span from playing Phoenix to playing Phoenix again, from June 30 to July 12, Clark scored 96 points with 62 assists, becoming the first WNBA player ever to have 90 points and 60 assists in a run of five consecutive games. Unsurprisingly, Clark was named WNBA Rookie of the Month for July.

．

For all the conversation about the antagonism Clark faced from her WNBA opponents, a notable moment of kindness was offered by Las Vegas Aces guard Jackie Young, a former Notre Dame star and 2024 Olympian, in a July 2 game in Vegas. Clark slipped as she was driving near the lane, sliding on her knees as the ball rolled out of bounds. With Clark still down, Young leaned over and began *untying* her shoes as she looked at Clark, who then was on one knee tying her shoe. Young tapped her on the arm to see if she was okay as Clark smiled back. By fiddling with her shoelaces, Young was stealing time for Clark to compose herself before play began anew.

"Just doing the right thing, just making sure she's good and just checking on her," Young said. "I gave her a little tap, make sure she's cool. Because, at the end of the day, you know, we just want to play this game, have fun, be healthy. Just giving her a little bit of time to reset, regroup, and just make sure she's okay."

．

The Fever were 11-15 going into the All-Star break, sitting in seventh place in the league, firmly in playoff position. Clark was leading the league in assists, with 8.2 per game, and leading all rookies in scoring, with 17.1 points per game. She had 5.8 rebounds per game as well.

Because almost everything in sports media needs to involve hot takes, an enticing conversation was going on about this very premature question: Who should become the Rookie of the Year, Caitlin or Angel? While a flashy point guard who can shoot and pass the ball like a dream will usually have an edge over an unstoppable rebounder, especially one with the statistics Clark had, some were on the Reese bandwagon.

TMZ Sports caught Dawn Staley in an airport as the All-Star Game neared. "So, you're going to try to put me into controversy, right?" she said. "They both are having great years. If I had to pick a Rookie of the Year at this time, today, it's Angel. Not a doubt. What she's been able to do with the double-doubles, but listen, the season is halfway through and Caitlin is coming. Oh, Caitlin is coming. . . . I say this, whatever team makes the playoffs, that's our Rookie of the Year."

•

The 2024 WNBA All-Star Game in Phoenix was not going to be your typical exhibition game; it was the US Olympic team's last test before leaving the country, and their best test, facing a WNBA team that featured the most impressive collection of talent in the world—other than the Olympic team itself. The selection process for the All-Star Game was 50 percent fan voting, 25 percent WNBA player voting, and 25 percent media voting.

One guess who received the most fan votes. It was Clark, of course. She received 700,735 votes, followed by teammate Aliyah Boston, with 618,680; A'ja Wilson, with 607,300 (she was already playing for the Olympic team); Breanna Stewart, with 424,135 (also on the Olympic team); and Angel Reese with 381,518.

In another sign of just how extraordinary Clark's popularity was, a year earlier, for the 2023 All-Star Game, Wilson was the top vote-getter. Her total? 95,860 votes. That "rising tide lifts all boats" phrase certainly was having its day; the public's fascination with Clark was carrying over to so many other players. They were being seen, and supported, as never before.

Clark started for Team WNBA, and while her three-point shooting was way off—she went 0-for-7—she dished out a rookie-record

10 assists, one shy of Sue Bird's overall record of 11, to help her team upset the Olympic squad, 117–109.

The last of those assists, with six and a half minutes left in the game, went to Angel Reese. The two rookies slapped palms on the way back down the court, a little glimpse into their relationship as teammates, not rivals.

"What you've been waiting for!" Ryan Ruocco exclaimed on the broadcast, which attracted an audience of 3.4 million, the largest ever for a WNBA All-Star Game. Everything was bigger around Clark; the horde of reporters gathered at her podium on Media Day looked like a Super Bowl turnout: boom microphones, cameras everywhere, media members packed ten deep.

After the game, as Clark bounded up the stairs to the interview table, she exclaimed, "I'm on vacation!" As she sat down with a big grin, she added, "All right, last time for a month, get your questions in."

"I honestly can't wait to not touch a basketball for a while," she said minutes later, laughing. "I think I've shot too many times in the past year." With these final words, she left the podium: "Everybody have a nice month."

•

Clark went on vacation to Mexico with teammates Lexie Hull and Katie Lou Samuelson. They of course popped up on social media; Samuelson shared a photo on Instagram of Clark and Hull lounging on a floating mat in the water with the caption, "Just a couple mermaids."

This was a thing, Hull explained. "I posted a video to TikTok when we were in Phoenix, and we were in the pool doing recovery and everyone was like, 'They're the mermaids.' It just stuck and people love it. We're here for it."

When the mermaids returned to Indianapolis, they plunged right into Christie Sides's mid-season training camp at Gainbridge. Ironically, they would have more time to practice then than they did before the season, when their schedule was so compressed and the start of the season so rushed. They also would have time to do something Sides had wanted to do before the season but time would not allow: team-building exercises, fun and games.

There was a Wiffle ball home run hitting contest, a putting contest, charades, balloon juggling, even a game in which the players wrapped Clark, among others, in toilet paper like a mummy. "Only a few of the games had to do with basketball," Sides said. "Just to hear them all laughing, that's what builds team chemistry."

Clark wanted to win every competition, of course. "Let's go! I'm made for this! Call me Babe!" she said as she drilled a Wiffle ball off the wall of the Fever practice gym.

"That's her fire, that's her passion," Sides said. "It's fun and contagious."

Reporters returned to talk to the players after practice one day. The mood was light. Clark actually interrupted her own interview when she was asked if she had played golf with teammate Grace Berger, whom the reporter said was a state champion high school golfer. Clark was startled. "Grace was? What?! Are we sure?" She wanted to find out right then and there. "Grace!" she shouted over the reporters' heads across the practice gym. "You were a state champion golfer? Why did you hide that from me?"

Clark said she hadn't played golf with anyone on the team—yet. "We can get 'em into it." Playfully, she added, "I want to see AB swing a golf club."

Sides said in an interview that Clark's sense of humor "really came out during the Olympic break. That's when everyone had time to get to know each other and build relationships that had nothing to do with what was happening on the basketball court in the heat of the moment. So, everything got lighter. I mean, she's a character, she's funny. She has a quick wit. I love humor, clever humor, and she is definitely somebody who has that gift."

Clark scheduled a couple of other trips while the Olympic Games were going on in Paris. She has a foundation—the Caitlin Clark Foundation—that is focused on education, nutrition, and sport. On August 2, Clark was in Des Moines to help distribute more than 350 backpacks filled with school supplies to public and parochial students. Her corporate partners helped make it possible: Nike provided the backpacks, Hy-Vee the school supplies, and Gatorade the water bottles.

A week later, in New York, she and boyfriend Connor McCaffery visited the Yankees clubhouse before a doubleheader with the Texas Rangers. "It was fun to see the amount of our guys that were kind of starstruck being around her," Yankees manager Aaron Boone said.

•

At the 2024 Summer Olympics, the US women's basketball team earned its eighth consecutive Olympic gold medal, winning all but one game by at least 13 points. That one was the last one, the gold medal game against France in which the United States trailed by as many as 10 points in the third quarter before coming back to escape with a ragged 67–66 victory.

In that gold medal game, Diana Taurasi and Caitlin Clark played the same number of minutes and scored the same number of points: zero and zero. One was courtside, sitting on the team bench. The other was in the United States, 4,000 miles away.

Interest from reporters and fans predictably fell short of what the team would have attracted with Clark. The opening press conference for the US women's team drew about 20 reporters, while the men's team attracted well over 100. For the team's first game in Lille, France, against Japan on July 29, Ben Golliver of *The Washington Post* reported that there were "plenty of open spots" in the press tribune and "only two dozen or so reporters" in postgame interviews. Attendance also was off: 13,040 for the US game, as opposed to more than 20,000 for each of the three other women's games that day.

Did interest among the media pick up for the USA–Australia semifinal game at Paris's Bercy Arena? It did not. There were only 18 journalists scattered around the massive interview area after the game, when the night before, for the US men's semifinal, the same area was packed with well over 100 reporters.

The TV viewership on NBC was good, but well below what it would have been had Clark been there: 7.8 million watched the US beat France. The game started at 9:30 a.m. Eastern on a Sunday morning, so that number was commendable, but it also was the worst viewership for a US women's basketball team gold medal game since 2008, according to NBC. In 2021 in Tokyo, the number was 7.9 million. In 2016 in Rio, it was 8.1 million. In 2012 in London, 10.2 million. Those games had different start times, so the comparisons were apples to oranges, but the numbers still tell the story of USA Basketball's missed opportunity.

Even the 2024 US women's soccer gold medal match, played the day before, starting in the morning as well, albeit at 11 a.m. Eastern, had 9.4 million viewers. That was the highest viewership for a women's gold medal soccer game since 2004. So, soccer was going up, and basketball was going down, begging the question: How many more millions would have watched had Clark been on the roster?

In December, *The Washington Post* listed USA Basketball's choice to not pick Clark for the Olympic team as one of "the very worst sports decisions of 2024."

# CHAPTER THIRTEEN

# "You Can't Take Your Eyes Off Her"

O ver 20 days and nights, across five months in the heartland of America and the home of the game of basketball, they streamed into the glistening downtown fieldhouse to see her. She is a magnet, pulling them in from around the country, and around the world. A trio of women who drove six hours from Decatur, Alabama, all wearing No. 22 T-shirts. A blogger from New Zealand who brought his family halfway around the world, including a six-year-old son who asked if boys were allowed to play basketball too. A father and daughter—so many fathers and daughters. The big guy wearing No. 22 who said he never would have been caught out in public in a women's jersey until, well, this.

What none of them knew, as they willingly and happily paid hundreds of dollars for tickets to watch her play, was that while they had rearranged their schedules to come see her, she was looking at them.

"It's one of my favorite parts of the day," Caitlin Clark said. "I drive here, it's two minutes from where I live, and there's always so many people on the side of the roads that have my jersey on or have Fever gear on." She especially noticed the dads and the young daughters. "That was literally me just a short time ago."

When the game is over, her fans gather by the exit of the players' parking garage, hoping to catch a glimpse of her in her car—and it's the same thing all over again. "I know a lot of people camp out when I leave. I never stop, so I'm sorry, but I usually try to get home. It's been a long day, but I really appreciate all the support, and it's definitely cool. People don't even know I'm driving by, and they're in my jerseys and stuff, and that's never anything that I take for granted."

•

Indiana Pacers communications executive Eddie White often escaped from Gainbridge Fieldhouse before Fever games to talk to fans who were walking to the arena from the parking lots. His question was simple: "Where are you from?" Four women had driven in from Canada. A couple from New Hampshire. Two fans from New Jersey. A couple from Wisconsin who just bought season tickets. "People from all over," White said, "there to see Caitlin."

The license plates tell quite a story for Fever legend Tamika Catchings. "You used to be able to pull up right before a game. Now the parking lots are full. All these Iowa license plates, Illinois, even Tennessee. They heard about her and now they want to see her."

"A lot of those people, they travel from really far to get here," Clark said. "There are a lot of people who come up to my parents throughout games, and people come from Vermont or are here from Buffalo, are driving all these ways to just have one experience in this gym with us. And for me, that's really cool. There was a young girl that my parents ran into. My mom was in the Kansas City airport, and [the girl] was coming to her first-ever Fever game, and she was just really excited. And my mom had one of my trading cards with her in her purse, and gave it to her, and she started crying.

"I actually ran into the little girl in the tunnel after the last game, so I think it just puts into perspective how special these moments are for people, whether they meet you or not, getting to enjoy this environment and this experience in the game is what makes really lifelong memories for them."

•

In the warmth of a mid-August late afternoon, Patrice Hill was walking along a sidewalk a block from Gainbridge with her two cousins who had driven with her from Alabama and another who had flown in from Washington, DC. "We're all huge Caitlin Clark fans," she said. "She's changed the game of basketball. I didn't even think about being a Fever fan until Caitlin got there."

"Never," said her cousin, Bri Watkins. "I was never a WNBA fan until her, when she made that mark in college. I just like her game."

Hill and her cousins are Black, and she was well aware of the racial overtones of this WNBA season. "Making it Black vs. white is just the world we live in, but if you're a basketball fan, it shouldn't matter about color when somebody's so great. Caitlin Clark is a great basketball player and she entertains me."

•

Mark Dalton, senior vice president for media relations for the NFL's Arizona Cardinals, came to Indianapolis for a preseason football game, but he, too, made time to come to Gainbridge. "I can't be 30 minutes away from seeing Caitlin Clark in person and not come here," he said. "I could see her in Phoenix, but I wanted to see her in Indiana. Certain celebrities and athletes have that certain air, she walks out on the court and there's a different air in the building. Michael Jordan, Wayne Gretzky, Tiger Woods—if you have a chance to see them with your own eyes, you do it. If you have a chance to see her, you have to come and do it."

•

Wherever Clark goes, everyone wants something from her, and she almost always delivers. An autograph. A selfie. A smile. An interview. An answer. A minute.

Kids gather along the railing at Gainbridge Fieldhouse or in opposing arenas, yelling her name. This is Clark's pregame autograph time for the children who adore her. She works the line like a politician running for office.

"First thing I'm looking for is the young kids. That's who I look to sign for, more than anything—young girls, young boys. That's who I want to make sure I can get to before anything. Obviously, I want to make time for everybody. That's really hard with the amount of people that are over there and wanting me to sign. But [I'm] definitely looking for the young boys and girls. I feel like I was just them wanting anybody's autograph."

One day, through no fault of her own, Clark missed a kid, a boy of about 10 holding a No. 22 jersey. There are so many little people packed together, arms outstretched, that no one can see them all. The boy burst into tears after Clark went by, but she had already passed him, so she had no idea as she made her way to the last of the children, then worked her way back toward the tunnel to the locker room.

Then she spotted him. She saw the boy in tears. She reached over. Startled, he produced the jersey, and she signed it. Success.

Around town, at games or events she attends, it's the same routine. A mother with a two-week-old asked Clark to sign the baby's white Fever onesie with a Sharpie.

"Is this the youngest to get an autograph?" the new mom asked Clark.

"I think so. I signed an ultrasound one time, but, yeah, an actual living-in-the-world [human], yes."

•

Clark ignited something in the country in places where no one would have expected it. Men who had rarely turned on women's college basketball now planned an afternoon or evening around her game. I found one of those men at Augusta National Golf Club, of all places, the private club that famously wouldn't allow women to become members until 2012 despite waves of negative publicity about its discriminatory stance.

In April 2024, right after the Iowa–South Carolina NCAA final, I asked club chairman Fred Ridley why he thought Clark had sent women's basketball TV ratings soaring to historic heights, while in women's golf, US star Nelly Korda had won four consecutive tournaments on the LPGA Tour but had garnered very little national attention.

"I think that every once in a while, somebody comes along that just captures the imagination of the sporting world," Ridley said during his traditional pre-Masters press conference. "And I say 'sporting world' because it really goes beyond basketball. I have to confess that in spite of my love of the game and the women's game of golf, I haven't watched a lot of women's basketball, but I watched the last three or four games that Iowa played this year. So, there you go. I mean, it's just the way she plays, the way Caitlin plays the game, her passion, her energy—it really just captures the imagination of the fans."

Ridley wasn't the only member of one of the oldest boys' clubs in the world—the men's golf establishment—to become a Clark fan. Two-time US Open champion Curtis Strange compared Clark to Tiger Woods, and then some.

"It's the whole package," Strange said in an interview for my *USA Today* column. "The TV camera likes them, which means we're going to like them. It's the smile, it's the look, it's the fitness, it's the way they go about it. With Caitlin, she comes across mid-court and you can't take your eyes off her. It's like going to a Mike Tyson fight—don't go to the bathroom in the first round, you're gonna miss the knockout. Don't take your eyes off her when she crosses mid-court because it might go up from anywhere."

•

Many were not taking their eyes off Clark. As the WNBA's break for the Olympics ended and games began again, the Fever released their mid-season report on Caitlin Clark's impact, and the numbers were staggering.

Videos produced by the team had more than 800 million views from April 15 through July 19, trailing only Inter Miami (Lionel Messi's team) across major US sports franchises during that time. No team in the NBA, NFL, NHL, MLB, or WNBA attracted more social media views. During that same time period, the Fever gained 1.3 million followers on social media to reach a total of 1.8 million, the most in the WNBA.

Ticket sales were up 265 percent over 2023, with Indiana leading the WNBA in both home and away attendance. Jersey sales for the Fever increased 1,193 percent since Clark arrived in Indianapolis.

"This is a historic moment, an inflection point for women's basketball, and there's nothing more fitting than Indiana being at the center of it all," said Mel Raines, CEO of Pacers Sports & Entertainment.

Meanwhile, the WNBA announced a new 11-year, $2.2 billion media rights deal with Disney, Amazon Prime, and NBC beginning with the 2026 season. The $200 million per year more than tripled the league's current media deal, which was valued at about $60 million annually. The new revenue could greatly increase the players' woefully low salaries.

It was no surprise, then, that the WNBA players association announced a few months later that the players would opt out of their current collective bargaining agreement with the league. That agreement lasts through October 31, 2025, giving the league and the union time to negotiate the next agreement.

•

As the crowds poured into Gainbridge Fieldhouse night after night, the woman who dribbled through the streets of Seattle to help start a WNBA franchise was sitting in her seat near the tunnel where the Fever come and go from the locker room, marveling at what she was seeing: full arenas, the playoffs potentially on the horizon, and a vast national following for her young star.

For 77-year-old Fever general manager Lin Dunn, practically every moment of the 2024 WNBA season was a revelation. She went to college at the University of Tennessee at Martin in the late 1960s. "There was no basketball team, no scholarships, no nothing. We did get to play a little bit of competitive badminton, and tennis, where we had maybe six competitions within the state. But they wouldn't start a basketball team. I went in and complained and whined about that."

UT-Martin did begin a women's basketball program—after Dunn graduated. The early star of that team was Pat Head, who would become much better known by her married name, Summitt.

In 1970, Dunn went off to her first coaching job at Austin Peay. She was paid $7,000 to teach physical education and absolutely nothing to coach three women's sports: basketball, volleyball, and tennis. She made an additional $500 for being the cheerleader sponsor, which meant she would drive the cheerleaders, and the school mascot, to all the football and men's basketball games.

The Austin Peay mascot is "The Governor," a top-hat-wearing character that looks a lot like Mr. Monopoly. One night at a men's basketball game at Eastern Kentucky, the student who wore the mascot costume got sick. With no other students around to replace him, Dunn put on the costume and became "The Governor."

"It's hard, hard, hot work," she said. "When people talk about mascots at games, I say, you have no idea what these mascots do because I've been one."

Dunn left Austin Peay for the University of Mississippi, where she coached volleyball, tennis, and basketball—and actually was paid to do it. Then she was off to the University of Miami to start the Hurricanes' women's basketball and volleyball programs, then to Purdue, where she took the Boilermakers to the Final Four in 1994, and then to the WNBA.

All that history, all that work, all those years no one cared—and now it was August 2024 and she was watching Gainbridge fill up once again for Caitlin Clark and her teammates.

"I really cannot believe this," Dunn said. "It's happening every game this season. I look up to the back corner of the arena, as high as the seats go, to the top row, and I can't believe my eyes. All those seats, all of them, filled for women's basketball."

# CHAPTER FOURTEEN

# "Confidence Is Everything"

A s the national anthem was being sung by the group Straight No Chaser at center court of Gainbridge Fieldhouse on August 16, Clark stood at the far end of a line of teammates, stirring. It had been nearly a month since the All-Star Game. The Phoenix Mercury were in town. That meant Diana Taurasi. That meant Brittney Griner. Clark couldn't wait. "Itching to get back out on the court" was the way she described it in the hours before. "We've been ready for it, and now you've got to come out and show the work that you've put in."

Clark believed that, while the Olympic break had helped tremendously with team bonding, she and the Fever had already been playing beautifully at times, sometimes even in long stretches, as they went 8-6 from the moment she was left off the Olympic team to the Olympic break itself. She was averaging more than 17 points per game and nearly 10 assists during that time. A monster had been awakened, indeed.

"I felt like I was starting to get in the groove," she said. "So, it was kind of weird. . . . I wanted to kind of keep playing. I felt like we were starting to find our flow together and be myself. And then you don't get to play for a month."

The Fever stood at 11-15, in seventh place, a good spot to be in when eight teams would make the playoffs, and such a change from the difficult days of May and early June. "I felt like those first 11 games in 20 days were really difficult, because I expect so much of myself, and I wanted to be so good," Clark said. "Everybody expected us to be great, and then you're 1-8, and everybody's frustrated, and we're like, 'Oh my gosh, what are we gonna do?' . . . I think it taught us all a lesson of being able to persevere and be resilient and show everybody that instant gratification isn't always the greatest thing in the world."

Soon enough, the players were gathering at mid-court for the opening tip. The first time the two teams had met, Taurasi and Griner had sought out Clark, standing alone, looking very much the new kid on the block. This time, Clark purposely and confidently went to them. Arriving behind Taurasi, she tapped her on the back to get her attention and gave her a warm hug, then worked her way around the circle to embrace Griner and Kahleah Copper, the Mercury's third Olympian, as well as the other two Mercury starters. If anyone doubted, Clark was now entirely comfortable in her surroundings, and totally in control of them.

Proof of this development came quickly. With less than three minutes gone in the game, Clark nailed her first three. By the end of the first quarter, she had scored 13 points. The entire Phoenix team had only 16 as the Fever led, 33–16. Clark did all this while missing nearly two and a half minutes of the 10-minute quarter.

•

"Holy cow!" Little more than six minutes into the game, Clark was motioning to Sides that she needed to be subbed out and come to the bench. "I need a quick minute here."

How was it possible that this 22-year-old could be winded in the first six minutes of her first game in a month? Could someone be too hyped up, too excited to be back? "Just gotta get a second to breathe," she said later. "We were playing fast and then my defense isn't as good and I'm kind of a liability for my team." She wasn't out of shape by any means. It was just that the Fever practices could not, she said, "replicate a real game."

Clark was back before the end of the first quarter. Less than 30 seconds into the second quarter, she made her third three-pointer of the game; Indiana had doubled up Phoenix, 36–18. Other than taking a two-minute breather in the third quarter, she played the rest of the game.

The Mercury would come back and take the lead from Indiana, 62–61, late in the third quarter, but the Fever wrested it back within 30 seconds, and won, convincingly, 98–89. This was the last of three games between the two teams for the year, and, surprisingly, the Fever had swept the series. Clark ended the game with a team-high 29 points, 4 three-pointers, 10 assists, and 5 rebounds. It was her 10th double-double of the season.

•

Coaches talk about their point guard being an extension of themselves on the court, but Sides also wanted Clark to experience the game, and make decisions about it, on her own. The time to make that come alive was over the Olympic break. During scrimmages, Sides would tell Clark—"and only her," Sides said—about what offense they were running in a particular drill so Clark could be the voice on the court, telling her teammates what the play was and where each should be.

"I would throw some things out there with some sets that we haven't run, so she had to think it through and put people in the right position," Sides said after the Phoenix game, having watched Clark do just that, finding the speedy Kelsey Mitchell time and again as the veteran hit 6 threes and shot 11-for-22 overall for 28 points.

"Kels got hot there, made a few in a row," Clark said. "So, you're just looking to find her, especially the way she runs the floor with her speed. I've always got my eyes up trying to look to find her. And I think she can tell when I want her to go backdoor, when I want her to come cut off the ball or anything like that. [There's] just that chemistry that you get used to playing with one another. It's taken time, but I think we're really starting to get it down."

Clark would later talk generally about the task at hand as a young point guard as she gained more control of the offense. "How can I put teammates into position to be successful, who's just made a shot, who needs a shot? Those are all things I think of as I go to call a play, all while trying to manage myself at the same time. It's a lot as a point guard, but that's what's fun for me. You get to pick apart the game of basketball and also try to make your teammates better and your team better at the same time."

Clark displayed remarkable confidence for someone her age in her willingness to constantly critique her own play. "Sometimes I overpass, but then, obviously, the turnovers. [She had five that night.] So, to just continue to find a way to try to limit the ones that are bad turnovers—a couple tonight that weren't the greatest—but you live and learn."

There was a certain symmetry to the moment, this post–Olympic break win against a team of such well-known stars. Clark said the team's first victory over Phoenix, on June 30, "boosted us into how we're playing basketball right now." Then they beat the Mercury again on July 12, and now here again in mid-August. "Confidence is everything," Clark said. "Confidence is good for the group, and it's also contagious."

•

Two days after the Fever's first win following the Olympic break, they earned their second, another significant victory, 92–75, over Seattle, a veteran team that had defeated Indiana the first three times they had played in 2024.

But across less than two minutes on the clock in the third quarter, with Indiana clinging to a small lead, all the good and the bad that Clark could muster was on full display. Taking a handoff after a rebound from Boston, dribbling just once, Clark, always looking ahead, always pushing forward, flung a pass from one foul line to the other, like a quarterback finding a wide receiver on a fly route, catching Mitchell in full stride behind the Seattle defense for an easy layup. That pass became her 226th assist of the season, the most ever by a rookie in WNBA history, passing the mark set by Sacramento's Ticha Penicheiro in 1998.

Mitchell didn't call Clark "Caitlin," or even "Clark." She called her "C-squared," as in, "I always say C-squared is one of those players where her IQ is going to take us a lot of places. So, you just really got a feeling when you fit in as far as knowing how to read and adjust off her. And once you make that adjustment, I think, obviously, it's really good basketball."

Two possessions later, Clark nailed her first three of the game after six misses, one of those lightning bolts that energizes the crowd the way nothing else in basketball quite can. On Seattle's next trip down the court, Boston was called for a foul, her third. Clark waved her arms angrily and argued with the referee. Then, coming back down the floor, Clark tried another three from the same spot she had hit from just 20 seconds earlier, but it bounced high off the front of the rim. Another miss. Exasperated, she punched the air with her right fist as she ran back on defense.

Seattle then threw the ball away, a positive development for the Fever, but Clark's body language said otherwise. Still angry about missing her last three-point attempt, she threw her arms into the air again, walked toward the basket, reached back with her right hand, and slapped the cushioned stanchion directly on the WNBA player logo.

The whistle blew. That was a technical foul, her fifth of the season. This was not good. Seven and you're suspended for a game—and the Fever still had 12 games remaining in the regular season.

Clark, incensed, pleaded her case with the officials. Boston tried to calm her with a touch of her chin, then took hold of one of her arms. Clark regained her composure enough to heave a high pass over smothering defenders to Boston to increase the Fever lead, but then went right back to jawing with the officials.

"Are you kidding me? Are you kidding me?"

Katie Lou Samuelson popped over to Clark, putting her arms around her and steering her away from the referee.

Clark's all-consuming passion was both exhilarating and troubling, so I asked her about it after the game: "Obviously, you were fiery, there's a lot going on . . ."

Clark: "Yeah, crazy."

"Can you describe what's going on in your brain at that moment . . ."

"Too much," Clark said, shaking her head. "I got a technical for basically being mad at myself because I missed the three, and then I went and hit the backboard, and [the official] told me it was disrespectful to the game of basketball.

"So, I don't know, it reminded me of the technical that I got in college, where I said, 'Damn it,' where it's, like, a personal frustration, had nothing to do with my team, had nothing to do with the reffing, had nothing to do with the other team. It was just because I'm a competitor and I felt like I should have been making more shots."

Clark then sarcastically noted that the Fever played much better after the technical foul was called. "But I think [the ref] fired me up to continue to play a lot harder. I thought we got a lot better after he did that, so I want to thank him for that."

The Fever were ahead, 43–38, when Clark was called for the technical foul. The rest of the way, Indiana outscored Seattle, 49–37. "It was a little chaos there for two and a half minutes, and I think I could have done a better job of kind of regaining my cool, but that's the fire and passion that just gets me going," she said. "It's just finding a way to channel that and use that. And I thought I did a really good job of that at the end of the third and the fourth quarter."

Nonetheless, Sides spoke with Clark about it afterward, and not for the last time. "I don't need Caitlin to sit out a game." But she also wanted Caitlin to be Caitlin. "She's just a fiery competitor. I don't want to take that away from her. That's the difference in who she is."

•

Caitlin Clark honed her skills and became a star playing for Coach Dickson Jensen and his All Iowa Attack AAU team from the sixth grade through high school.
(Courtesy of Kolby Jensen)

After turning down Notre Dame, Caitlin Clark chose to stay in Iowa to play for veteran head coach Lisa Bluder. Together, they took the Hawkeyes to two consecutive NCAA finals.
(© Joseph Cress/*Iowa City Press-Citizen*/USA TODAY NETWORK via Imagn Images)

Caitlin Clark scored 41 points to lead Iowa to an upset victory over No. 1 South Carolina in the 2023 Final Four, then did what she loves to do—celebrate with her many fans. She says she adores them as much as they adore her.
(© Kevin Jairaj-Imagn Images)

A rivalry is born: LSU's Angel Reese follows Caitlin Clark around the court and shows Clark where her championship ring will go in the final seconds of the Tigers' 102–85 victory over Iowa in the 2023 NCAA final. (© Zach Boyden-Holmes/ USA TODAY NETWORK via Imagn Images)

Caitlin Clark and the Hawkeyes drew 55,646 fans for an exhibition basketball game in the school's football stadium—Kinnick Stadium—to start her senior year. It was the largest crowd in women's basketball history. (Nick Rohlman/*The Gazette* via AP)

Caitlin Clark's 33-foot, 6-inch three-pointer broke the NCAA Division I women's all-time scoring record on February 15, 2024, at Carver-Hawkeye Arena. The spot is now marked with the number 22. (© Joseph Cress-Imagn Images)

Caitlin Clark was 10 when she received a hug from Maya Moore at a Minnesota Lynx game in 2012. Twelve years later, as captured by ESPN, Moore surprised Clark at the game in which she broke Pete Maravich's NCAA Division I all-time scoring record. Of course, the two exchanged another hug. (© ESPN)

General manager Lin Dunn, left, and coach Christie Sides, right, with their No. 1 draft pick on her first day in Indianapolis, April 17, 2024. (© *The Indianapolis Star-USA TODAY NETWORK* via Imagn Images)

Young fans and innovative signs are a staple at Caitlin Clark games. At Gainbridge, families aren't necessarily from the Indianapolis area, or even the Midwest. New York and New Jersey were in the house on August 18, 2024. (Courtesy of Christine Brennan)

Caitlin Clark says one of the most important things she does is connect with boys and girls before and after games, signing dozens of autographs. Few pro athletes devote as much time as she does to children and families on game days. (Courtesy of Christine Brennan)

One of the most discussed moments in American sports in 2024: Chennedy Carter's hip check of Caitlin Clark on June 1, 2024. Clark's reaction? She kept calm, didn't retaliate, and made the free throw that helped decide a close game. (Photo by Brian Spurlock/Icon Sportswire via AP Images)

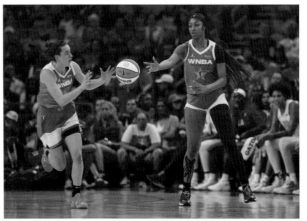

Caitlin Clark and Angel Reese were teammates, not rivals, in the 2024 WNBA All-Star Game. They worked together when they were on the court at the same time, and a fourth-quarter Clark assist to Reese was one of the highlights of the game, won by the WNBA All-Stars over the US Olympic team. (© Mark J. Rebilas-Imagn Images)

They looked out for her, they laughed with her, they loved being on the receiving end of her passes, and they celebrated her milestones. On September 4, Aliyah Boston and NaLyssa Smith join Caitlin Clark after Clark's second triple-double of the season. (© Grace Hollars/*IndyStar*/USA TODAY NETWORK via Imagn Images)

Kate Martin was Caitlin Clark's best friend at Iowa. In September, she came to Gainbridge Fieldhouse with the Las Vegas Aces as a rival and opponent of Clark, yet she still ended up talking about her. (Courtesy of Christine Brennan)

After the Fever's big victory in Chicago on August 30, Indiana backcourt mates Kelsey Mitchell and Caitlin Clark met the press in a small room not far from the court. (Courtesy of Christine Brennan)

Caitlin Clark's fiery competitiveness led to several technical fouls throughout the season, and to a new name for her teammates: the De-Escalation Committee. Fever players did whatever they could to keep their star rookie out of trouble, including bear hugs and interventions. (© Grace Hollars/*IndyStar*/ USA TODAY NETWORK via Imagn Images)

Connecticut's DiJonai Carrington answers questions at the Mohegan Sun Arena on September 24 between Games One and Two of the Sun's play-off series with the Fever. This is a still image from my video of our interaction when I asked her about her fingers hitting Caitlin Clark in the eye. (Courtesy of Christine Brennan)

WNBA commissioner Cathy Engelbert spoke and answered questions for 27 minutes before Game One of the WNBA Finals on October 10 in Brooklyn. She never once mentioned Caitlin Clark's name. (Courtesy of Christine Brennan)

Tamika Catchings, a league MVP and 10-time All-Star selection who led the Fever to the 2012 WNBA title, still lives in Indianapolis and owns three tea cafés called Tea's Me. She joined a staff member behind the counter in September 2024. (Courtesy of Christine Brennan)

Caitlin Clark was a hit on the golf course, drawing big galleries during an LPGA pro-am. She also played in the PGA Tour's John Deere Classic Pro-Am in Silvis, Illinois, in 2023, with her AAU coach Dickson Jensen as her caddie. (Courtesy of Kolby Jensen)

Caitlin Clark has become a popular speaker at conventions and conferences, many of them focused on women, often talking about the opportunities for girls and women in sports and in our culture. (Photo by Marla Aufmuth/ Getty Images for Massachusetts Conference for Women)

In early November, Caitlin Clark, a devoted "Swiftie," went to two Taylor Swift concerts on consecutive nights in Indianapolis. By mid-January, she was sitting with Swift in her suite at a Kansas City Chiefs playoff game. Clark grew up cheering for the Chiefs, following them even "before [they] were really good." (Perry Knotts via AP)

Caitlin Clark watches her No. 22 jersey rise to the rafters at Carver-Hawkeye Arena on February 2, 2025. Iowa had announced that it would be retiring her number at the end of her historic college career. (© Julia Hansen/*Iowa City Press-Citizen*/USA TODAY NETWORK via Imagn Images)

There was one final scene, a coda to the emotions of the game and what Clark brings out in her opponents, and herself. With the game won and nearly over, as a time-out was called, Clark was walking near the Seattle bench, waving an arm to get the fans going, when Seattle's Skylar Diggins-Smith veered into her and gave her a little shove. Clark kept walking to her bench and appeared to pay no attention, but the same could not be said for social media, which replayed and dissected Diggins-Smith's moment with Clark for days afterward. It was just another example, small though it might have been, of some veteran players' disdain for Clark, especially when they were losing to her.

Emotions rose again as Sides and Seattle coach Noelle Quinn met for a long discussion along the sideline while Clark tried to get closer to the tête-à-tête before being gently coaxed back to her bench. Still watching Sides and Quinn, Clark yelled "Stop crying!" from a safe distance, words the Seattle bench never could have heard, before laughing as Samuelson positioned herself between Clark and any further trouble, locking fingers with her as they both smiled, while Lexie Hull, who put on a show with 6 three-pointers of her own and a career-high 22 points, put a reassuring hand on Clark's shoulder.

All of this action to keep Clark from getting into further trouble, and another technical, was akin to a couple of older sisters looking out for the youngest. There would soon be a name for this effort, which included Boston, Samuelson, Hull, Mitchell, and Wheeler. It was invented by a fan on X: the Caitlin Clark De-Escalation Committee.

But what exactly was going on between Sides and Quinn? "They said Caitlin had gone into their bench area and they didn't appreciate that," Sides recalled later. "The conversation was very respectful on both sides. But when we talked, we didn't know that Caitlin had been pushed into their bench area. I mean, she literally was pushed into the area from how Skylar was coming off the court. You see it on the broadcast."

As soon as the game was over, Clark found Sides in the coaches' conference room and explained it all to her before Sides could watch a replay.

"I didn't do what they're telling you I did," Clark told Sides, who believed her, of course.

"She felt bad for it," Sides said, looking back. "It wasn't her fault."

Muffet McGraw, Diggins-Smith's college coach at Notre Dame, also saw the replay. "Skylar is a competitive player," she said. "Things like that happen in the moment between two competitors, but there's such a spotlight on Caitlin that it got so much more attention."

Indeed it did; it was the most watched WNBA game ever on ABC with 2.2 million viewers.

•

Due to the vagaries of the 2024 WNBA schedule, the red-hot Fever immediately had to take nearly a week off before playing again. They flew to Minneapolis for a Saturday-night game that they knew would be a challenge against a team that was simply too good for them, and lost to the Lynx, 90–80. Clark played well again, scoring a team-high 23 points with 8 assists, becoming the fastest player in league history to score at least 500 points and record 200 assists.

But the game and its result were almost incidental that night. If sports, at their most basic, are about kids playing a game, and role models who hopefully never disappoint them, and dreams that come true, this was that night for Caitlin Clark. It was the night that the Lynx retired the great Maya Moore's jersey and hung it from the rafters, and Clark was thrilled to have a front-row seat for all of it. "You can't really script it any better," she said.

It all started with the pregame press conferences. The stars appeared, one after another, in one tiny, overheated Target Center room packed with cameras, microphones, and reporters. First up was Cheryl Reeve, the Lynx coach who also was the US Olympic coach who had singled out Clark before the Olympics. With those Olympics now over, Reeve was singing a very different tune about Clark.

"You're all standing here, I don't think it's just for Maya Moore's jersey into the rafters—at least, I hope some of you are here for that—but every city that [Clark] is in, I thought it was really cool her senior year of college to see that take hold. It wasn't just the Iowa fans. It wasn't just they sold out. She became a road show. I don't want to slight anybody in college, but I don't remember seeing that in my time. And that's held true. We've wanted a player or a league that can sort of transcend some of these spaces and have a road show. And Caitlin Clark and some of the rookies give us that, obviously—Caitlin, you know, being the headliner."

Reeve praised the way Clark plays. "The single best thing that she does, that young players don't do, is she plays at an incredible pace, and pace can get you really, really far. Pace and passing, I think, are her two greatest things. I know the sexier part is probably the logo three. But the pace and the passing is what makes her exceptional."

Was this really the woman who had wanted to do anything but talk about Clark the last time the two teams played six weeks earlier?

Reeve also gave Clark her highest compliment: She made Clark and Moore interchangeable talents, at least for one night. Asked about having both in the same building, Reeve said, "Well, I wish one was playing for us—either one."

Next up was Clark, who had to squeeze past Reeve as she made her way into the room that Reeve had just exited. She had idolized Moore from the next state over as a girl who loved sports, and now here she was, one of the most publicly appreciative athletes in sports, in this arena on this night.

"Maya was definitely that person for me, and she was obviously tremendous. . . . Just the passion and the joy that you could always see her play with, she always had a smile, she was competitive, she was fiery, but she was just a solid basketball player. And then, obviously, a solid individual, and those are the main reasons why I loved her so much."

Moore, now 35, helped lead the Lynx to four NBA titles, but that's only part of her story, as Clark alluded to. In 2019, Moore stepped away from her storied career to work for the release of Jonathan Irons, a family friend who was in prison. In 2020, Irons's conviction on a 1997 burglary and assault charge was overturned by a judge who determined that he had been wrongly convicted. Moore and Irons now are married and have a son.

"Obviously, she doesn't play basketball anymore," Clark said, "and everything that she does for the world is way cooler than what she did on the basketball court."

Moore came last. She said that over the course of her career, so many children came up to her to get an autograph or a hug, as now happens with Clark, that there was no way for her to remember or know who they were, including a 10-year-old girl from Iowa. "It's just really, really cool to think about one of those little girls became Caitlin Clark."

After the game, back in that same room, Clark was still talking about Moore. "She's courtside and you look over, that's a childhood idol. You've got to pinch yourself a little bit at times and be thankful for the moment."

Once she was finished with her press conference, Clark, wearing the commemorative Maya Moore T-shirt every player and spectator had been given, slipped back into the darkened arena to sit in the first row and catch about a half hour of the on-court ceremony honoring Moore. Her friend, photographer Bri Lewerke, snapped several pictures of Clark intently listening to the testimonials for Moore. But she caught something else in the frame: a half dozen young girls wearing No. 22 jerseys and T-shirts in the stands behind Clark.

So, there was Moore, and Clark, and those young girls: past, present, and future, the stepping stones of Title IX.

Later, Clark quietly left her seat, stepped back through a corridor under the stands, grabbed a late dinner from the team's catered Mexican spread in the hallway near their locker room, and headed to the bus. Even with the loss, it had been a perfect night.

•

Winning games again for the Fever started two days later. The Atlanta Dream, a team not nearly as mighty as Minnesota, moved their game with Indiana from their 3,500-seat venue by the airport to State Farm Arena, the Hawks' downtown NBA home, and filled it with a new record crowd for a WNBA game in Georgia: 17,608, just a tad more than the 17,575 that showed up the other time the Fever were in town, in June.

The Dream celebrated the attendance record by posting the news on their big scoreboard with pictures of three of their stars. That's what you do with news like that: You take credit for it and thank your fans, even if a significant portion were wearing Clark T-shirts and jerseys. Of course, they didn't put a photo of the real reason they drew a record crowd—the only reason they drew a record crowd. No team would publicly thank someone on the opposing team, but obviously the full house was there for Clark.

"You see this crowd," said Atlanta coach Tanisha Wright, "we understand that a big part of this has to do with Caitlin Clark and the brand of basketball she has brought here and she's been playing." Then she pivoted to her team, just a half game out of the final playoff spot as the game began. "We have some great players as well who have done an amazing job playing a great brand of basketball these last couple of games."

This was the bind the WNBA found itself in. Who praises an opponent for doing what you can't do: fill your home arena with fans who otherwise wouldn't be there? It was such a bizarre dilemma for teams that wanted to beat Clark and the Fever. Wright handled it as well as anyone. Don't fight it. Acknowledge it. Move on.

For Clark, as routine as these sellouts were, she was still enthralled by them. "I'm only 22 years old, but I act like I'm 10, so I don't know, I feel like I'm just a kid that plays basketball and has a lot of fun, and for me, coming into these arenas and these environments, I look around and it's incredible. I don't show up and expect these crowds. For me, that's not anything that ever gets old. Especially as a young girl who grew up going to games, I would have come to a game in a building like this and seen this type of crowd, I think I would have been kind of in heaven."

•

Clark signed autographs and heard the wild cheers—and she also heard a strange silence late in the first quarter, when, for the second time in the season, she crumpled to the floor and stayed down, lying in pain, with what turned out to be a scary but otherwise inconsequential rolling of her left ankle.

The arena was buzzing as Indiana led by three, and then there was practically no noise at all for the 30 seconds she was down. Boston, always looking out for Clark, immediately leaned over, putting both hands on Clark as she lay on the court.

Once play stopped, Mitchell and NaLyssa Smith joined Boston in their concern for Clark. Soon, Erica Wheeler had left the bench to assist the others in helping Clark to her feet. The crowd applauded, and Mitchell applauded with them. The notion that this team didn't have her back, or that somehow the Black players were envious or jealous of her, was being disproved on a daily basis.

On the bench, Clark was asked if she wanted to go back to the locker room. The last thing she wanted to do was to go back to the locker room. "No, please, just tape it right here. Let's go."

As she explained later, slightly chagrined, "I saw the replay. I look really soft. It wasn't that bad of a turn, but it hurt. So, sometimes you just need a second. If you've ever sprained your ankle, it just kind of stings for a little bit. So I was good."

Clark missed just three minutes of game time. She was back to start the second quarter, finishing with 19 points and 7 assists in an 84–79 Fever victory. "You're not a real basketball player if you haven't sprained your ankles a bunch. That's when you know."

•

In the victory over Atlanta, Clark had two turnovers. Only two. She stepped out of bounds halfway through the first quarter and threw a pass out of bounds in the middle of the third quarter. That was it. It matched her lowest total of the season, and it would tie the lowest for all the games yet to come. Clark and Sides talked specifically about that number— two—after the game. "She was really proud about that," the coach said.

Then Sides emphasized what she had said all season: The high number of turnovers wasn't just Clark's fault. "She has a vision that sees things that sometimes other players on the court just don't see; sometimes they're just not ready. That's where we've grown. I think now our players are starting to understand what she sees and putting themselves in those positions to catch those passes that she's making."

•

Connecticut was next, back home in packed-to-the-rafters Gainbridge on a Wednesday night in late August. Included in the massive crowd were recently returned Olympic stars Simone Biles and Gabby Thomas. Clark and her teammates applauded when the gold medalists appeared on the big screen during a break in the game, then posed for photos after the game. The prized picture of Clark with Biles and Thomas popped up on social media accounts from *Glamour* to *People*, from ABC to the *Today* show.

That was fun, but this was Connecticut, that physical, no-nonsense, defensive-minded club that had given the Fever fits so far this season. The two teams had met three times, and Connecticut had won all three. "This is a team that we felt we hadn't really given a game to at all," said Clark, who had just been named Eastern Conference Player of the Week, a rarity for a rookie.

Just as they had in the previous games, Clark and the Sun's DiJonai Carrington spent a lot of time with one another: glaring at, guarding, and trying to one-up each other. Late in the first half, Clark ran Carrington into her teammate Alyssa Thomas, then, with Carrington down on the court, lying on her stomach, Clark nailed a three.

Late in the third quarter, Clark got the better of Carrington again, dribbling twice, then stepping back outside the three-point line to create enough space to send an arcing 26-footer over Carrington's outstretched arm for a 62–56 Indiana lead.

Thirteen seconds later, Carrington hit a three of her own. *Touché.* As she ran back on defense, she put her right index finger to her lips, shushing the crowd. But Clark answered immediately, flying the length of the court for a driving layup as Carrington vainly defended her.

Carrington and Clark were made for each other, both tough and willing to battle, including the occasional histrionics. The two had developed some history. More was to come.

The Fever didn't lose this time. They won, 84–80. It was their first victory over the Sun in more than three years, snapping an 11-game losing streak. Even more important, this was nine wins in the last 10 home games for Indiana. The Fever were growing up before the nation's eyes, so unlike the team that lost that first game in mid-May.

"It feels like a different season," Clark said. "I feel like I was a completely different player then. I feel we were a completely different team then. . . . We didn't even really know our identity as a team and how we wanted to play basketball. I was trying to figure out my teammates. My teammates were trying to figure out me and how we're going to put everything together to make it work. We're night-and-day different."

For her part, Carrington wasn't quite done with the Fever. Not long after the game ended, she posted this on X: "the indiana fever have the nastiest fans in the W. ew."

Carrington didn't elaborate. She didn't say what happened, if anything. There were no incidents reported that night at the game.

Less than four hours after she posted about Indiana's fans, at 2:18 a.m., Carrington sent out another message. She shared an awful post showing the infamous picture taken at the time of George Floyd's 2020 murder, with Clark's face superimposed on the police officer, Derek Chauvin, and Carrington's on Floyd:

imagine thinking George Floyd's murder is a joke. all because of a basketball game. this is so sick.

It was terrible. But, sadly, it's also what social media, especially X, had become. Loathsome images and disgusting, hateful comments—racist, misogynistic, homophobic—weren't confined to the WNBA. Every public figure was a target for something or other. Black women often were targeted more than others. What was new, what made it different this season, was the frequency and intensity of the toxicity that the WNBA players were facing with the vastly increased attention on the league this year. The players were not used to it and had not been prepared for it.

•

The press conferences for the two biggest names in women's basketball were back to back on Friday night, August 30, inside the Chicago Sky's 10,387-seat Wintrust Arena in the city's South Loop. Caitlin Clark first, then Angel Reese. If Clark and Reese were the players of the hour, the Rookie of the Year race was the question of the hour. What did they think of the competition for the award?

Not much. "I think me and Angel would both give you the same answer," Clark said. "We don't wake up and think about individual awards. I know that's what all of you think we do. We don't. That's what everybody wants to make this about, but both of our teams are competing for playoff spots. That's our main focus. That's a selfish thing to just care about an individual award. She would give you the same exact answer. I'm sure she has given you the same exact answer."

Clark was right. "We don't either care about the Rookie of the Year," Reese said, "but I think you guys have made it a big thing. We haven't. So, just continue to work within our team. We both want to win, we've been wanting to win, that's what we've done in our collegiate career. We played against each other last year and the year before in the March Madness tournament, so we're just trying to do whatever it takes to win. That's what's important right now."

Whatever they or anyone thought of the Rookie of the Year conversation, it ended that night. Clark, already on a tear since the Olympic break, took over Chicago's gym and made it her own, scoring the most points she had in any game to that point in the season, 31, while becoming such an obsession for Reese's Chicago teammates that they completely melted down late in the game, fouling her time and again as the game was out of reach.

•

It was "Barbie Night" in Chicago, a promotion in honor of Reese, the Sky's "Bayou Barbie." Every fan received a pink T-shirt, and when Chicago jumped out to an early 13-point lead, it seemed to be the perfect evening for a Windy City celebration.

Then Indiana started running, playing at a speed Chicago just could not handle. Near the end of the first quarter, with the Fever having clawed back to within six, Indiana's Temi Fagbenle poked the ball away from Reese under Chicago's basket. Clark picked it up and started racing down the court as Fagbenle turned on the afterburners. Clark dribbled to half-court and threaded a beauty of a bounce pass to Fagbenle; she made the layup, was fouled, made the free throw—and the lead was down to three.

The second quarter showed all of Clark's promise. She hit an open logo three after a pass from Wheeler to tie the game, 26–26. Half a minute later, Clark splashed another three from 25 feet to put Indiana ahead, 29–26. The cheers were so loud—Fever fans were revealing themselves in every section of the arena—that ION play-by-play announcer Lisa Byington said, "It's almost like it's home court here in Chicago for the Fever." Where had we heard that before?

The Fever never trailed again. Clark often talks about playing "pretty basketball" filled with precise passes and plenty of pace. This was that.

Near the end of the first half, Clark blew to the hoop for a driving layup. "Did that go in? Did that go in?" she teased the fans. It went in. Indiana was ahead by nine.

The second half went just as well for the Fever. Only a minute in, Clark stepped back from 6'7" fellow rookie Kamilla Cardoso for another spectacular three. As the Sky called time out, Clark made her way to the Indiana bench with glee, first running, then skipping, then leaping high into the air. A still picture of that moment symbolized her month of August: pure joy and satisfaction with her play. She couldn't wait to get back to her bench, slapping hands with all her teammates who were smiling as much as she was, with Wheeler dancing a little jig.

The Sky soon began unraveling. First, Chicago's Michaela Onyenwere was called for a Flagrant 1 foul for not giving Clark room to land safely after a three-point attempt. Clark made all three free throws. Then, in the fourth quarter, with the Fever up by 23 points, two consecutive fouls were called on the Sky's Diamond DeShields, both in the same spot on the court, on inbounds plays in which DeShields pushed Clark out of bounds not once but twice. After the first one, Clark made the free throw, and Indiana was inbounding again when DeShields did the exact same thing. No time expired on the clock. Just one shove after another resulting in another made Clark free throw. Clark's mantra at these moments is simple: Don't react. Be all business. Make the free throw. Rack up the points.

Less than a minute later, Clark was on the run down the court when DeShields ran to her side and barreled into her, sending Clark flying. That was Chicago's second Flagrant 1 foul of the half on Clark, who scrambled to her feet and immediately ran toward her bench, not wanting to get into any trouble. No retribution. No talking. Just a quick dash out of there.

However, as the officials watched the replay to see just how bad it was, Clark uttered a few choice words, with perhaps more to come, while wandering around with her teammates by the bench. Wheeler was close by with a towel in hand. The last thing the Fever wanted was for Clark to get a technical, so Wheeler put the towel over Clark's mouth, pie-in-the-face style. "It had to be done," Wheeler said later with a twinkle in her eye.

Clark took the hint and pulled her jersey up over her mouth as she continued to talk to her teammates and coaches. There was no way she was going to get in trouble if no one could read her lips. And her lips definitely were still moving.

"We were all just trying to keep Caitlin calm in that moment," Sides said later. "They were fouling her when it was out of reach. It was like a movie, I was just trying to get her away and to where I could keep her safe and get her out of the gym."

In the maelstrom, Clark was given two free throws for the DeShields flagrant foul. She made them both, for her 30th and 31st points, as the Fever went on to a 100–81 victory, their third of the year against Chicago, with one loss. Clark became the first player in league history to register more than 30 points with 12 assists and 5 threes in a game.

The *Chicago Sun-Times* had forecast the drubbing in two classic tabloid headlines that morning: "Fever & a Headache" and "A Clark & Stormy Night." It was Indiana's third straight win and fifth out of six since the Olympic break, allowing the Fever to reach the .500 mark for the first time since the start of the season. They had now moved up to sixth place in the WNBA standings, ahead of Phoenix.

It was Clark's 11th double-double and her third game with at least 25 points and 10 assists, the most in a season in WNBA history. It was one of her best games of the year, and considering the opponent, the most gratifying. "I remember saying earlier this season, I know there's gonna be a moment where we look back on this later in the season and be, like, 'This 1-8 start is gonna help us somewhere down the line.' And I think this is now that moment," she said.

Only when Clark was out and the game was lost did Reese get enough points (10) and rebounds (11) to record another double-double. Nonetheless, it was a milestone: her 23rd of the season, a WNBA rookie record.

# CHAPTER FIFTEEN

# The De-Escalation
# Committee

Clinching a playoff spot in any sport usually brings celebration on the court, confetti from the rafters, and champagne in the locker room. It's not the end of the season by any means, but it's a statement, a way to gauge progress. It's a measurement the Indiana Fever had failed to meet since 2016. So, how did Caitlin Clark celebrate the moment the Fever clinched a playoff spot on the evening of Tuesday, September 3?

"I went to sleep."

It was late, and Clark was at home in her apartment in Indianapolis, watching two WNBA games out west: Chicago at Las Vegas and Atlanta at Phoenix. As the games wound to their conclusions, their significance was clear. Losses by Chicago and Atlanta would put the Fever, and the Mercury, into the playoffs. That's exactly how things played out. The Aces easily defeated the Sky, 90–71, and the Mercury beat the Dream, 74–66.

Clark is a night owl, so she likely would have been watching those games no matter what they meant: "I stay up late, so it's not really unusual." When the games ended so favorably for the Fever, Clark said her reaction was simple: "I turned it off and I went to sleep. I didn't even check my phone until the next morning."

Asked the next day if it bothered her that clinching a playoff spot—which would have been unthinkable after their poor start in May—didn't happen in real time at a Fever game, Clark shook her head. "No, honestly, it was like, 'Uhhh, whatever.' . . . I'm not really into the party. . . . Obviously, this is a big moment for this organization. . . . But, at the same time, I came in with the expectation that this is what's going to happen. For me, this isn't a party. I feel like it's a great accomplishment, but there's so much more left to be done. Yeah, we made the playoffs. There's [still] six regular-season games. I'm not just happy to be in the playoffs, I think we have the type of team that can win and advance, going one game at a time."

She did take pleasure in one aspect of the late-night events: knowing her team was going to be in the playoffs more than two weeks before they began. "It doesn't have to come down to the wire for us."

•

Even if Clark wasn't necessarily in a celebratory mood, there was more to be pleased about beyond making the playoffs when she arrived at Gainbridge Fieldhouse for that night's game with the lowly Los Angeles Sparks.

It was as if Christmas had come early for her. Clark was now the toast of the league. She became the first player in league history to win the Rookie of the Month and Eastern Conference Player of the Month honors in the same month (August), and she was named Eastern Conference Player of the Week for a second consecutive week. But she had something else on her mind—someone else, actually. After a couple of sentences about how "cool and special" her honors were, Clark's attention turned to her teammate Kelsey Mitchell, who also had a terrific August, scoring more than 20 points in each of the six games. She wasn't asked a question about Mitchell; she just wanted to talk about her.

"I felt like Kels probably should have got a little love," Clark said. "I honestly thought she probably should have been Player of the Month.

Just what she was doing, and the clip [at which] she was doing it. . . . So, I feel very fortunate to play with her. Honestly, I'm not even trying to be corny; like, I really think she deserved it. So, I think sharing that with her, I feel lucky to have a backcourt mate that has been through this for seven years and has really helped me and let me flourish, and the same with Christie."

She mentioned Sides because her coach had been named WNBA Coach of the Month, the first time a Fever coach had won the honor. Sides praised both Mitchell and Clark and mentioned how pleased she was that Clark gave Mitchell a shout-out.

•

In the midst of all the accolades, the Fever had a game to play that night, against Los Angeles, a game in which there were more accomplishments for Clark. She became the fastest player in league history to reach 100 three-pointers in a season, prompting TV analyst Debbie Antonelli to exclaim, "Caitlin, go ahead and shoot till your arm falls off!"

Clark recorded her second career triple-double in a 93–86 victory: 24 points, 10 rebounds, and 10 assists. She became the first rookie and just the fifth WNBA player with multiple triple-doubles in a season.

But it almost didn't happen. As the game was drawing to a close, she was in double digits in points and assists, but not yet rebounds, with nine. With 11 seconds remaining, the Sparks' Kia Nurse missed a three-pointer, and as it bounced off the rim, the person who was there to grab it was, lo and behold, Clark. The sellout crowd went wild—people bursting out of their seats, leaping into the air—much crazier than the reaction for any rebound in a game that was already decided should ever sound.

Clark was asked afterward if she was aware the rebound was for a triple-double. No one need ask this woman questions like that. Of course she knew. "It's right next to the scoreboard, so I think everybody's pretty aware of what's happening," she said, laughing. "Somebody had to get the rebound, and I was actually the closest one to the ball, so . . ." The next closest person to the ball was Aliyah Boston. But as Clark jumped to grab the ball, Boston immediately put her hands in the air as if to say, "I'm not touching that."

"We always joke about stealing each other's rebounds," Clark said.

Meanwhile, Mitchell was trying to figure out why the crowd was going crazy. She stood under the basket with a perplexed look on her face. Once the clock expired, Clark walked over and the two shared a laugh.

Clark did give Boston a gift of another sort with seven minutes left in the game. As she tore down the court with Boston running with her, she drove to the basket, then sent a stunning behind-the-back pass to Boston for the easy bucket, and a foul. Clark screamed and skipped away, delighted. "I like sprinting," she said afterward. "I already told you guys."

"She likes to run," Boston confirmed.

That Clark-to-Boston connection was known by another name: "CC to AB." Or, as Mitchell playfully called Clark, "C-squared," so the combo could be called "ABC-squared." Bridging the racial divide that seemed to have snared so many people in this season of all seasons, the two No. 1 draft picks had become good friends who always looked out for each other.

"*You* are amazing," Clark regularly said to Boston on the bench before games.

"*You* are amazing," Boston always replied.

Boston explained: "It was Caitlin's idea."

Do you do it every game? "Every game," Boston said.

It makes sense that Clark would initiate a little ritual like this. She is, by nature, an unfailing optimist. No matter how badly things were going early on, for her team or for her personally, she ended almost every interview with a dash of perspective, with something good, with a positive look ahead. And so it was with this pregame pep talk, which was captured on camera after the WNBA's Olympic break.

"You're going to be amazing because you *are* amazing," Clark said to Boston, delighting in the conversation. "Thank you, you too!" Boston said, a smile exploding across her face.

These two, creating their own burst of positivity in the pressure cooker of this most unique of sports seasons.

The up-tempo Fever were on fire. Their record after the Olympic break moved to 7-1, and they were 17-8 since that 1-8 start. "We're just a competitive group of individuals," Clark said. "Nobody wants to lose; it's not fun, especially in front of these fans. A lot of them, they only get to see the Fever play one time. They spend a lot of money to come here and watch us and have fun with us. You want to give them a show every single time."

•

Clark's scintillating play was quieting most of her critics, but women's hoops trailblazer Nancy Lieberman still decided an impassioned defense of Clark was warranted. "What Caitlin Clark has done for the game is generational," she said behind the microphone for Indiana's game at Dallas a few days earlier. "As a baller to a baller, I just want to say thank you to you, Caitlin Clark, for just lifting our game up. . . . You're going to make all these women multimillionaires one day, like Tiger did, like Michael Jordan did. And we shouldn't hate on her, we should celebrate her, not tolerate her."

Lieberman spoke about the spectacle of "hundreds of fans lined up" before the game to see Clark, calling her an "enormous superstar of the game. We prayed to have the media that's going on right now, my generation, and it's happening right now."

As a postscript, Lieberman said Clark was in her top five for MVP voting. Weeks earlier, some were making the case for Clark to finish second to Reese for Rookie of the Year. Now, momentum was building not just for Clark to sweep to a huge Rookie of the Year triumph, but also to be one of the five ranked choices on MVP ballots.

•

Clark and her teammates were riding high as they approached the most treacherous portion of the conclusion of their season. The Fever had won five in a row for the first time since a six-game winning streak in 2015, when they made it to the WNBA Finals. But in a six-game home stand, trouble was on the way.

The highly regarded Minnesota Lynx were arriving, and after a brief respite against Atlanta, the Las Vegas Aces would be the opponent—twice. Sides, Clark, and the Fever were thinking of the two Aces games as a preview of a playoff series, not necessarily because they'd be playing Las Vegas, but because the two games in three days in the same arena mirrored what the first round of the WNBA playoffs, a best-of-three format, would look like.

As confidence grew for Clark and the Fever, there were high hopes that these three games were "very winnable," as Clark said—all of them. It turned out they were not winnable at all. None of them.

•

Had the season ended on September 6, Indiana and Minnesota would have met in the first round of the playoffs. Minnesota, 24-9, would have been the third seed and Indiana, 18-16, the sixth. As their game began, Indiana jumped out to a fast start, leading 27-19 after one quarter and 50–45 after two. Clark scored 17 points in the first half. Things were clicking; the Fever looked like they not only belonged in the playoffs but were rolling right into them.

Then it all fell apart. The third quarter was a disaster for the Fever. They were outscored, 29-12. And, with the pressure on, Clark lost her composure. She threw her arms into the air after missing a short jump shot, then waved for the crowd to continue booing after she was called for a foul. When a foul was called on the Lynx a couple of minutes later, she sarcastically quick-clapped while walking toward the official who made the call.

Things went from bad to worse. Near the close of the third quarter, a Clark drive to the basket was thwarted by Minnesota standout Napheesa Collier, who blocked her layup attempt, sending Clark to the floor with no foul call. And there Clark stayed, lying on the court, in the lane, slowly getting up as the game went on without her.

*The Athletic's* James Boyd described the moment: "The game was going on, but Caitlin Clark chose not to be a part of it. The Indiana Fever superstar wasn't watching from the sideline Friday against the Minnesota Lynx; she wasn't stuck in foul trouble or nursing an injury. She was in the middle of the action, lying on the court, and had simply given up. It was as if Clark was in a video game and the game player's controller died. But this wasn't virtual. This was the real thing."

After Minnesota scored with its five-on-four player advantage, Clark, now standing, was waiting for her team to come back to her. Soon, a foul was called on the Lynx and Clark again began her fast clapping, all but tempting the referees to call a sixth technical foul on her. That was enough for Sides. At 1:54 of the third quarter, in came Wheeler, out went Clark. As Wheeler entered, she spotted Clark close to one of the referees, so, in a classic veteran move, she stepped between the two of them and began chatting up the ref as Clark walked to the bench.

Minutes later, the fourth quarter began, and just like that, Clark was back—composed and ready to go. "Just kind of a mental reset," she said. "It felt from my standpoint that the third quarter kind of got away from us. Get a quick breather knowing I'm going to need myself to find a way to have a big fourth quarter for us."

Two Clark assists in the first two minutes led to three-pointers by Lexie Hull and Mitchell, and the Fever had cut the Lynx lead in half, from 12 to 6. Clark had a three of her own two minutes later to bring the Fever within 3, then found Boston for a layup.

One-point game, 78–77, Minnesota. This was the moment for the Fever, and for Clark. With 5:17 remaining, Clark stretched to defend the Lynx's Alanna Smith on a jumper and stuffed her shot, grabbing the ball. The crowd, already on its feet, now was leaping with Clark as she sped down the court. She thought she saw an opening to thread a bounce pass to Temi Fagbenle down low. If it worked, if they connected and Fagbenle scored, the Fever would be in the lead.

Clark released the ball, but the middle was too clogged with Minnesota defenders near Fagbenle. The angle was just not there. The pass was picked off, the opportunity gone. Clark's imagination had gotten the better of her. Said Sides: "She came right to the bench and talked about it: 'That was a bad pass. Bad decision.'"

"My turnover in transition is what really ended the momentum for us," Clark said later. "I got a block and steal and we're running in transition and honestly made just a really bad read."

The Fever ended up losing the game by 11.

Conversation about Clark's behavior in the third quarter continued after the game—including from Clark. "I think there's a line, and sometimes your passion, your emotion can get to you, but that's not something I would ever change," she said. "Frustrating . . . I thought I got fouled . . . I think I could have done a little bit better job controlling my emotions. I think it started bad for us and continued to snowball."

"She's just so passionate," Sides said, "and her competitive spirit reminds me of Diana Taurasi. When she is upset or mad, that's what we've been working on, trying to figure out how to get past those moments. I was worried she was going to pick up a T [technical foul] in that third quarter, and thank goodness that she didn't, but that's growth, and she's got to learn that in those moments, I need my point guard to have a cool head, get us to whatever we need to be in offensively. And then, if it's not a foul call that you thought, you got to get back in transition and help our team get stops. We're working on those things."

Former Notre Dame coach Muffet McGraw, who knew Clark from the recruiting process, said at moments like this, she was "worried about her, just the pressure of everything. I know she always would say, 'It's not pressure, I don't feel all that.' But mental-health-wise, when you look at what Simone Biles had gone through at the Olympics, I hope she's okay. I hope she's found a way to get away from all of it, because I think when those things are acted out like that, I think that was just a lot of pent-up other stuff. But I can't imagine what it's like to be in her shoes, to have all that on her back, so you can understand how occasionally she's going to lose it."

Clark's AAU coach, Dickson Jensen, said Clark's competitive drive is the reason behind the outbursts. "Everybody gets on her about talking back to the officials, and saying she has these attitude issues, and in all due respect to all of them, it's really just her competitiveness," Jensen said. "I mean, very deep down, when the game is over, she's saying, 'I'm not holding any grudges against you. That's a game, right?' And people look at that as if, 'Oh, she's a baby.' No, she really wants to win. And you look at the calls that she complains about over the years, and I bet she's arguably correct on 90 percent of them."

Said Sides: "It was a real fine line to let her be her, because she's different. And what I told her was, you can operate in those moments and be able to still turn it on and keep playing at a high, high level when there's some chaos involved, but other players on your team might not be able to bounce back as fast to get their focus back. That was our conversation that I would try to have with her: You operate in this chaos. That fuels you and your game elevates in those moments, but with some teammates, it might not have the same effect."

•

It's safe to say that no athlete in the nation was interviewed more in 2024 than Caitlin Clark. She was always playing and always available.

That was a good thing because in early September, there was a lot to talk about.

A day after Angel Reese announced she had suffered a wrist injury during a game and would miss the rest of the season, Clark came in for her press conference before the September 8 Atlanta game and was asked right away about the injuries in the rookie class, especially Reese's news.

"It's obviously, definitely sad, anytime you see anybody go down with an injury, especially people that you came into this league with, whether it was Cam [Brink, injured earlier in the season], whether it was Angel, and especially Angel—like, you want to see her finish out this year, obviously, she's had a historic year, and she's done some incredible things.

"For me, getting to play against her, her motor is up there, if not the best in the league; like, she just doesn't stop working. So, you know, congratulations to her, I thought she had a tremendous year, and I thought she came to the league and really did what she's done well her entire career, as long as I've known her. So, it's definitely devastating. That's never anything you want to see from a player."

•

Three days later, Clark was back in the Fever press conference room talking about a very different subject. After the first and only debate of the 2024 presidential campaign between Vice President Kamala Harris and Donald Trump, Taylor Swift posted a long message on Instagram. In it, she endorsed Harris and also urged her 280 million followers to educate themselves on the candidates, register to vote, and consider voting early. Clark, a big fan of Swift's, was one of millions who liked Swift's post as soon as she saw it.

Swift's comments obviously were big news, coming as they did in the midst of a polarizing political season. But media outlets also were focusing on the celebrities who liked the post, Clark among them. She was being mentioned in online stories and social media posts along with Oprah Winfrey, Jennifer Aniston, Viola Davis, and Kylie Kelce. Whether she wanted to be or not, Clark had become part of the post-debate Swift story.

So, in her pregame press conference the next day, September 11, before the first of two home games with Las Vegas, I asked her about it.

"Caitlin, you liked an Instagram post last night from Taylor Swift that got a lot of attention. And I'm just curious if you could tell us what that post meant to you, and if you are, in fact, potentially going to endorse Kamala Harris?"

"I think for myself is, I have this amazing platform," Clark replied, "so I think the biggest thing would be just encourage people to register to vote. This is the second time I can vote in an election, at age 22—I could vote when I was 18—so I think do that. That's the biggest thing I can do with the platform that I have, and that's the same thing Taylor did, and I think continue to educate yourself with the candidates that we have, the policies that they're supporting. I think that's the biggest thing you can do, and that's what I would recommend to every single person that has that opportunity in our country."

Analysis continued for a while on social media, of course. Was this Clark's first foray into politics, or was she just a Swiftie liking a post about voting, a message—VOTE—that was on the warm-up T-shirt she often wore, as all WNBA players did? There also was online criticism of my question, coming as it did right before a big game. Clark went on to have a difficult time against the Aces, going 1-for-10 from three-point range and 6-for-22 overall for 16 points in a demoralizing 86–75 loss to the two-time defending champions.

Did the issue bother her? Clark never said. As always, she just moved on.

•

While that first game with the Aces was frustrating for Clark and the Fever, the second one two days later turned out to be a lost opportunity for a young team trying to make a statement about its promise for the playoffs.

Just four minutes into the game on Friday, September 13, Clark missed two free throws, a rare occurrence for a 90 percent free throw shooter. Moments later, she was called for a foul. As her momentum carried her under the basket, she slapped the stanchion, the one at the other end of the floor from the one she hit in August. The whistle blew. It was another technical, her sixth of the season. One more and she would have to sit out a game.

"I think I could have done a better job keeping my emotions in check," she said later, "but at the same time, like, really? I mean, it's a rule, so they have to call it. I get it. It's just tough."

It was a first half of frustration for Clark; she was held scoreless. In the second half, she scored 18. She added 9 assists, including one that broke the WNBA's single-season record for assists—not a rookie record, but the record for all players—set by Connecticut's Alyssa Thomas the previous season.

Clark noted the crowd's reaction when she broke her scoring drought with a layup early in the third quarter. "The cheer they let out when I made that first layup, you could tell it was like, 'Ah, finally, this girl could score again.'"

Just as they did against Minnesota a week earlier, the Fever hung around. With little more than a minute to go, they were within two—and Clark was launching a 31-foot bomb. Had it gone in, the Fever would have been in the lead, but it was just short, hitting off the front of the rim, then bouncing off the backboard. That was Indiana's last and best chance. The Aces won, 78–74.

Clark always replays shots and moments in her head after a game. "You go back and think about what we could have got there, what we couldn't have got, and I thought it was a great shot, honestly. If you make it, every single person loves it. And honestly, I thought it was in. It's like, ah, it was right there. As a competitor, you definitely want that, and I think the roof probably would have blown off."

Clark said she rarely is surprised by the result of a three-point shot when it leaves her hands. "I usually know. Sometimes you'll see me pointing if I can tell it's a little bit off. The ones that are annoying are the ones that feel really good and then don't go in, but at the same time, that's a positive because you feel good, your shot feels good, the mechanics feel good. It's almost like, how is that not going in?"

•

It wasn't all seriousness for Clark. Time and again, she cracked up her teammates with humor during practices, or when she continued to rely on them for help when she got herself into a jam on the court.

It's the rookies' job to sing "Happy Birthday" at the end of practice or shootaround to anyone celebrating a birthday on that day, and on September 13, it was Lexie Hull's birthday. The idea is to have the singing come from the rookies—plural. But there was only one rookie left on the Fever roster: No. 22. As Clark prowled inside a circle of her teammates on the court, belting out her dramatic, loud, and off-key rendition of "Happy Birthday," she added comments along the way.

"Guys, sing," she said, waving her arms like a conductor. A few did. Most did not. This was her job, not theirs.

After more singing, Clark stated the obvious: "We need to get more rookies!" Then she picked up Hull and paraded her around inside the circle. Uproarious laughter ensued.

"Having fun and smiling is a huge reason why we've been able to find so much success, and why people have also enjoyed watching our group," Clark said. "You can tell we have a lot of fun out on the court. We play basketball the right way. We celebrate our teammates' success, and I think that's what overall has brought us even more team success. . . . I've said many times, it doesn't feel like a job. I feel like a little kid, and I know everybody kind of gets a kick out of me at practice. We try to keep it light and fun, and I enjoy coming to practice. I don't know if everybody says that, but I do. I love practice."

Sides and her teammates talked glowingly about the joy of having Clark around. "She's really a funny, funny person," Sides said. "She has us laughing a lot out on the practice court."

Or in the middle of a downtown Indianapolis street. On a May 1 team photo shoot with Indianapolis's Monument Circle behind her, with the street closed and lights and cameras (and action) all around, Erica Wheeler and NaLyssa Smith both draped big necklaces with their numbers on them around Clark's neck. Aliyah Boston stepped in to hold Clark's hair as Smith worked on the clasp. Now that was teamwork.

•

But the league leader in Clark silliness was the Caitlin Clark De-Escalation Committee.

As Clark approached the dreaded magic number of technical fouls—seven—that would force her to miss one regular-season game, her teammates came to her rescue time and again. Wheeler did it earlier with the pie-in-the-face move in Chicago and her maneuver to get between Clark and the referee in the Minnesota game.

Then came the sixth technical, when Clark hit the stanchion in the Las Vegas game. This meant that if she was called for a technical in the last home game of the year against Dallas, she would have to sit out the final game of the regular season at Washington on September 19. No one wanted that: not the Mystics, who had moved that game to huge Capital One Arena, not the WNBA, not Clark, and certainly not Sides, because that Washington game was going to be the final tune-up before the playoffs.

In the Dallas game, Clark was called for a loose ball foul after she drove to the basket and ended up in a heap. She wasn't happy. Boston grabbed her and turned her away from the officials. "That's not a foul," Clark yelled as she circled around the court. Wheeler came in as reinforcement and skipped and jumped in front of Clark to redirect her.

Later in the game, Clark drove in for a layup and thought she had been fouled, but no foul was called. As Dallas called a time-out, Clark stood near mid-court, threw her arms into the air, and screamed for a foul.

On the bench, Katie Lou Samuelson flew into action. She sprinted across half the court, took a big hop, and planted herself in front of Clark, just a couple of inches away from her, and stood there, not moving, nose to nose. This was a basketball intervention. If that seventh technical was dangerously close to being called, it did not get called. Clark and Samuelson then walked to the Fever bench for the time-out.

"If we can keep her from getting technicals, that is always positive," Samuelson explained. "She's just always chirping, but it's good, and she knows it, too, so it's easy to laugh about it and play off it too."

There was one more troublesome moment that Wheeler took care of a few minutes later. As Clark sprinted down the court, she was fouled hard in transition, resulting in a free throw. Right after the contact, Wheeler wrapped Clark in a precautionary bear hug. "I de-escalate a lot of things around here," Wheeler said. "She's passionate about the game; the ref is the ref. I can see [her] taking it a little farther, and I'm already standing up and ready to de-escalate it, and she allows me to."

Clark definitely allows it. She called it "babysitting," happily so. When sports photographer Bri Lewerke posted a photo on Instagram labeled the "CC de-escalation committee," Clark replied, "Bruh," with a dozen sideways laughing-crying emojis. Boston also chimed in: "We work overtime," with two more laughing-crying emojis.

"I love that she got energized," Sides said. "They all know what's at stake with Caitlin, and they know she's doing incredible things. She's just special, and these guys know that's her passion, that's her fire. And they all know when she's reached that point and when we need to have a little assistance to come out there. And I appreciate that. I saw Katie Lou running to stand right in front of her, all the way from the bench. That's just good team chemistry stuff, that's just trying to make sure their teammate doesn't do anything that doesn't allow her to play in our last game against Washington."

Despite all the concern, Clark figured that the referees might just look the other way. "I didn't think they were going to give me a technical at any point tonight. I would have been really sad for people in Washington, DC. I didn't want to do that. I try my best, but my teammates do a really good job. They think it's funny."

But it wasn't always funny. "I still thought there were a couple moments there where I could have been a little bit better," Clark said, "but now it's basically over. I don't have to worry about that anymore, but I don't want to be getting technicals at all, and my mom doesn't want that for me, either."

Despite all the extracurricular activity in the Dallas game, Indiana won its 20th game of the season, 110–109, ensuring at least a .500 record, which was quite an accomplishment for the young Fever squad. Clark had the highest point total of her young career, with 35. And the technical foul pressure was completely over; she knew that even if she happened to be called for a technical in Washington, it wouldn't carry over to the playoffs, so she was safe. The day turned out to be a total success.

•

During the shootaround the day of the game in Washington, Samuelson was called into duty again. Clark was doing what she always does, running around, laughing and jawing, wanting to win every drill. Next thing anyone knew, she was lying on the court, face down, and Samuelson was lying on top of her, pinning her down, pro wrestling style.

"She's a kid sometimes, and she keeps everything light, but sometimes you gotta put her in place," Samuelson said afterward. Clark slapped her open hand on the court—"tapping out," in wrestling—and Samuelson let her go, acknowledging the sense of accomplishment the Fever felt in protecting their prized rookie: "We made it through without getting seven [technicals], so I think that was our goal as a group and we did it."

At that shootaround, like all shootarounds, the players end by heaving half-court shots. Those moments create delightful social media posts for Clark's fans, and Clark desperately wants to win every time. When someone else makes a shot, and a celebration breaks out, Clark sometimes rushes in: "No, we're not done here! We're not done here!" She wants to take her shot. Sometimes it goes in.

•

During that Dallas game, on a Sunday afternoon, the hometown Colts were playing at the same time in Green Bay. It was easy to imagine fans staying home to watch the NFL rather than trekking downtown for the WNBA. Every other year, sure. Not this year. Not this team. Not with this player in the building. The attendance was 17,274. Gainbridge Fieldhouse was filled to capacity.

But Indy had nothing on DC four days later. The largest crowd in WNBA regular-season history, 20,711, filed into Capital One Arena on a Thursday night to see Clark. She played for only 20 minutes and scored just 8 points with 8 assists as Sides took out her starters in the third quarter with Game One of the playoffs just three days away. Some spectators groused about that a bit afterward, but this wasn't a surprise. Anyone buying a ticket had to know the Fever didn't need to win the game and most likely would clear their bench, which is exactly what happened in a 92–91 Washington victory.

"This is what we've been hoping for, forever," Indiana's NaLyssa Smith said of the record crowd. "You never get used to it, just always showing up and playing in front of sold-out crowds. I mean, shout-out, Caitlin. Shout-out, Caitlin. We appreciate her for this."

•

The evening before the Mystics game, Clark had been visiting Lexie Hull's room in the team hotel at The Wharf, Washington's trendy waterfront neighborhood, when she decided to show off her baseball play-by-play skills:

"And that ball's hit to the shortstop. Rojas throws over to first base, and that's not going to be enough. That's an infield single by Contreras."

Clark's voice was deeper and more serious than usual. She was trying to sound like an announcer in a TV or radio booth rather than a basketball player sitting on a hotel room bed calling the Philadelphia Phillies–Milwaukee Brewers game being played on Hull's TV.

Hull pulled out her phone and videotaped Clark's performance for social media. "It was too funny not to record," Hull said later.

A few highlights: "Swings, a chopper, right down the first base line, Harper fields it, and then that's an out! That's one out. Runner advances to second."

A bit later: "And that brings us to the top of the fifth, with the Phillies leading, 1–0. We'll be back in a minute with a 30-second break. Thanks for tuning in."

With Hull laughing in the background and Clark herself chuckling off and on, the budding announcer then leaned over and went face-first into the bed.

I asked her about it a few days later. "I told Lex that sometimes I'll just commentate some games and she's like, all right, we'll do it right now. . . . It was pretty funny. I messed up a few times. That's a hard gig."

A fan of all sports, Clark said she has been keeping an eye on the Phillies of late with her boyfriend, Connor McCaffery, who grew up as a fan of the team. Her favorite teams stretch from the Midwest to the East Coast. "I still like the Cubs. I like the Yankees. I'm not, like, a diehard of any baseball team. My dad was a big Royals fan growing up because Kansas City was the closest professional sports team to where I grew up. I liked the Chiefs before the Chiefs were really good, too, so I'm not a bandwagoner either. . . . I don't know if commentating's in my future, but who knows? Maybe one time, for fun, somebody will let me do it."

The offers popped up on social media almost immediately. Tom McCarthy, the TV announcer for the Phillies: "You have a future, and by the way, any downtime you have, you're up in the booth whenever you want. Bring Connor too. He likes the red."

The Brewers chimed in as well: "Let's get you on our broadcast for real, @CaitlinClark22, hit us up."

Who didn't get a kick out of this previously hidden Clark talent? MLB teams certainly did. They, of course, wanted to capitalize on her unprecedented ability to draw attention to any sport she touched, especially from girls—an audience men's professional sports often fail to attract. It was like anything else Clark did. People couldn't get enough of it.

# CHAPTER SIXTEEN

# The Playoffs

As Caitlin Clark and her Indiana Fever teammates traveled to the Mohegan Sun Casino and Resort for the team's first playoff game since 2016, it was not lost on Clark, or anyone with the Fever, that she would be playing the first postseason game of her professional career in the same arena, on the same court, shooting from some of the same spots, as she had four months earlier in the first regular-season game of her pro career.

That game in Connecticut on May 14 was memorable for many reasons—most of them bad—for Indiana and Clark. In a blowout loss, kicking off that dreadful 1-8 start to the season against a murderer's row schedule, Clark scored 20 points, which is very good for a rookie in her first game against one of the strongest defensive teams in the league, a defense that gave her so much respect they were in her face from the get-go. But because she was so new, and because her teammates barely knew her, and because the Sun were so relentless, Clark ended up with 10 turnovers that night. She would not have that many again all season, but what happened on that floor started a national conversation that Clark could not shake for some time, even though it turned out to be epically misleading.

Now it was September 22, and she was back with an entirely new storyline. Her day had begun fabulously; she was gathering awards by the armful. She finished fourth in voting for the WNBA Most Valuable Player, an award won appropriately and unanimously by Las Vegas star A'ja Wilson. Clark also collected three honors from the Associated Press: Rookie of the Year, unanimously; All-WNBA First Team; and All-Rookie Team. After results like that, there was no doubt that the big rookie prize, the WNBA Rookie of the Year award, would be hers soon enough.

"It's pretty night-and-day from where we first started," Clark said of how far the team had come. As for herself and her honors, Clark was unmoved. "It's cool, but at the same time I don't really care. My life is very unaffected by that."

·

Game One of the best-of-three playoff series was not even 90 seconds old when Clark dropped to the court in pain, holding the right side of her face. Ryan Ruocco was on the call for ABC: "Clark gets hit in the face by Carrington and is down. Caitlin Clark is down. No call as Connecticut takes advantage and Clark is still down after taking a shot following the pass to Boston."

Clark had been circling around the three-point line when she tossed a pass to Aliyah Boston at the top of the key. DiJonai Carrington, who was guarding Clark, threw her right hand into the air to try to swat the ball, and as her arm came down, television replays showed her fingers hitting Clark in her right eye. Because a foul wasn't called, Carrington took off for an easy layup with Clark still lying on the court.

The game was then stopped, allowing Clark to regroup on the bench before she came back in without missing a second of playing time. Soon, her eye was turning black and blue; she played the rest of the game with a shiner and ended up having a poor shooting night, going 2-for-13 from three-point range and 4-for-17 overall in a trying 93–69 loss—a score that was even worse for the Fever than their 21-point loss in the May season opener. "We just played a crappy game," Clark said.

But Clark was adamant that the poke in the eye had nothing to do with it. "Obviously, got me pretty good in the eye. I don't think it affected me, honestly. I felt like I got good shots, they just didn't go down. Obviously, a tough time for that to happen. I got some really good looks. I had two, three pretty wide-open threes in the first half that you usually make."

But as for her eye, she wanted to be clear: "It didn't bother me. Obviously, it didn't feel too good when it happened."

•

As the Fever prepared for this series, they talked about how their youthful exuberance might help to carry the day. They were buoyed by what had worked over the past month, a Clark-fueled adrenaline rush of a run leading to a 9-5 post-Olympics record, including their 84–80 victory over Connecticut in Indianapolis on August 28. Clark and her backcourt sidekick Kelsey Mitchell had finished the summer on a tear, with a supporting cast that rose to the occasion time and again, including some magnificent play by Boston and Hull, among others.

Could that be the formula for success in a short series against a far more experienced foe? Connecticut's players came into Game One having played a combined 222 playoff games. The entire Fever roster had played 19 games; their starting five had never played a second in the playoffs.

The answer to that question was obvious as the game wore on: Not on this day. Connecticut was too physical, too good. Everything the Sun did worked. Coach Stephanie White had a trick up her sleeve for Clark, deciding to make a defensive switch after losing the last game to Indiana, putting 6'4" veteran DeWanna Bonner on the six-foot Clark.

"So much about this game is about comfort, it's about rhythm, it's about timing, it's about all those things," White said. "How can you make an adjustment that disrupts some of that? . . . It gave us a different look at the point, and I really liked that." Clark ended with

11 points, 8 assists, 4 rebounds, 3 steals—and tied for her season low
with 2 turnovers.

"Welcome to the playoffs," a Fever official said with a sad shrug in a
back hallway after the game. That was meant cynically, of course—but
a lot of people *were* welcomed to the playoffs thanks to Clark. Her
playoff debut drew 1.84 million viewers on ABC, going up against
NFL games on a Sunday afternoon. It was the 24th WNBA game of
the season to reach at least one million viewers, 21 of which featured
Clark, according to *Sports Media Watch*. The TV audience for the
Fever–Sun game dwarfed that of the three other WNBA playoff games
that day: 403,000, 410,000, and 461,000, all on ESPN.

•

Do-or-die Game Two for the Fever came three days later, again in
Connecticut. The first two games of the first round of the WNBA
playoffs were hosted by the higher seed, meaning the Fever would
have to win to go back to their sellout crowd in Indy for a deciding
Game Three. Until then, they were holed up in Uncasville. It was a
long wait. Clark said she had spent five consecutive days inside the
sprawling Mohegan Sun complex. Her hotel room was inside the
complex. The arena was inside the complex. The walk to the arena from
her hotel room was inside the complex. She and every player who had
ever had a road game with the Connecticut Sun were living the classic
line from the Eagles' "Hotel California": *You can check out anytime you
like, but you can never leave.*

To take a break from the arena and their hotel rooms, athletes and
team personnel would wander through the vast mall that was under the
same roof as the arena and the casino complex. Coaches were spotted
buying ice cream. Some made the trek to Starbucks. The Fever coaching
staff, including coach Christie Sides and president Dr. Allison Barber,
met one night for dinner at Sol Toro, a Mexican spot inside the vast
labyrinth of shops, restaurants, and stores. At another table was PR

director Ryan Stevens, with several reporters who were covering the Fever in the playoffs.

As for Clark, she'd had just about enough time inside that big, airtight entertainment bubble. She wanted to see the sky. She wanted to breathe fresh air. So she did.

"It was my first time outside in five days yesterday, I realized," Clark said an hour and a half before tipoff for Game Two. "So, that probably wasn't too healthy, but whatever, I went to Mystic, Connecticut. I went to dinner with my parents last night. So, a very cute little town, went to some cute Italian restaurant, so, that was good. It's good to get outside and get some fresh air and see some grass.

"You don't realize that when you leave your hotel room—and obviously, we walked the back way to practice—so, you're never outside, you're never smelling fresh air. So, probably should have done that a little earlier, but glad I did it yesterday."

Then Clark said out loud what many in the WNBA believe: The Sun's home base, an hour drive from the Hartford airport and not close to any big city, is not a particularly desirable place to play.

"I think our team's made light of the situation," she said. "And obviously, this isn't an ideal spot, not much around other than a casino and some shops, but we've had a lot of fun together."

•

The ball was right where her teammates wanted it—in Clark's hands.

There were little more than four minutes remaining in Game Two on Wednesday night, September 25, when Boston handed the basketball to Clark, who was slicing behind her. The Fever were losing, 70–68. They'd been beaten badly three days earlier in Game One. This was a best-of-three series; two losses and you were done.

So, the clock was counting down, not just to the end of the game, but to the finish of Clark's nearly yearlong run to the very top of American sports, a magical joyride the likes of which no female athlete—and, for that matter, no male athlete—had ever quite experienced. Twelve straight months of Caitlin Clark basketball games, a year in the headlines, in the spotlight, in the news. From October 2023 at Iowa to September 2024 in the WNBA, 12 months of historic TV numbers and sellout crowds, of riveting conversation and revealing controversy, of proving so many people wrong, and making so many people, especially young, athletic girls, so incredibly happy. No female athlete had ever had such a profound effect on attendance, social media, TV viewership, and merchandise sales on a sport and a league in so short a time.

To ensure her rookie season didn't end right then and there, Clark, whose eye appeared to be fine and barely bruised, had to do something, and she had to do it fast. Time was running out.

Competitive to her core, powered by a deep well of confidence, she knew this was her moment. "You get used to this pressure," she had said three weeks earlier, looking ahead to the playoffs. "I think at times, you can definitely feel it a little bit, but you just remind yourself you've been in these moments before, and fall back to the confidence of the work that you put in."

Clark quickly darted to her left. She dribbled with her left hand as she slid along the top of the circle, ending up on the left side of the court, her defender racing over to try to get to her in time. Clark was exactly where she wanted to be. Left side. Beyond the three-point line. If she had a favorite spot on the court, this was it, 26 feet from her target.

Up she went in that pogo-stick three-point-launch position of hers. The ball was on its way. Left leg straight up, then straight back down. Right leg askew. Arms high in the air. Wrists cocked.

Arms still in the air. Waiting, waiting. "Clark for the lead . . ." It was the familiar, anticipatory voice of Ruocco, who had called so many of Clark's three-pointers in the NCAA Tournament, then in her first few months as a professional. He was the soundtrack for the most famous thing she does.

At that moment, ESPN's audience had built to a WNBA cable record 3.4 million viewers. The scoreboard clock was running down. 4:01 . . . 4:00 . . . Ruocco's voice was rising. The ball was falling toward the basket, curling inside the rim, funneling down, rippling the net.

"You bet!" Ruocco exclaimed.

"Indiana has come all the way back, a 12–2 run."

The arena erupted. The Fever were now ahead, 71–70. This was Connecticut's home court, the 8,910-seat arena built deep inside the casino complex, just a couple minutes' walk from the incessant lights and sounds of the slot machines. But this was Clark, so that meant that even an away game felt like a home game, especially at moments like this. Whole sections of Indiana fans, many in their Clark T-shirts and jerseys, leaped to their feet. This had been happening all season, for every Fever road game, yet there always was something new and surprising when it occurred because this was never supposed to happen in sports, game after game, week after week, especially with a franchise like the Sun, a long-standing organization in a state that was crazy about women's basketball, a team that had built a very strong and loyal fan base of its own. But Clark was the human gateway to the women's game for countless new fans, so old rules and perceptions went out the window in the WNBA in this year of all years.

•

ESPN couldn't stop showing the replay of Clark's three-point shot. It was a massive moment in a close game, but it was more than that. It was what viewers tuned in to see. To millions of fans, Clark is synonymous with one thing: the long three-pointer, called the "logo three" even if it isn't officially from a logo in the center or at the side of the court.

"Big shot!" said Rebecca Lobo, the Hall of Fame analyst who had been behind the microphone for many of Clark's games in college and in her rookie year. "Big. Big shot."

With that basket, Clark became the first rookie in WNBA playoff history with at least 25 points, 5 rebounds, and 5 assists in a game. And she wasn't done yet. But unlike so many other times this season when Clark celebrated a magical shot, she did not pump her fist when that three slipped through the cords of the net. She did not wave an arm to fire up the crowd. No, she simply let her arms fall and started to run back, hard, on defense. She had more work to do.

•

Connecticut soon answered. Sharp-shooting guard Marina Mabrey made a triple of her own a half minute later, and the Sun were back in front by two. This was the ebb and flow of playoff basketball at its most frenetic and crucial moment.

Back came the Fever with a layup from one of the few veterans on the roster, Temi Fagbenle, who was alone coming down the lane after Clark tried and missed another three. The game was tied, 73–73, with 3:13 to play.

After a Connecticut miss, the Fever were back on offense. Nearly a minute and a half after her three, Clark fired a bounce pass to Boston underneath the basket for a layup that put the Fever back up by two, 75–73, with 2:41 left. Clark to Boston, a pass and a bucket, at such a crucial moment trying to keep their season alive. The Fever had a chance. Check that: They had more than a chance. With a couple of minutes left, they were winning.

Would Clark pull off what so many had seen her do in college at Iowa, lifting a team well beyond what was expected of it? On ESPN, Ruocco spoke for hundreds of thousands of sports fans: "Will it be her final game until April? Or will she play Friday night in a do-or-die Game Three?"

Was this the end of the line for the most impactful and popular women's basketball player on earth? Or was the story of this unprecedented year in women's sports still being written?

•

After Boston's layup, Bonner came right back with a drive to the hoop. Tied again.

Now it was Indiana's turn. Clark found Fagbenle at the top of the key as the Sun fans chanted, "Dee-fense. Dee-fense." But the noise was just as loud, perhaps louder, for the Fever. The Sun had rushed two defenders at Clark, leaving Boston wide open for a layup on a laser of a Fagbenle pass—77–75, Indiana, with two minutes remaining.

Bonner responded 10 seconds later with an arcing three-pointer to put Connecticut up by one. "High-level entertainment," Ruocco said.

After an Indiana turnover with 1:28 to go, Bonner's three-point attempt hit the back of the rim and bounced high into the air. Boston tipped it to Fagbenle, who tossed it to Clark. Down the court she came with a minute to go, firing a half-court pass to Mitchell, dancing along the three-point line. She had her shot. She took it. It banged off the front of the rim.

But the rebound came right back to Mitchell. She leaped as if she were going up to shoot, but kicked a pass back to—no one in a Fever jersey. No teammate was there, only the Sun's Bonner.

It was a terrible mistake in the moment, compounded when Mabrey, left alone, nailed a 26-foot three-pointer with 46 seconds to go. The Fever went into a time-out now down, 81–77. As Clark came off the court, she slapped the seat of a chair on the bench in frustration.

Mitchell missed another three moments later, and that was just about it. Clark did have one final prayer of a shot, one last long three, down 85–79 with 15 seconds to go—from almost the same spot as the three that connected with four minutes to go—but it hit off the back of the rim and bounced off the top of the backboard and out of bounds as Clark threw up her arms in disgust.

So, the answer was no, Clark was not taking this team any further, not this time. The Fever lost, 87–81. The experienced Sun swept the first-round playoff series, two games to none. Clark finished with a game-high 25 points, with 9 assists and 6 rebounds. Despite making only 3 of her 12 three-point attempts, she kept her composure and played a very good game.

As the clock hit 0:00, Clark walked toward the Fever bench, alone, but not for long. Erica Wheeler, of course, was making her way toward her and was the first to greet her, putting an arm around her—and a hand out at an advancing cameraman to keep him away for a moment.

In the huddle, Wheeler grabbed Clark around the side of her neck and held on, looking into her eyes, making sure she was okay. Within moments, Clark left the court, appearing 22 minutes later in a press conference with Sides and Boston.

•

When athletes meet with reporters after a loss, there are always thoughtful pauses and melancholy glances. But when that loss also ends the season, the finality begins to set in the moment the questions start coming. It's over, the players know. It's really over. And so it was for Clark.

"Obviously, it's a tough one, especially because we climbed all the way back in and definitely had our opportunities late, and then a few different miscues, and it's back to a two-possession game," she said. "We couldn't quite get over the hump there. . . . It's a good little taste of what's possible for this organization and for this franchise. And there's a lot for us to hold our heads high about. We're a young group, a pretty inexperienced group, but we came together and had a lot of fun playing with one another."

Then she grew a bit wistful. "That's sometimes the worst part of it, is you feel like you're really playing your best basketball, then it has to end."

As a pro, she had come full circle; her Fever season had ended where it began, meaning the most unexpected 12 months in women's sports history were over, from Iowa's outdoor exhibition game in Kinnick Stadium on October 15, 2023, to September 25, 2024: All the records, the historic TV viewership, the unprecedented sellouts—it was over. Clark was now finished playing basketball in the public eye until May 2025.

"Basketball has really consumed my life for a year, so I feel like it'll be good for me to kind of reflect back on everything that's happened," she said. "I feel like I didn't even have time to really reflect on my college career, because it ended so fast, and then I came here and was trying to give everything I could to this team and kind of move on and put all that behind me and help this team get back to the playoffs.

"So, I feel like taking some time for myself and really enjoying that and reflecting back. And, you know, it was special. There were a lot of things that this group accomplished that a lot of people probably didn't think was possible after the start we had to the season. So, it'll definitely be probably a little weird for me over the course of the first couple weeks. And then I'm sure I'll get bored and pick up a basketball again."

It was natural to ask Clark what was next. It was the first time in a while that no one was sure of the answer. "I was focused on beating the Connecticut Sun," she said. "I haven't thought too far down the line. I don't know what I'm going to do tomorrow. I don't know what I'm going to do the next day. Maybe play some golf. That's what I'm going to do until it gets too cold in Indiana. I'll become a professional golfer."

Some thought she was being serious. She wasn't, but that didn't mean some golf wasn't in her future. Boston, standing in for Clark's millions of fans, had the last word on that idea.

"Not too much, babe, right?" she said. "Keep it basketball."

CHAPTER SEVENTEEN

# Controversy

Little more than 36 hours after the Fever's season ended, at 1:41 p.m.
Eastern on Friday, September 27, the Women's National Basketball
Players Association posted a lengthy statement on social media:

### A MESSAGE ON BEHALF OF THE 144

This week was dedicated to celebrating and amplifying A'ja, Caitlin,
DiJonai, and Napheesa for their hard work and truly exceptional
performances all season long. We were not going to distract from
their successes, nor would we dim the glow of the spotlight that
centered them. They have earned that focus and celebration.

But we will take this moment now to stand up for them and the
rest of our members. Every single one of them.

Because we call B.S.

To unprofessional members of the media like Christine Brennan:
You are not fooling anyone.

That so-called interview in the name of journalism was a blatant
attempt to bait a professional athlete into participating in a narrative
that is false and designed to fuel racist, homophobic, and misogynistic vitriol on social media.

You cannot hide behind your tenure.

Instead of demonstrating the cornerstones of journalism ethics like integrity, objectivity, and a fundamental commitment to truth, you have chosen to be indecent and downright insincere.

You have abused your privileges and do not deserve the credentials issued to you. And you certainly are not entitled to any interviews with the members of this union or any other athlete in sport. Those credentials mean that you can ask anything, but they also mean that you know the difference between what you should and should not.

We see you.

Our relationship with the media is a delicate one that we will continue to strengthen because the media is essential to growing the game. No one knows that better than we do.

But the players are entitled to better. They are entitled to professionalism.

We call on *USA Today* Network to review its Principles of Ethical Conduct for Newsrooms and address what we believe is a violation of several core principles, including seeking and reporting the truth. *USA Today* Sports should explain why a reporter with clear bias and ulterior motives was assigned to cover the league. We also urge the league to review its policies and take measures to prevent such issues, protecting the integrity of the game and its players.

Terri Carmichael Jackson
Executive Director

•

Two hours later, *USA Today* took its turn posting on social media.

Journalists ask questions and seek truth. At *USA Today*, our mission is to report in an unbiased manner. We reject the notion that the interview perpetuated any narrative other than to get the player's perspective directly. Christine Brennan is well regarded as an advocate for women and athletes, but first and foremost, she's a journalist.

Roxanna Scott
*USA Today* Sports Executive Editor

•

How did we get here? This is what happened:

Almost exactly three days earlier, just before 1:20 p.m. on Tuesday, September 24, between Games One and Two of the Fever–Sun playoff series, DiJonai Carrington walked across the court at the empty Mohegan Sun Arena to speak with a knot of reporters there to interview both teams after their respective practices. Social media was running wild with videos and photos of Carrington's fingers hitting Clark in the eye, with unsubstantiated claims and insinuations that Carrington had tried to injure Clark.

There also were other videos making the rounds on the internet in which Carrington and teammate Marina Mabrey were seen laughing later in the game, including Mabrey motioning with her fingers. It appeared that they were mimicking former NBA star Carmelo Anthony's gesture celebrating a three-point shot, but the internet was rife with questions, comments, rumors, and innuendo about all of it, and since social media had driven so much of the conversation around the WNBA this season, there was only one way to give the athlete in question a chance to clear the air, and that was to ask Carrington about it.

So I did.

"DiJonai, when you went and kind of swatted at Caitlin, did you intend to hit her in the eye, and if so—or if not, either way—could you talk about what happened on that play?"

"I don't even know why I would intend to hit anybody in the eye," she replied. "That doesn't even make sense to me. But no, I didn't. I didn't know I hit her, actually. I was trying to make a play on the ball and I guess I followed through and I hit her, so obviously it's never intentional, that's not even, like, the type of player that I am."

I followed up to give her a chance to address the issue of the other videos getting quite a bit of attention online. "Did you and Marina kind of laugh about it afterwards? It looked like later on in the game they caught you guys laughing about it?"

"No, I just told you I didn't even know I hit her, so I can't laugh about something I didn't know happened."

In my long career, I've asked hundreds of questions that were far more challenging and potentially controversial than those. This is what journalists do. We ask questions, specific questions, sometimes difficult questions. In all cases, the athlete has an opportunity to take the questions any way he or she prefers, to fight back, to tell their side of the story, whatever they want to do.

I would ask any male athlete what I asked Carrington, so why wouldn't I ask a female athlete those questions? I posted the video of my questions and Carrington's answers on social media; it received millions of views. By covering this story seriously, I was giving the WNBA the respect it deserved, just like the NFL or the Olympics. I was doing my job.

•

Fifteen minutes after I asked Carrington those questions, *ClutchPoints'* Matthew Byrne asked Clark during her on-court media availability what she would say to "the crowd of people that think a hit like that was intentional."

Clark laughed. "It wasn't intentional by any means. You just watch the play. It wasn't intentional."

Byrne's post on X received hundreds of thousands of views. Clark's answer was now available in the public domain for one reason: Byrne asked the question.

•

Just a couple of minutes after Carrington's interview session was over and she walked away, I was standing near the other reporters at the side of the court when her teammate DeWanna Bonner walked toward me.

"You disrespected my teammate," she said.

I put out my hand and tried to introduce myself, but Bonner did not want to shake it.

"You attacked my teammate," she said.

I motioned to my phone in my hand. "Can I tell you what I said?" I was happy to show her the video I had just taken of Carrington's answers to my questions. I again tried to introduce myself since Bonner and I had never met, but Bonner wanted no part of that. "You attacked my teammate," she said again.

I tried to introduce myself once more. "I asked her a question to give her a chance to respond to a controversy."

"You disrespected my teammate," Bonner said again, walking away.

Bonner never raised her voice, nor did I. It was the kind of tense but predictable conversation I have had dozens of times over the length of my career with professional athletes, especially in the National Football League. When a journalist is doing her job properly, and an athlete is doing hers or his properly, they sometimes will not get along. This happens relatively often in big-time sports.

•

No more than 10 minutes before the Carrington interview, I had chatted with Connecticut Sun head coach Stephanie White on the court. We had both been on an ABC News Live show a few months earlier, talking about the Caitlin Clark Effect, so it was nice to catch up for a few minutes and exchange cell numbers.

Knowing how fraught the playoffs can be, and now possessing White's number, I decided to text her to let her know what happened in case she or her players wanted to discuss it with me.

"Your players are mad at my questions," I wrote. "Happy to discuss anytime. My questions gave DiJonai a chance to clear the air on a controversial topic. It was Journalism 101. I tried to introduce myself to DeWanna three times and tell her what happened but she just wanted to criticize me which of course is her right. Just fyi. Thanks."

Little more than an hour later, White replied. "Thanks for the heads up."

Five hours later, a WNBA official called me in my hotel room in Uncasville, about a mile from the arena. The official had been informed by the Connecticut Sun public relations staff about my questions to Carrington and Bonner's response. The league official told me that the Sun PR people had told Carrington that she should not have gone to a teammate to confront a credentialed reporter, but rather should have come to the PR people, who could have handled the situation.

Then the WNBA official brought up my questions to Carrington. "I have a simple test about whether questions are appropriate or not," the official told me. "They should not be vulgar, rude, or inappropriate. Your questions were not vulgar, rude, or inappropriate. Your questions were fine.

"Unfortunately, most of our players have zero idea what real media exposure is," the official continued. "They don't know what real coverage is, they have been shielded at college and then they come to the WNBA not knowing what real questions are. Frankly, our players just don't get it."

The official requested their name not be used due to the sensitive nature of the issue.

•

At 11:30 the next morning, Wednesday, September 25, eight hours before Game Two, Carrington wasn't on the court. She wasn't in the locker room. She wasn't looking at game film.

No, on the day she was named the WNBA's Most Improved Player, Carrington was poking her head through a gap in the black curtains surrounding a catering area backstage at the arena, raising her voice at three journalists sitting at a table.

Indianapolis *Fieldhouse Files* Fever beat writer Scott Agness, *Indianapolis Star* Fever beat writer Chloe Peterson, and I were in the otherwise empty catering area, waiting for the Fever shootaround to end on the court nearby, when Carrington surprised us with her appearance between the curtains.

"Why are you talking shit about NaLyssa?" she blurted out loudly, referring to her partner, NaLyssa Smith, the Fever forward.

The question surprised the three of us because no one was saying anything personal or derogatory about Smith. Agness and Peterson had been discussing a bit of Fever strategy they had just noticed on the court but had been asked not to divulge publicly—that Smith was going to be replaced in the starting lineup for Game Two by veteran Temi Fagbenle.

"You're saying she's a bad teammate!" Carrington yelled.

Then she looked specifically at me. "I walked past and I heard you talking shit about NaLyssa! It was you, out of your mouth!"

Carrington, of course, had been outside the curtains while Agness and Peterson had been talking about the change in the Fever starting lineup. I invited Carrington to come inside the curtains to sit down and speak with us. She refused, but she was still talking quite loudly, so much so that her voice was carrying through a back hallway of the arena.

Connecticut Sun manager of communications Alexandra Maund later said that her colleague, public relations specialist Caroline O'Keefe, heard the commotion and told Maund to find out what was happening. "Caroline comes running over to me, 'DiJonai's yelling at somebody,' so I ran over and grabbed her away," Maund said.

The Sun's Marina Mabrey also heard Carrington, and she ended up rushing toward her teammate as well. They were on the outside of the curtains around the catering area, but visible to us through gaps in the curtains. We watched them convince Carrington to stop talking and walk away.

Obviously surprised by this development, Agness, Peterson, and I immediately replayed the conversation around the table that preceded Carrington's arrival through the curtains and agreed that no one had said what Carrington said she heard.

•

That wasn't the end of it. Thirty minutes later, with Agness, Peterson, and me now back on the court, waiting to interview the players, Smith walked by, then came back toward the court moments later with her cell phone pressed to her ear. Carrington had left a voicemail for Smith relating her version of the catering area story, according to a Fever official.

Smith strode toward me. "Do you have something to say to me?" she asked.

"I'm always happy to talk to you," I replied.

She scoffed and walked away.

Within minutes, back under the stands in a dark hallway, WNBA communications director Sam Tager was standing with Agness and me. Smith walked by us, looking at me. "What did you say?" Smith asked. "What did you say?"

I told her that no one—Agness, Peterson, or I—said anything negative about her.

"You are lying," Smith said to me and walked away.

Tager shook her head: "This is like a bad game of 'Telephone.'"

Minutes later, Maund said she wanted to hear the entire story, and I was happy to tell it, so she gathered Fever PR director Ryan Stevens, Tager, Agness, and me around a backstage table. Each of us taped the conversation. I retold the details, and Agness added his, which corroborated mine. Peterson was on deadline, so she wasn't with us, but she later confirmed the same details.

At the end of our meeting, Maund said, "Jen [Rizzotti, the Sun president] is on her way in right now, and I'm going to talk to her about it. . . . I'll see what she wants to do. . . . You may be hearing from us, but I appreciate your honesty."

An hour later, a WNBA official who was not in Connecticut called me to say they had listened to the audio recording from our meeting about the incident and were going to follow up with the Sun about Carrington's behavior.

•

The news of the players union wanting to banish me for asking a question and a follow-up exploded not only in sports social media but also in the mainstream media. Over the next few days, I was supported. I was lectured. I was cheered. I was excoriated.

A sampling:

Soccer legend Megan Rapinoe, whom I have known and covered for more than a decade, said this about my questions on her podcast: "That feels racist."

Lindsay Gibbs, who runs a women's sports newsletter, posted on X: "Wild to see reporters I grew up admiring, trailblazers of the industry, become hacks in real time."

Carrington herself reposted the WNBA players association statement, adding "@cbrennansports, goofy."

Those who were angry with me believed that the WNBA was not the same as other sports leagues and required different kinds of questions—ones that took into account possible racial backlash before they were asked. There was concern that the two questions I asked could lead to social media attacks on Carrington and other Black players.

Others thought the questions were appropriate, allowing Carrington to deal with a controversial topic on her terms, in her own words.

Tom Jones, senior media writer for *The Poynter Report*, a daily media newsletter: "Brennan was doing her job, a job she has done well and fairly for decades. In this case, she went directly to Carrington, as is the journalistically responsible thing to do."

*The Boston Globe*'s Tara Sullivan: "Absurd on its face, and laughingly uninformed and hypocritical in each of its five pages posted to social media last Friday, the statement indicted the WNBPA far more than it could ever hurt Brennan, a trailblazing journalist who has been on the ground covering women's sports for more than four decades. . . . The WNBA and its players keep fumbling their golden opportunity with a string of ill-advised decisions and PR gaffes exposing them as not being ready for prime time."

CNN's Jake Tapper and I discussed the players' call to ban me on his show, *The Lead*, on September 30. Tapper ended the segment this way: "Whoever wrote that statement for the WNBA players union should probably read a little bit more about Christine Brennan before accusing her of buying into anything having to do with homophobia or racism or sexism, because those are horrible blights on our culture that you have been fighting against for decades."

Annie Costabile, the *Chicago Sun-Times'* WNBA reporter, said she understood how race and politics always have played a role in coverage of the league, but that threatening to take a journalist's credential was never the answer: "Early on covering the beat, I experienced a sense of being protective of the players because I saw firsthand how disrespected the sport was collectively," she said. "I thought respecting the sport and the players meant being protective over being fair. I was wrong. Respecting women's sports doesn't mean we should cover the league in a soft manner. These women are athletes, the ultimate competitors, and they deserve the same coverage, including critical coverage, that we give to all sports. That's the mark of true equality. Sometimes when we have these conversations about coverage of the WNBA, you have to ask, are we treating it as a sport, or as a charity?"

•

It seemed that everyone had something to say about the Carrington situation and the call to banish a journalist—everyone except the leadership of the WNBA.

WNBA commissioner Cathy Engelbert's public silence was explicable at least in part because she was already in trouble with her players. On September 9, in a CNBC interview, she was asked about the "darker, more menacing" tone around race and sexuality among the fan bases in the Caitlin Clark–Angel Reese rivalry on social media.

Instead of condemning the vitriol, Engelbert said, "There's no more apathy. Everybody cares. It is a little of that Bird–Magic moment, if you recall from 1979, when those two rookies came in from a big college rivalry, one white, one Black. And so, we have that moment with these two. But the one thing I know about sports, you need rivalry. That's what makes people watch. They want to watch games of consequence between rivals. They don't want everybody being nice to one another."

Engelbert also acknowledged the perils of social media, saying she tells players, "If someone's typing something and you wouldn't ask their advice, ignore it."

Condemnation of her words came quickly. The WNBPA's Terri Jackson issued a statement a day later: "Here is the answer that the Commissioner should have provided to the very clear question regarding the racism, misogyny, and harassment experienced by the Players," she said. "There is absolutely no place in sport—or in life—for the vile hate, racist language, homophobic comments, and misogynistic attacks our players are facing on social media.

"This is not about rivalries or iconic personalities fueling a business model. This kind of toxic fandom should never be tolerated or left unchecked. It demands immediate action, and, frankly, should have been addressed long ago."

Trying to contain the controversy, Engelbert went on social media to clarify her remarks, writing, "To be clear, there is absolutely no place for hate or racism of any kind in the WNBA or anywhere else."

This was the backdrop against which the players association's call to ban me played out. It was an effort that failed. I was not banned. My *USA Today* editors included my name on their credential request for the WNBA Finals, I received a credential, and I covered Game One in Brooklyn.

Engelbert, Rizzotti, Carrington, and Smith all declined to comment about these developments for this book through their spokespeople. Jackson did not return text and voicemail messages seeking comment.

•

At its core, this controversy was about the portrayal of prominent female athletes on social media, especially Black female athletes. If there's one thing we all know and can agree on, it's that social media often displays the worst of us. X is a cesspool. Other websites and platforms can be equally terrible. They usually are worse for women than men, and even worse for Black people, especially Black women.

This is not news. It's not a secret. A quick look at X will give you all the information you need. Major companies and organizations know it. The Indiana Fever knew it as the 2024 season began and encouraged their players to get off social media as soon as the team saw how awful some Caitlin Clark fans were being toward the mistakes and miscues of Fever players, especially Aliyah Boston, and how ugly Clark haters were being toward Clark herself.

No one should have been shocked by what was happening. As a top WNBA official told me, "This happens everywhere. Why are our players so surprised? Why are they not prepared for it?"

•

The Sun had just won Game Two and clinched their playoff series with the Fever when veteran Connecticut forward Alyssa Thomas condemned Indiana fans in her postgame press conference:

"In my 11-year career, I've never experienced the racial comments [like those] from the Indiana Fever fan base," she said. "It's unacceptable. . . . I've never been called the things that I've been called on social media and there's no place for it. . . . We don't want fans that are going to degrade us and call us racial names. . . . We don't want to go to work every day and have social media blown up over things like that. It's uncalled for, and something needs to be done, whether it's them checking their fans or this league checking. There's no time for it anymore."

Sun coach Stephanie White defended her team in her press conference, but noted that the issue of social media abuse is an all-encompassing topic. "We've seen a lot of racism, sexism, homophobia, transphobia throughout the course of our country. Sport is no exception, and it's unacceptable, to be quite honest. . . . It's a lot of teams in our league and a lot of athletes, not just in our league, that get attacked like this. We continue to encourage them to silence the noise, control what they can control."

Fever coach Christie Sides spoke a few times during the season about how difficult it was for her team to endure racially tinged hatred on social media as well, and she discussed this again after Game Two in the same press conference room.

"The outside noise that these guys had to endure . . . There's a lot of hurtful, hateful speech out there that's happening, and it's unacceptable. This is basketball and this is their job and they're doing the best they can. And when it gets personal, to me, there's no reason for it, and these guys have to listen and watch that. Social media is their life. This is what they do. They have to read and see these things constantly."

The WNBA released a statement after the game: "The WNBA is a competitive league with some of the most elite athletes in the world. While we welcome a growing fan base, the WNBA will not tolerate racist, derogatory, or threatening comments made about players, teams and anyone affiliated with the league. League security is actively monitoring threat-related activity and will work directly with teams and arenas to take appropriate measures, to include involving law enforcement, as necessary."

Interestingly, the only known issue involving the behavior of a fan toward a player during the Fever–Sun series actually occurred against Clark. During Game Two, Clark asked for a Connecticut fan to be removed from his seat close to the court for undisclosed language and/or behavior. Security officials talked to the spectator, then allowed him to return to his seat. The WNBA would not comment for this book on what the fan said or did.

During Fever exit interviews on September 27, veterans Kelsey Mitchell and Erica Wheeler appeared together, and when asked about Thomas's comments, they both said they "don't condone" what she described.

But Wheeler said that she and her teammates, having been subjected to intense scrutiny all season, were not exempt from racial taunts. "Our ears have been blocked out longer than most people, if that makes any sense. . . . We probably got it, too, we just don't care about it. . . . I don't care about it because it's a fan who's probably sitting on the couch doing nothing, so I don't care."

Clark also spoke about the issue in her exit interview that day: "It's definitely upsetting. Nobody in our league should be facing any sort of racism, hurtful, disrespectful, hateful comments, and threats. Those aren't fans, those are trolls, and it's a real disservice to the people in our league, the organization, the WNBA. But there are a lot of really good fans whether they've been fans for 20-plus years or whether they're new fans in our league. I think continuing to uplift this league in a very positive light is the best thing that we can do."

"Social media has changed the game for the better and the worse," said Associated Press national women's basketball writer Doug Feinberg. "Obviously, with all the nastiness that goes on on social media, but also I think it's helped grow the game, because 10 years ago, someone makes a great play, you may have to wait until that night or the next day to see it on *SportsCenter*. Whereas now, within five or 10 minutes—or 30 seconds—the highlight's already on social media and the wow factor is there right away. And that wasn't the case before, and that's helped grow the sport positively. Of course, negatively, people are making comments that they wouldn't make to their face. The old phrase, 'there's no such thing as bad press'? This is taking it to the limit."

# CHAPTER EIGHTEEN

# Overtime

On Friday, September 27, the day that Caitlin Clark and the Indiana Fever would have hosted Game Three of their first-round playoff series, Indianapolis was a ghost town. Hurricane Helene was making its way north, sending sheets of rain sweeping through the empty plaza surrounding the soaring glass windows of Gainbridge Fieldhouse. The Fever team store, stocked with playoff merchandise and every size and color of No. 22 jersey, was open, but the only people inside were two reporters and two employees.

Fever officials had dreamed of what might have been, the hyped-up, emotional, capacity crowd that would have arrived that night, hurricane be damned; the opportunity for Clark to lead Indiana in a playoff game at home, to perhaps win that playoff game and take the Fever into the second round—it was all there, until it wasn't, due to the two losses in Connecticut.

Instead, the players were filing into the press conference room for their exit interviews before heading home, looking back on the season and looking ahead to 2025, which seemed like a very long way away. Clark arrived just before 10:30 a.m. and was soon talking about the message Christie Sides and the other coaches delivered in the locker room after the quick departure from the playoffs: "You have to let this kind of burn inside of you, and let it kind of bother you in a way that it's going to drive you through the off-season."

Answering questions for 13 minutes, Clark spoke about how the playoff series loss would motivate her: "We believe we can build this place into a championship contender. That's what I believe. . . . I'm going to do everything in my power to help this organization get there. But you gotta let it hurt you a little bit and really drive you throughout the off-season."

Less than a week later, on October 3, Clark's off-season brightened when she won the award that had basically been hers since she launched herself out of the Olympic break: she was named WNBA Rookie of the Year. She received 66 out of 67 votes from a national panel of sportswriters and broadcasters. Angel Reese received the other vote. The person who voted for Reese never revealed themselves, but certainly received quite a bit of attention, very little of it good. "It should have been unanimous," said ESPN's women's basketball studio analysts Chiney Ogwumike, Andraya Carter, and Carolyn Peck, almost in unison.

Clark's statistics were extraordinary, especially considering the withering defensive pressure she endured all season. She averaged 19.2 points, 5.7 rebounds, and a league-high 8.4 assists per game. She finished the season with 337 assists, a new WNBA record, 21 more than Alyssa Thomas, who set the previous league record in 2023. Clark also set rookie records for points in a season, with 769; three-pointers, with 122; and triple-doubles, with 2. No other rookie has ever had one. Her 122 threes led the league as well. Clark also made the WNBA All-Rookie Team with Angel Reese, Kamilla Cardoso, Rickea Jackson, and Leonie Fiebich.

With the Fever having dispersed for the season, the organization put out a video of congratulations to Clark from her teammates. They included Erica Wheeler: "Super proud of you man, how you just block out the noise and handle your business and also have fun with it. . . . You're breaking all the records, bro. I don't know what else you're gonna do."

Katie Lou Samuelson: "As much as you like to joke around all the time, and our team likes to joke around all the time, this is an amazing accomplishment. You have had such a historic season. I'm proud to call you my teammate. . . . I know this is one of many awards you will win."

Kelsey Mitchell: "C-squared, what's up, friend? . . . You've changed the world in so many ways. You've done it with so much grace. I'm so happy to take the floor with you. . . . From me to you, I'm always going to be a fan, always going to be in your corner, I'm always going to be in your backcourt. Congratulations, kid."

Later in October, Clark became the first rookie since Candace Parker in 2008 to be named to the All-WNBA First Team, joining A'ja Wilson, Napheesa Collier, Breanna Stewart, and Alyssa Thomas. As Nike said in a post honoring Clark, "Is there a rookie record for rookie records?"

•

While Clark was collecting awards and looking ahead to the spring and summer of 2025, there was still plenty of basketball to be played—by other players. The WNBA playoffs marched on, working their way to a marquee New York Liberty–Minnesota Lynx matchup in the Finals, and while the TV viewership numbers were much better than they had ever been, they paled in comparison to what Clark had drawn in her two playoff games.

For instance, Game One of the Liberty–Lynx series, on October 10 in Brooklyn, was watched by 1.1 million viewers on ESPN. It was the most-watched Game One of the Finals in league history, up 57 percent from Game One of the 2023 Finals. But it also was less than half the audience that watched Clark's final game of the season. Game Two of the Fever–Sun series attracted 2.5 million viewers overall, peaking at 3.4 million.

As the Liberty–Lynx series went on, it drew more interest and more viewers, cresting at 2.15 million for the deciding Game Five, won by the Liberty. It was the most-watched WNBA Finals game since 1999, but of course was still less than what Clark attracted in her second playoff game. It also was only the sixth-most-watched WNBA game of the year, behind four Fever games and the All-Star Game—all of which, of course, involved Clark.

The numbers really were remarkable. The WNBA regular-season viewership statistics were a rout, according to Fox Sports' Michael Mulvihill: Clark's games averaged 1.178 million; all other games, 394,000.

Attendance mirrored TV viewership: The Fever's average attendance of 17,036 fans was the most in WNBA history, according to AcrossTheTimeline.com, easily ahead of the second-place New York Liberty's 12,730.

Even more surprising, the Fever's average home attendance in Clark's rookie year was better than the average home attendance of five NBA teams in the 2023–24 season: their hometown partner Indiana Pacers, the Atlanta Hawks, Washington Wizards, Memphis Grizzlies, and Charlotte Hornets. First, there was the 2024 NCAA women's final topping the men's final by 4 million viewers, now this. Clark was taking women's sports to previously unthinkable heights.

In December 2024, *The Indianapolis Star* reported that Clark was responsible for 26.5 percent of the WNBA's league-wide activity during the 2024 season, including attendance, merchandise sales, and television. One of every six tickets sold at a WNBA arena could be attributed to Clark, the *Star* said.

Clark's economic impact on the city of Indianapolis was $36 million, Dr. Ryan Brewer, associate professor of finance at Indiana University Columbus, told the *Star*'s Dana Hunsinger Benbow. Earlier in 2024, the NBA All-Star Game's impact in Indy was $400 million, Brewer said, meaning Clark's value was nearly 10 percent of the NBA All-Star Weekend.

"That's for one year. We're talking about one player," Brewer said. "The numbers are so staggering. They don't even seem real."

The *Star* wasn't the only newspaper measuring the Caitlin Clark Effect. On October 13, *The Washington Post* published a full-page story and graphic in its Sunday sports section: "By any measure, Clark's impact was huge," read the headline, with the subhead "Fever rookie's stats, popularity and record TV ratings and attendance dramatically changed the WNBA."

As the *Post*'s Ben Golliver wrote, "Never before has a WNBA star managed to be a household name in so many households."

Yet, throughout the WNBA post- and off-season, the league found itself curiously out of step with the nation's fondness for Clark. On October 10, before Game One of the WNBA Finals in Brooklyn, Commissioner Cathy Engelbert spoke for 27 minutes in a press conference about the historic developments in the 2024 season and never once mentioned Clark's name.

Calling the season "the most transformational year in the WNBA's history," Engelbert talked glowingly about the record or near-record levels of viewership, attendance, merchandise sales, and digital engagement. "You saw some teams upgrade . . . arenas for certain games this year, and I thought that was a sign and signal as attendance has grown across the league that we can play in bigger arenas. . . . We had our highest-attended game ever, over 20,000, in Washington this year."

Clark, of course, was the reason for most of those moves to larger arenas, and her presence definitely was the only reason Washington had the biggest crowd in WNBA regular-season history on September 19. Engelbert sprinkled the names of various WNBA players throughout her press conference, among them: Napheesa Collier, Sabrina Ionescu, Breanna Stewart, Leonie Fiebich, Aliyah Boston, and A'ja Wilson. But no Clark.

Through her spokespeople, Engelbert was asked to be interviewed for this book several times in late 2024 and early 2025. Every request was declined. In March 2025, I asked again, specifically wondering why Engelbert, on October 10, failed to mention Clark's name when referring to the unprecedented season highlights that happened because of Clark.

On March 10, Engelbert replied in a text message sent through a spokesperson:

"You're asking me why I didn't mention Caitlin Clark during my WNBA Finals press conference? I didn't mention any players in that press conference other than some of those from the Liberty and the Lynx who were participating in the Finals."

Engelbert did mention two players who were not participating in the Finals: Aliyah Boston and A'ja Wilson. She talked about them when mentioning WNBA players in commercials: "There's virtually not a sporting event you can turn on where one of our players is not in an ad spot. That was not happening five years ago. Look at Aliyah Boston and Sabrina and A'ja and so many of our players in these ad spots."

Engelbert's March 10 text continued: "I have stated many times that Caitlin is a generational talent and there is no denying her impact—not only in the WNBA but beyond the world of sports. We have also always stood by the belief that our league is not about any one player but about the collective talent, teamwork, and dedication of all the athletes who continue to elevate the game and inspire generations. Just because Caitlin's name is not mentioned in every interview or press conference does not mean we do not recognize, celebrate, and fully support her—both as an athlete and, even more importantly, as a person."

•

A week and a half before the WNBA Finals, Engelbert, in an interview with *60 Minutes* correspondent Jon Wertheim for a piece on Clark and the WNBA, was asked to describe "the Caitlin Clark phenomenon." Engelbert replied, "She's clearly an unbelievable player, came in with an unbelievable following, has brought a lot of new fans to the league. If you look at our historic season around our attendance, our viewership, Caitlin—Angel, too, Angel Reese, Rickea Jackson, Cameron Brink—this class of rookies, we will be talking about them a generation from now."

Wertheim followed up. "I notice when you're asked about Caitlin a lot, you bring up other rookies as well."

"No league's ever about one player," Engelbert replied. "That player could get hurt or whatever, so I think it's just to give recognition that in sports, people watch for compelling content and rivalries. And you can't do that alone as one person."

By practically any measure, Clark was that one person.

•

On December 10, 2024, Clark was named *Time* magazine's Athlete of the Year. Even though the award has been around for only six years, it has become prestigious because it has been given to some of the biggest names in sports: the 2019 US Women's National Soccer Team, LeBron James, Simone Biles, Aaron Judge, and Lionel Messi. Having a player in that kind of company would make most leagues proud. But longtime Washington Mystics owner Sheila Johnson was not pleased with *Time*'s decision.

"Why couldn't they have put the whole WNBA on that cover and said the WNBA is the league of the year because of all the talent that we have? Because when you just keep singling out one player, it creates hard feelings," Johnson told CNN sports anchor Amanda Davies on December 13.

Johnson also said this during the interview: "It has taken the WNBA almost 28 years to get to the point where we are now. And this year, something clicked with the WNBA, and it's because of the draft of the players that came in. It's just not Caitlin Clark, it's [Angel] Reese. We have so much talent out there that has been unrecognized, and I don't think we can just pin it on one player."

Johnson certainly was aware that her team specifically benefited from the public fascination around Clark's arrival in the WNBA. Johnson's Mystics moved both of their 2024 home games with Indiana from their 4,200-seat arena to the 20,000-seat Capital One Arena, selling out both of those games, including that record crowd of 20,711 on September 19. Those two games accounted for 31 percent of the Mystics' total home attendance in 2024.

Asked about Johnson's comments, Engelbert said in the March 10 text message: "That really is a better question directed to Sheila, but what I will say is that we respect that everyone is entitled to their opinion. As a league, we are always in favor of WNBA players, both past and present, getting the recognition they richly deserve, which is why we are so committed to telling and sharing their stories—and we will continue to do so. Caitlin had an extraordinary year, breaking records, being named a WNBA All-Star, earning the WNBA Rookie of the Year award, and receiving *Time*'s Athlete of the Year—a well-deserved honor, and we applaud her."

Asked several times about her CNN interview for this book, Johnson did not respond, but a spokeswoman did reply to an email: "Sheila doesn't have anything further to contribute regarding the subject."

Observing all of this, from the early slights by Diana Taurasi, Breanna Stewart, Sheryl Swoopes, and more, to the Chennedy Carter hit and to the playoff and postseason drama, was Muffet McGraw, the venerable Notre Dame coach who sent 20 players to the WNBA during her 38-year coaching career—and also coached Engelbert at Lehigh.

"I thought that the players could have embraced the idea that 'Hey, this is great for us too,'" McGraw said during an interview on December 18, 2024. "'More people are going to see us play, too, and we're going to benefit from this and pack the house, so this is great for the game.' I think they missed the boat. . . . It did appear to be more petty jealousy than anything else."

Meanwhile, in the *Time* article, Clark went further than she ever had on the subject of her race. "I want to say I've earned every single thing, but as a white person, there is privilege. A lot of those players in the league that have been really good have been Black players. This league has kind of been built on them. The more we can appreciate that, highlight that, talk about that, and then continue to have brands and companies invest in those players that have made this league incredible, I think it's very important. I have to continue to try to change that. The more we can elevate Black women, that's going to be a beautiful thing."

There was yet another major year-end honor for Clark. She received the Associated Press 2024 Female Athlete of the Year award, which is significant always, but especially so in an Olympic year, when women like gymnast Simone Biles and swimmers Katie Ledecky and Torri Huske were among the biggest stars at the Games. Clark became only the fourth basketball player to be honored by the AP since the Female Athlete of the Year award was first presented in 1931, joining Swoopes (1993), Rebecca Lobo (1995), and Candace Parker (2008 and 2021).

•

When Clark mused in the playoffs about becoming a professional golfer, she was kidding. But when she showed up to play in the pro-am at Annika Sorenstam's LPGA tournament in the Tampa area on November 13, crowds swelled, videos went viral, the golf community fell in love with her—and she proved she could play.

Clark hit more good shots than bad, took mulligans when she wanted, and included the fans whenever she could.

"Get it in the hole, kid!" a spectator yelled.

"Don't get your hopes up," Clark replied.

She joked about giving away her shoes—pink Nike golf shoes with gold spikes—if a wayward shot hit a fan. She kicked up her heels on the green. She drew raves from Golf Channel commentators who aired numerous highlights of her round.

One of her drives—her first of the day—landed only about 20 yards behind top-ranked golfer Nelly Korda's, and right down the middle of the fairway. She hit deft approach shots, made a 15-foot par-saving putt to the delight of the spectators gathered around the fifth hole, and showed a soft touch around the greens.

Clark even added a comment on Instagram about a video taken by someone in the gallery as her shanked tee shot on the third hole flew right at them, sending a few fans ducking for cover but hitting no one: "This is the greatest video ever."

But the biggest takeaway was her gallery. It was massive for an LPGA pro-am. The golf world was smitten. When Clark dived into the crowds to sign autographs after her round, the scene looked Tiger-esque—that is, if Tiger Woods had ever wanted to spend time with fans the way Clark does.

Golf Channel reporter and analyst Karen Stupples summed it up on air: "Just speaking to the fans in general, they are just so happy to be here and to be able to watch her do anything, even if it's not basketball."

The social media interest in Clark's day on the golf course was intense. The LPGA had seven million social media impressions that day, while media coverage on social and X about Clark earned an additional 27.3 million impressions, according to sports analytics company Zoomph.

Clark played golf off and on throughout the fall, but she decided not to play more competitive basketball. She turned down Unrivaled, the 3x3 women's league playing in Miami over the winter, and also declined an offer to participate in a three-point shooting contest at the 2025 NBA All-Star Game, preferring to focus on the WNBA All-Star Game's three-point contest in Indianapolis in July 2025.

That doesn't mean Clark wasn't working on her game. She was in the weight room, and the gym, throughout the fall, winter, and spring. On January 22, 2025, her 23rd birthday, she made 50 of 54 shots from three-point range on the Fever's practice court. When she wasn't practicing, she often was attending sporting events, instantly becoming the most popular person in the arena when spotted courtside or on the scoreboard's big screen. She supported the Butler University men's basketball team and assistant coach/boyfriend Connor McCaffery; the Indiana Pacers; the Iowa Hawkeyes women's team; and the Indy Ignite women's professional indoor volleyball team in its inaugural season. She appeared onstage as a speaker at conferences and events, and went to not one, but two Taylor Swift concerts, back to back, in early November at Indianapolis's Lucas Oil Stadium.

Things soon escalated for Clark in Swift's world. She was invited to be a guest on the popular *New Heights* podcast hosted by Travis Kelce, Swift's boyfriend, and his brother, Jason, then joined Swift in her suite at the Kansas City Chiefs' playoff game against Houston on January 18, 2025.

"She's unbelievable," Travis Kelce gushed about Clark as he was interviewed at the Super Bowl. "She's the funnest one to watch right now, and one of the best basketball players I've ever seen. . . . I just have nothing but great things to say about who she is as a person. Just so welcoming and just so warm as an individual that she can have a conversation with anybody. She's cut from the same cloth as me in that regard. Us Midwesterners, we tend to just accept everybody with open arms."

•

Less than a week before appearing with Swift at the Chiefs game, Clark was dealing with a troubling and dangerous situation. A 55-year-old Texas man was arrested at an Indianapolis hotel on January 12, 2025, after he allegedly sent numerous threats and sexually explicit or violent messages to Clark via social media, according to court documents.

"Been driving around your house 3x a day . . . but don't call the law just yet, the public is allowed to drive by gainbridge . . . aka Caitlin's Fieldhouse," the man messaged Clark. "I'm getting tickets. I'm sitting behind the bench," read another message.

Clark told police she feared for her safety and altered her public appearances and patterns of movement because of the threats. Prosecutors wrote that the posts "caused Caitlin Clark to feel terrorized, frightened, intimidated, or threatened" and caused her to have "reasonable fear of sexual battery."

"No matter how prominent a figure you are, this case shows that online harassment can quickly escalate to actual threats of physical violence," Marion County (Indiana) prosecutor Ryan Mears said. He also praised Clark for reporting the threats. "It takes a lot of courage for women to come forward in these cases, which is why many don't. In doing so, the victim is setting an example for all women who deserve to live and work in Indy without the threat of sexual violence."

•

On February 2, 2025, Iowa retired Clark's No. 22 jersey in a ceremony in front of another sellout crowd at Carver-Hawkeye Arena. Before the game, Clark offered another window into her mindset when asked in a press conference about facing so much scrutiny over the past 18 months.

"I just try to remind myself every single day how grateful I am to be in the position that I am. I try to treat everybody the same way that I would want to be treated. . . . I think having a small circle around me of people that I really trust, and those are the people that you can always count on and lean on, is what's been so important for me over the past year. But also . . . I feel like one of my greatest skills is, I really don't care. I don't. I don't care. I believe in myself. I'm confident in myself. I'm confident in my teammates. I try to instill that in them. I'm confident in the coaching staff on whatever team I was on, whether that was here, whether that's at the Fever now, and you just rely on those people."

•

In the off-season, major change came to the Fever. The leadership of the franchise liked what it saw in 2024, but wanted more, and wanted it now.

All three of the team's top leaders were replaced: three women left, three women arrived in their place. Fever president Dr. Allison Barber announced that she was leaving at the end of the 2024 season to help create the country's first girls' sports and leadership complex, named Marvella after the wife of late Indiana senator Birch Bayh, known as the "Father of Title IX." Marvella Bayh, a tireless advocate for women and girls, died of breast cancer in 1979 at 46. The complex will be located in northwest Indiana.

Barber was replaced by Kelly Krauskopf, the longtime Fever president and general manager who in 2018 became the Pacers' assistant general manager, the first woman in NBA history to hold an executive basketball management role. The Fever had become such a plum job that making the move from the NBA back to the WNBA made complete sense.

For general manager Lin Dunn, it was time—time to step into an advisory role with the team to make way for new general manager Amber Cox, a highly regarded sports executive in soccer and the WNBA.

And the biggest change of all: the Fever surprisingly announced on October 27, 2024, that they had "parted ways" with Coach Christie Sides. Krauskopf thanked Sides for leading the team "through an integral transition period over the last two seasons," calling her "an incredible representative of the Fever and our community."

Sides's only public comment at the time appeared on X. "Leave it better than you found it," she posted, adding a peace sign.

•

The day after Sides was fired in Indiana, Connecticut coach Stephanie White announced that she was leaving the Sun. Four days after that, on November 1, the Fever announced they were hiring White to replace Sides. White is an Indiana native who played for the Fever from 2000 to 2004, was an assistant coach with the Fever from 2011 until 2014, and head coach in 2015 and 2016. White was the one coach the Fever leadership wanted to lead them. Had she not been available, it's likely Sides would still be coaching the team.

The Fever roster that White was taking over was changing considerably. While veteran Kelsey Mitchell re-signed with the club, eliciting a celebration in the Gainbridge lobby that included a hug from Clark, newcomers included three-time WNBA champion and former

Fever No. 1 draft pick Natasha Howard, as well as Connecticut veteran DeWanna Bonner.

Some of the big names leaving the team were NaLyssa Smith, Katie Lou Samuelson, Temi Fagbenle, and Erica Wheeler. Watching Wheeler go was particularly poignant given how selflessly she had looked out for Clark. But with that momentous rookie year now over, Wheeler had done her job.

•

For the first time in five seasons, March Madness went on without Caitlin Clark. UConn won the national title over South Carolina; TV viewership for the NCAA final dropped significantly from Clark's 9.9 million in 2023 and 18.9 million in 2024 to 8.6 million, but was still up from pre-Clark days, showing a sustained level of interest in the women's game. Clark herself showed up at the Big Ten tournament in Indianapolis in early March—as a spectator, cheering on her former Iowa teammates from a courtside seat.

She also continued to make forays into the wide world of other sports. Invited by the NFL to its owners meeting in Florida, Clark appeared on a panel with Serena Williams to talk about the explosion of interest in women's sports.

"I think both of their perspectives were really valuable for our ownership to understand, to sort of learn from them," said NFL commissioner Roger Goodell, adding of Clark, "She's already an icon at a very young age."

But with the 2025 WNBA season fast approaching, no matter how many outside engagements Clark had, she always ended up returning to the practice court at Gainbridge Fieldhouse with her Indiana Fever coaches and teammates. There she was, right where she belonged: on a basketball court, the ball in her hands, standing behind the three-point line, ready to take her shot.

# Acknowledgments

Writing about Caitlin Clark and her immense impact on women's sports was a fascinating project at this time in my career, but it still required quite a team to help tell the story. Lucky me, I was able to rely on a group of all-stars every step of the way.

Thank you to the wonderful people who stopped what they were doing to read early drafts, in some cases twice: Amy Brennan Swaak, Cathy Dunlap, Peter Barzilai, Christine Spolar, Matthew Byrne, Melissa Isaacson, and Tony Reid. Dunlap also offered invaluable research assistance.

Thanks as well to the many colleagues and friends who offered advice, support, and even a comment or a quote to help make this book better: Harry Edwards, Lesley Visser, Bob Costas, Jackie Mac-Mullan, Michael Wilbon, Craig Fenech, Kevin Blackistone, Richard Lapchick, Rick Nixon, Carol Stiff, Jeff Millman, Wright Thompson, Scott Dochterman, Kyle Sagendorph, Jenna McKernan, Cameron Papp, Kristin Huckshorn, Michele Himmelberg, Kevin Modesti, Barb Reichert, Phil Hersh, Vicki Michaelis, Kelly Whiteside, Glenn Kardy, Ross Greenburg, Evan Jaenichen, Jeff Barker, Mark Hyman, George Solomon, Nick Lowery, Bob Corwin, Zachary Draves, Mark Borchardt, Jill Schuker, Kathy Popper, Levan Bezhanishvili, Laurie Saxton, Willie Weinbaum, Meredith Geisler, Barry Geisler, Peter Land, Mike Burg,

Robin Sproul, Judy Woodruff, Al Hunt, Polson Kanneth, Margaret Talev, Sandy Evans, Steve Hoffman, Leah Hoffman, Becky Timmons, Marty Aronoff, Tom Rieck, Jeff Metcalfe, Amy Walter, Kathryn Hamm, John U. Bacon, and Larry Mark.

I want to thank the many communications and public relations professionals from both the TV and basketball worlds who helped with a viewership number, a statistic, or an interview, including Greg Hughes, Dan Masonson, Katie Callahan, Julie McKay, Santa Brito, Michael Terry, Lauren Douglas, Giggy Maxwell, Abbey Zepper, Olivia Kuby, Autumn Hair, Ketsia Colimon, Carly Ebisuya, Liam Branley, Alexandra Maund, and Caroline O'Keefe. Thanks also to the WNBA's Ron Howard and the NBA's Mike Bass and Mario Illuzzi.

Now to the Indiana Fever: Thank you to Caitlin Clark, Mel Raines, Allison Barber, Lin Dunn, Christie Sides, Ryan Stevens, Mina Denny, Eddie White, Hillary Spears, Karima Christmas-Kelly, Fran Robinson, and Jackie Maynard for your cooperation and assistance in this project. Thanks as well to Clark's agent, Erin Kane, and her publicist, Rachel Walsh. While *On Her Game* is an unauthorized biography, I'm so appreciative of how the entire Fever organization helped in ways big and small to facilitate my access and reporting. All the players, led by Clark, answered every question I asked; my thanks not only to Clark but also to her teammates Erica Wheeler, Lexie Hull, Kelsey Mitchell, Katie Lou Samuelson, Temi Fagbenle, Aliyah Boston, Grace Berger, and Kristy Wallace.

Athletes, coaches, officials, and sports leaders offered their valuable time for interviews, including Tamika Catchings, Lisa Bluder, Muffet McGraw, Kate Martin, Briana Scurry, Brenda Frese, Tara VanDerveer, Dickson Jensen, Kristin Meyer, Val Ackerman, Donna Orender, Donna Lopiano, Donna de Varona, Billie Jean King, Ilana Kloss, Julie Foudy, Amy Wilson, Joe McKeown, Meghan McKeown, Nancy Lieberman, Dan Hughes, Peg Burke, Pam Ward, and Debbie Antonelli.

In the Fever press room, my thanks to Bob Kravitz, Scott Agness, Chloe Peterson, Matthew Byrne, Malcolm Moran, Madie Chandler,

Tony East, James Boyd, Lew Freedman, Bri Lewerke, Dana Hunsinger Benbow, Paisley Gray Reaves, Tasha Jones, and Brad Brown.

Many on the WNBA beat were helpful, including Michael Voepel, Rachel Bachman, Annie Costabile, Alexa Philippou, Katie Barnes, Maggie Vanoni, Kareem Copeland, Geoff Magliocchetti, Mel Greenberg, and Pat Borzi.

At *USA Today*, many thanks to Caren Bohan, Roxanna Scott, Nicole Poell, Mike Freeman, Steve Berkowitz, Josh Peter, Dan Wolken, Nate Davis, Mike Brehm, Susan Page, and Lark-Marie Anton, among many other wonderful professionals. When the WNBA players association called for me to be banned from covering the league for asking a question and a follow-up in September 2024, Bohan and Scott reacted quickly, making a strong statement in defense of journalism in general and my work in particular. I am grateful for their support. As noted in the book, a few of the stories and quotes in these pages first appeared in my columns in *USA Today*.

I also want to acknowledge and thank the terrific colleagues I'm honored to work with at ABC News, CNN, and *PBS News Hour*.

Thanks, too, to Andrew Blauner for his friendship, advice, and strong belief in this book.

This was my fourth book with Scribner, and the team there was as extraordinary as ever. Every step of the way, I was encouraged and supported by my terrific editor, Rick Horgan. Thank you, Rick. Assistant editor Sophie Guimaraes went above and beyond to make sure everything came together, no small feat when we were moving at breakneck speed. Paul Samuelson expertly led the publicity charge, while Ashley Gilliam Rose did the same on the marketing effort. Counsel Victor Hendrickson provided valuable legal advice and a few important editing suggestions as well. Thanks also to production editor Katie Rizzo, publicity director Maya Rutherford, art director Jaya Miceli, interior designer Kyle Kabel, and Brian Belfiglio for his sage early advice.

A special thank-you to three terrific editors and leaders at Scribner: former publisher Nan Graham, who gave her blessing to this book;

Marysue Rucci, Scribner's new publisher with whom I worked closely in the mid-1990s when she was beginning her career as an assistant in the publishing world; and the great Lisa Drew, who brought me into the Scribner family thirty years ago and changed not only my career, but my life.

Finally, I want to thank my wonderful family for their support and encouragement, always: Kate, Tom, Brad, Jennie, Leslie, Danielle, Brad, Max, Amy, Derrick, Peter, Helena, Jim, Angela, Henry, Kathryn, Ralph—and Teddy, who will be picking up a basketball for the first time soon enough.